ADVANCES IN PERSONALITY ASSESSMENT
Volume 5

ADVANCES IN
PERSONALITY ASSESSMENT
Volume 5

Edited by
Charles D. Spielberger
University of South Florida

James N. Butcher
University of Minnesota

LEA LAWRENCE ERLBAUM ASSOCIATES, PUBLISHERS
1985   Hillsdale, New Jersey   London

Lawrence Erlbaum Associates, Inc., Publishers
365 Broadway
Hillsdale, New Jersey 07642

Library of Congress Cataloging in Publication Data

ISBN 0278–2367
ISBN 0–89859–559–2

Printed in the United States of America
10 9 8 7 6 5 4 3 2 1

Contents

Preface

The richness and diversity of the field of personality assessment is reflected in the contents of this volume. In keeping with the general goals of the Series, individual chapters report authoritative reviews and advances in theory and research in a number of areas. These include applications of personality assessment to significant social problems, methodological studies, and reports of recent investigations using traditional objective and projective personality measures and newly developed assessment instruments.

The volume begins with a comprehensive review of the assessment of alcoholism and drug abuse with the Minnesota Multiphasic Personality Inventory. Noting the social and economic costs of substance abuse in the United States, Edwin I. Megaree examines MMPI studies of the personality characteristics of individuals with alcohol and drug abuse problems. Research findings with the standard clinical and validity scales, and with special MMPI scales designed to detect persons with alcoholism and drug dependence, are reviewed and critically evaluated. The results from studies of alcoholism and drug abuse are compared, commonalities and differences among these studies are noted, and methodological problems that must be taken into account in interpreting the research findings are discussed.

In Chapter 2, Norma Deitch Feshbach summarizes the results that emerged from a series of studies of the effects of chronic maternal stress and socialization practices on children's behavior. These findings provided the impetus for the development of three innovative psychometric instruments designed to assess chronic stress in the parents of young children. Correlates of the scales developed by Feshbach and her colleagues, and evidence of their reliability and validity based on cross-cultural research are also reported.

Although anger, hostility and aggression are central concepts in many theories of personality, there has been surprisingly little research on the assessment of anger. Increased interest in this area has been stimulated by evidence that anger/hostility is a major component of Type-A coronary prone behavior. In Chapter 3, Mary Kay Biaggio and Roland D. Maiuro review a variety of approaches that are currently used to assess anger and hostility. Objective, projective and behavioral measures of anger and hostility are critically evaluated and compared. Psychophysiological and biochemical correlates of anger that have been identified in laboratory investigations are also reviewed.

Over the past 20 years, Ernest S. Barratt has conducted extensive research on the nature and assessment of impulsiveness. In Chapter 4, Barratt outlines the systems theory model of personality that has guided his research. He then describes the voluminous evidence he has obtained from laboratory and clinical studies and observations of everyday life behavior that clarifies the psychological, social and biological basis of impulsiveness and its effects on performance. Characteristics of persons who differ in impulsiveness and the effects of impulsiveness on information processing, psychomotor task performance, and cognitive and psychophysiological responses are also examined.

In Chapter 5, Donald L. Hamann reviews the research literature on anxiety and musical performance. After noting numerous methodological deficiencies in this research, he reports the findings of an extensive research program in which he has investigated the effects of state and trait anxiety on musical performance. Interesting findings of relationships between anger and musical performance are also reported. Situational and task-related variables, for example, solo and group performance conditions and the experience and degree of mastery attained by a particular musician, were found to interact with anxiety and anger in influencing musical performance.

The personality characteristics of psychologists, psychiatrists and social workers who had been accepted for training in a psychoanalytic psychotherapy program are reported in Chapter 6. In this unique study Theodora M. Abel, Samuel Role and Vega A. Lalire evaluate and compare the responses of the candidates to the Behn-Rorschach Test within the context of the Rapaport and Exner scoring systems. Similarities and differences among the three groups were identified and interpreted on the basis of the extensive clinical experience of the investigators.

The final chapter by David M. Buss examines the stability of personality dispositions (traits) over an extended time period within the context of the Buss-Craik Act Frequency Theory of interpersonal dispositions. Multitrait, multimethod assessment of 200 specific acts over a six-month period revealed impressive consistency as evaluated by individually-computed stability coefficients and group trends. The robust stability of personality dispositions will be reassuring to assessment researchers who assume that personality traits are relatively stable and capable of predicting specified behaviors over time.

Diversity in research methodology associated with differing theoretical orientations is readily apparent among the investigators who have contributed to this volume. By bringing together the clinical observations and research findings of investigators with widely different points of view, the editors sincerely hope that this series will facilitate the development of an integrated and comprehensive body of knowledge that encompasses all facets of personality assessment.

Charles D. Spielberger
James N. Butcher

1 Assessing Alcoholism and Drug Abuse with the MMPI: Implication for Employment Screening

Edwin I. Megargee
Florida State University

It is difficult to comprehend the human and economic cost of alcoholism and drug abuse. Gerstein (1981) has reported that estimates of the excessive mortality directly attributable to alcohol via diseases such as cirrhosis ranged from 18,000 to 35,000 deaths in the United States alone in 1975; in addition an estimated 43,000 to 60,000 deaths from homicide, suicide, and accidents were indirectly attributed to alcohol by knowledgeable sources.

There is, of course, no way to assess the human cost of these deaths. Writing in the *American Psychologist,* U.S. Senator Dan Quayle (1983) spelled out the economic impact of alcoholism and drug abuse:

> The price we pay for health care, days away from work, and lost productivity as the result of addiction and alcoholism is about the same as the amount requested by (the) President to run the 400 programs of the Department of Health and Human Services—$70 billion . . .
>
> There are more than 100 million people currently employed in the United States. Between 5% and 10% of the work force suffers from alcoholism . . . It is estimated that 3% to 7% of the employed population use some form of illicit drug, ranging from marijuana to heroin, on a daily basis . . .
>
> Employees with a drinking or drug problem are absent 16 times more than the average employee, have an accident rate that is four times greater, use a third more sickness benefits, and have five times more compensation claims while on the job. Forty percent of industrial fatalities and 47% of industrial injuries can be traced to alcohol abuse. (p. 455)

Problems associated with alcohol and drug abuse are not limited to the private sector. According to Sen. Quayle (1983), "The General Accounting Office

1

estimates that among federal workers, alcoholism alone costs the taxpayer $700 million annually" (p. 457f). A recent worldwide survey of Army personnel revealed that 11% of the E-1 through E-5 soldiers could be classified as "alcohol dependent" and 4% as "drug dependent"; 27% of those surveyed reported work impairment and 11% serious adverse consequences as a result of alcohol use in the preceding 12 months, while 22% reported work impairment and 11% serious adverse consequences resulting from drug abuse (Burt, 1982; Burt & Biegel, 1980).

Impaired judgement or alertness can be particularly hazardous for military personnel whose jobs call for them to operate highly complex, potentially lethal, machines and weapons. Everyone involved in landing a jet fighter on an aircraft carrier, submerging a nuclear submarine, launching a missile, or coordinating a parachute drop, needs to be functioning optimally or many lives can be lost. In the civilian sector, intoxicated or impaired personnel have no business in an operating room, a police car or, perhaps most chilling, the control room of a nuclear power plant. Yet people under the influence of alcohol and/or drugs work in all of these settings (*Newsweek*, Aug. 22, 1983, p. 54).

There is no immediate prospect that this situation is likely to improve. Quayle (1983) reported that, ". . . 1 out of every 10 seventh graders today is a problem drinker, and 1 out of every 11 high school seniors uses marijuana daily," (p. 458) and Nathan (1983) labeled our efforts at preventing the deleterious effects of alcohol and drug abuse a "failure." Given this state of affairs, employers in many settings, especially those involving high-risk occupations such as law enforcement and the military, have asked whether screening techniques could be used to identify those individuals who currently have problems associated with alcohol or drug abuse or are likely to develop such problems in the future.

Past and present behavior is, of course, the surest guide to the future, and employers who could afford the time and effort involved in conducting full background investigations, including interviews with applicants' friends and acquaintances, as well as thorough medical examinations, including biochemical tests for the presence of various substances, could no doubt identify some applicants who have already developed a substance abuse problem. Polygraph interviews could identify some others. But in the typical screening situation, particularly that which involves large numbers of applicants and limited amounts of time, such expensive, time-consuming techniques are impractical.

It would be simpler to use one of the many direct assessment techniques such as the Alcadd test (Manson, 1949), the Iowa Scale of Preoccupation with Alcohol (ISPA) (Mulford & Miller, 1960), the Khavari Alcohol Test (Khavari & Farber, 1978), or the Michigan Alcoholism Screening Test (MAST) (Selzer, 1971). These are self-report paper-and-pencil instruments that inquire straightforwardly about the subjects' drinking patterns. Unfortunately such techniques rely on the applicants' willingness to reveal potentially damaging information. Goldberg (1974) characterized the MAST as a test, ". . . which appears to work wonders at detecting those who admit drinking a good deal. . ." (p 354).

For these reasons, assessment personnel have focused on the potential contribution of indirect measures of personality characteristics that might predispose people to develop problems related to substance abuse or chemical dependencies. As our most widely used clinical assessment device, the Minnesota Multiphasic Personality Inventory (MMPI), has been suggested as an instrument that might be used in such screening. This review will survey the literature on the assessment of alcohol and drug abuse with the MMPI, with particular reference to its suitability as a preemployment screening device.

THE MMPI AND ALCOHOL ABUSE

The MMPI performance of alcoholics has been studied in a variety of inpatient and outpatient settings. Several comprehensive reviews of the literature on the use of the MMPI among alcoholic samples appeared in the late 1970s and the reader is referred to them for more detailed and comprehensive surveys of the literature prior to 1978 (Butcher & Owen, 1978; Clopton, 1978; Miller, 1976; Owen & Butcher, 1979).

Performance of Alcoholics on the Regular Clinical Scales

One of the most pervasive questions in the literature on alcoholism and substance abuse has been whether alcoholics and/or other chemically dependent people have distinctive constellations of personality characteristics. Some investigators have used the MMPI to seek a common "alcoholic personality" pattern. Others have administered the MMPI to determine if it could be used to differentiate alcoholics from psychiatric patients; from other substance abusers; or from normals. Still others have used the MMPI to evaluate alcoholism treatment programs and to determine if it is possible to differentiate alcoholics who remain in therapy from those who drop out. Most of these studies have reported the average MMPI profiles of their subjects. A potpourri of these mean profiles is presented in Table 1.1, along with the associated three-point codes as calculated by the present reviewer.[1]

The 35 samples in Table 1.1 range in size from 20 to 1,009; in all 4,884 subjects' MMPIs are represented. Most of the samples have mean ages over 40, considerably older than the people applying for most entry-level positions.

---

[1]A "three-point code" consists of the numbers of the three highest MMPI clinical scales: Scale 1 = Hypochondriasis (Hs), 2 = Depression (D), 3 = Hysteria (Hy), 4 = Psychopathic Deviate (Pd), 5 = Masculinity/Femininity (Mf), 6 = Paranoia (Pa), 7 = Psychasthenia (Pt), 8 = Schizophrenia (Sc), 9 = Hypomania (Ma) and 0 = Social Introversion (Si). In case of ties, scales are listed in numerical order and underlined. Punctuation marks are used to signify elevation, '' indicates all those scales to the left of the mark that equal or exceed a T-score of 80, ' signifies they equal or exceed 70, — denotes 60, and / marks 50. All mean profiles are K-corrected.

TABLE 1.1
Mean MMPI and Three Point Codes of Thirty-Five Samples of Alcoholics

Study	Sample	N	Sex	Race
1. Bean & Karasievich, 1975	Pts tested 5th day of treatment	207	M	-- --
2. Black & Heald, 1975	Servicemen in treatment program	40	M	-- --
3. Button, 1956	Alcoholic pts	64	-	-- --
4. Curlee, 1970	Inpatients at Treatment Center	100	M	-- --
	Inpatients at Treatment Center	100	F	-- --
5. English & Curtin, 1975	V.A. Inpatients	25	M	-- --
	"Skid Row" Halfway House	25	M	
	State Hospital Inpatients	25	M	
6. Goss & Morosko, 1969	Outpatients St. Hosp. Inpts.	200	M	
7. Hill, Haertzen & Davis, 1962	State Hospital Outpatients	184	-	W
8. Holland, Levi, & Watson, 1981	V.A. Inpatients	79	M	-- --
9. Horn & Wanberg, 1969	Inpatient alcoholics	1009	M	W
10. Hoyt & Sedlacek, 1958	Chronic alcoholics in treatment	177	M	W
11. Huber & Danaby, 1975	Pts who completed VA treatment	67	M	
	Pts who quit VA treatment	35	M	
12. Krauthamer, 1979	Middle class private inpatients	30	F	W
13. Lachar, Gdowski, & Keegan, 1979	Inpatients who volunteered for treatment	65	M	49%W 51%B
14. Laudeman, 1977	Young men who volunteered for treatment	27	M	-- --
15. MacAndrew, 1978	Alcoholics in treatment	195	F	
16. MacAndrew, 1979	Young men arrested for drinking offenses	91	M	
17. O'Leary, Donovan, & Hayes, 1974	V.A. Inpatients	100	M	
18. Patterson et al, 1981	VA pts. beginning alcohol treatment	272	M	W
		56	M	B
19. Penk, Charles et al., 1982	616 chronic alcoholic VA inpts admitted to alcoholic treatment program; divided into five groups according to age	81	M	-- --
		152	M	-- --
		165	M	-- --
		186	M	-- --
		45	M	-- --
20. Schroeder & Piercy, 1979	VA pts. in alcohol treatment	920	M	-- --
21. Soskin, 1970	VA pts. in voluntary treatment programs	41	M	
		41	M	
22. Zelen, Fox, Gould, & Olson, 1966	Committed inpatients	20	M	
	Committed inpatients	20	F	
	Voluntary clinic patients	20	M	
	Voluntary clinic patients	20	F	

Scales 4 and 2 were the most prominent in these averaged profiles. The elevation of these mean profiles was clearly in the clinical range, with one or more mean scores over 70 in most samples, but the degree of pathology among these older alcoholics was considerably less than that associated with the samples of youthful drug abusers to be discussed later.

A detailed examination of these profiles reveals some other interesting findings. The mean MMPI profiles of female alcoholics did not differ systematically

Mean Age	VALIDITY SCALES			CLINICAL SCALES										Three Point Code
	L	F	K	Hs	D	Hy	Pd	Mf	Pa	Pt	Sc	Ma	Si	
47	48	67	49	73	75	68	74	61	63	71	71	65	56	241'
38.9	48	64	49	61	68	62	70	58	60	64	64	67	53	4' 29-
--	53	55	55	57	63	56	69	57	53	56	53	55	51	42-15/
47.7	46	60	53	57	68	62	67	61	62	66	61	66	51	247-
46.8	50	60	53	56	69	63	69	45	62	65	63	58	56	247-
43.1	46	66	46	67	80	67	76	61	65	77	73	63	60	2"84'
47.2	35	60	55	59	68	60	74	57	59	62	63	55	55	4'28
39.2	46	60	48	62	75	62	69	55	65	64	65	58	58	2'468-
43.7	48	62	50	63	74	64	74	60	61	67	66	62	57	24'4
44	49	59	51	58	66	59	69	55	59	59	58	58	--	42-67/
42	50	65	51	62	72	64	73	59	64	69	70	64	56	428'
43	47	62	49	63	73	64	73	--	62	67	65	62	--	24' 7-
--	--	--	--	55	61	58	62	52	52	57	52	45	--	42-31
46.5	47	59	51	64	69	65	70	59	58	62	60	61	55	4' 23-
	48	62	50	66	74	65	75	56	61	67	65	58	58	42' 1-
29.51	50	57	56	51	52	56	60	44	55	52	58	60	53	49-8
42.2	50	65	47	64	74	64	69	60	--	67	71	65	--	28' 4-
--	--	--	--	53	57	56	69	54	64	60	69	65	52	48 9-
40.8	47	63	50	61	70	66	75	43	66	67	68	63	58	42'8
19	50	68	51	54	58	56	62	57	65	60	71	70	--	89' 6-
47.5	47	64	50	67	73	66	70	61	60	66	67	66	55	24'8-
47	49	66	49	72	76	68	73	60	62	69	70	65	57	241'
41	50	68	49	69	73	64	73	59	63	67	71	70	54	248'
≤30	49	72	48	66	75	65	78	60	67	73	78	73	56	472'
31-40	48	72	47	70	77	68	78	62	66	73	77	69	58	427'
41-50	49	66	50	73	77	70	74	60	63	69	70	66	57	241'
51-60	50	66	50	72	76	69	71	58	61	68	69	64	55	214'
≥61	52	65	52	71	72	67	66	58	59	67	69	60	56	21'8
45	48	62	49	65	75	66	72	59	60	68	65	72	56	249'
46	47	61	51	63	75	66	75	58	61	69	62	58	56	24' 7-
45.6	46	60	51	61	71	65	72	57	61	66	63	62	54	42' 7-
39.8	49	56	55	56	64	61	70	--	58	59	56	57	--	4' 23-
41.4	54	53	56	51	57	68	68	--	60	55	55	55	--	46-3/
39.9	46	66	51	64	76	65	76	--	61	75	75	65	--	2478'
40.4	51	73	50	6?	72	67	78	--	66	68	72	64	--	428'

from those of their male counterparts, but blacks generally obtained more benign profiles than whites. Socioeconomic status appeared to have an ameliorating effect, the most benign profile being obtained by Krauthamer's (1979) middle- to upper-middle class women tested in an expensive private clinic.

Despite these differences, a number of reviewers have commented on the overall consistency of the mean MMPI profiles found among alcoholic samples (Butcher & Owen, 1978; Clopton, 1978; Hoffman, 1976; Miller, 1976; Owen &

Butcher, 1979). The most recent of these reviews, (Owen & Butcher, 1979) commenting on profiles such as those in Table 1.1, noted:

> The first, and primary, characteristic noted about problem drinkers is the typically high elevations on Scale 4 (Pd). Scale 4 reflects personality characteristics which are sociopathic in nature, that is an apparent inability to learn from past negative experience, difficulty in establishing long term stable relationships, lack of expressed anxiety, and difficulties with authority (Dahlstrom, Welsh & Dahlstrom, 1972). Since 1943 (Hewitt), it has been shown time and time again that elevations on scale 4 characterizes (sic) samples of alcoholics, whether one looks at simple single scale elevations or overall configuration. This consistency appears to hold true regardless of sex, subcultural or cross-cultural origin or inpatient or outpatient status. . . . If one reads each of the 90 studies on the MMPI and problem drinkers since 1972 (Owen, 1979), scale 4 elevations would be found, regardless of the primary focus of the study. The ubiquitous nature of scale 4 elevations has been amply noted by other reviewers as well (Clopton, 1978; Graham, 1978; Hoffman, 1976; Butcher & Owen, 1978).
>
> Not only are problem drinkers similar, with respect to the MMPI, on scale 4 elevations, but on other scale elevations as well. When composite MMPI profiles are drawn, showing the average MMPI profile of a given sample of problem drinkers, striking similarities are seen. Specifically, scales 2 and 7 are often predominant in the configuration as well as scale 4 . . . Elevations on these scales indicate a component of anxiety, sadness, and emotional stress. Again the consistency of this overall pattern is not limited to white, American problem drinkers. For example, Butcher and Pancheri (1976) compared groups of alcoholic and nonalcoholic men in the United States, Switzerland, and Italy, using a discriminant function analysis, and found that MMPI scales 2, 4, and 7 discriminated between the problem drinkers and normals in all three countries. The problem drinkers in each country were similar to each other, in spite of cultural and language differences. Kristianson (1976) found elevations on scales 2 and 4 to be characteristic profiles (sic) of two samples of problem drinkers in Sweden. Kline, Rozynko, Flint, and Roberts (1973) report elevations on clinical scales 4, 2, and 8 to be prevalent in their sample of American Indian problem drinkers. (pp. 68–69)

Can this distinctive pattern of elevations on MMPI scales 4, 2, and 7 as noted in the above review and in Table 1, be used to diagnose or forecast alcohol abuse? Not with sufficient accuracy that would justify its implementation in a screening program. There are three problems involved: (1) lack of specificity; (2) profile heterogeneity; and (3) postdiction as opposed to prediction. Let us discuss each in turn.

Lack of specificity.   Although the average MMPI profiles obtained from a variety of samples of alcoholics consistently manifest elevations on scale 4, and often secondary elevations on scales 2 and 7 as well, this code type is not uniquely associated with the development of drinking problems. Recently incarcerated criminals, acting-out neurotics, and a number of other clinical groups may also have individuals with this profile pattern. (Of course, if one is more interested in identifying individuals who are likely to present employers with problems than in singling out those people who will develop difficulties specifically related to alcohol abuse, this lack of specificity is less troublesome.)

Profile heterogeneity. Although the previously cited reviewers agreed on the consistency of the averaged profiles reported in the literature, they also unanimously pointed out that there was considerable diversity and heterogeneity among the individuals whose profiles were averaged in these studies. The fact that alcoholics consistently produced the same mean profile does not necessarily imply that there is a single homogeneous alcoholic personality, any more than the fact that every can of V-8 juice tastes the same implies that there is a single vegetable, V-8, from which the juice was extracted.

Hodo and Fowler (1976) for example, reported that although the mean profile for Horn and Wanberg's (1969) 1009 alcoholic subjects was in the classic 42' pattern, 79% of the individual profiles had some other two-point code. Similarly, McLachlan (1975b) reported that the MMPIs of the 2200 detoxified chronic alcoholics he studied scattered across 22 separate two-point code types. Although the 24/42 code type was the largest single grouping, it accounted for only 13% of the profiles. Recently other investigators have reported similar findings (Holland, Levi & Watson, 1981; Schroeder & Piercy, 1979). Clearly, considerable heterogeneity underlies the apparent uniformity of the typical mean profile.

Another index to the diversity of alcoholics' MMPI profiles is the number of homogenous subtypes that have been reported. One of the earliest studies (Goldstein & Linden, 1969) identified four alcoholic subtypes, each with its own distinctive MMPI profile; 45% of the subjects in their original sample and 42% in their replication sample could be classified into one of these four types. Several subsequent studies have also delineated four subtypes (Bean & Karasievich, 1975; Conley, 1981; Donovan, Chaney & O'Leary, 1978; Loberg, 1981; Stein, Rozynko & Pugh, 1971; Whitelock, Overall & Patrick, 1971), but other investigators have reported finding three (Rohan, 1972); five (Mogar, Wilson & Helmes, 1970); seven (Eshbaugh, Hoyt & Tosi, 1978) and eight (Skinner, Jackson & Hoffman, 1974) profile types. Of course, as Loberg (1981), who replicated Goldstein and Linden (1969) and Bean and Karasievich's (1975) clustering on a sample of 109 Norwegian alcoholic inpatients noted, the number of groups obtained is heavily dependent upon the clustering procedure used.

Postdiction vs. prediction: Cause or effect? Even if the MMPI profile patterns noted in the studies thus far reviewed were uniquely associated with alcoholism and problem drinking, it is questionable whether they would be useful in screening young adults, especially those applying for employment. For example, scale 2, reflecting anxiety and depression, was found to be characteristically elevated among the chronic alcoholics studied. Did this anxiety and pessimism precede or follow the problem drinking? Was it a cause or an effect? As King (1978) pointed out, "Many investigators make the mistake of attributing aberrant profiles of alcoholics and other drug abusers to personality factors that precede drug ingestion . . . when they could just as easily and perhaps more likely be a result of drug ingestion and subsequent life problems" (p. 935).

There is good reason to believe that many of the characteristics associated with chronic alcoholics' MMPIs stem from the problem drinking. The two studies in Table 1 using young men arrested for drinking offenses (Laudeman, 1977; MacAndrew, 1979) reported lower mean profiles than those using older chronic alcoholics; moreover, they both lacked the distinctive elevation on scale 2 typically found in chronic samples. The fact that Penk, Charles, Patterson, Roberts, Dolan and Brown's (1982) chronic alcoholic VA inpatients who were under 30 had elevated profiles suggests that the chronicity of the drinking pattern rather than age per se elevates the mean profile.

More cogent evidence was provided in a comparison of MMPI profiles obtained before and after problem drinking developed. Capitalizing on the fact that for many years virtually all the students who matriculated at the University of Minnesota were required to take the Minnesota Multiphasic Personality Inventory, a team of investigators sifted the records of two of the major Minneapolis alcoholism treatment centers for patients who had once attended that university. After tediously searching thousands of records they managed to identify a small group of white male alcoholic patients who, years earlier, had taken the MMPI as freshmen before they had developed a drinking problem.

Comparing 32 of these prealcoholic profiles with those of 148 randomly selected classmates, Loper, Kammeier and Hoffman (1973) found their prodromal profiles were significantly higher on scales F, Pd, and Ma. However, Kammeier, Hoffman and Loper (1973) reported that the prealcoholic profiles obtained when the men were 20 year old freshmen were lower on each and every one of the clinical scales than the retests obtained 13 years later, after they had developed serious drinking problems. Whereas the early mean profiles were quite benign, with mean T-scores ranging from 48 to 61, the later ones were elevated, with T-scores ranging from 56 to 74. This investigation suggests that much of the elevation noted in studies of serious problem drinkers follows the onset of the drinking. For those who would use the MMPI to predict alcohol-related problems among young adults, this finding is most discouraging.

MMPI Alcoholism Scales

A number of special scales to assess alcoholism or identify alcoholics have been published in the last 20 years. Table 2 provides brief descriptions of seven such scales; Al (Hampton, 1953), Am (Holmes, 1953), Ah (Hoyt & Sedlacek, 1958), MAC (MacAndrew, 1965), ARev (Rich & Davis, 1969), ALF (Finney, Smith,

TABLE 1.2
The MMPI Alcohol and Drug Scales[a]

Scale/Year	Name	Original Derivation Sample			Mean Age	SD	No. Items
Hampton, 1953	A1	AA members (N=84)	vs.	Normals (N=84)	44		125
Holmes, 1953	Am[b]	Inpatient alcoholics (N=72)	vs.	Minnesota normals			59
Hoyt & Sedlacek, 1958	Ah	Inpatient alcoholics (N=98)	vs.	Normals (N=139) & other inpatients (N=54)			68
MacAndrew, 1965	MAC	Outpatient alcoholics (N=300)	vs.	Psychiatric out-patients (N=300)	42	9.19	49
Rich & Davis, 1969	AREV	Combination of items on previous scales					40
Finney et al., 1971	ALF	Combination of issues of previous scales					85
Rosenberg, 1972	AROS	Combination of items on previous scales				8.8	27
Atsaides et al, 1977	ICAS	Inpatient alcoholics (N=70)	vs.	Neurotic Inpts.		10.62	8
Panton & Brisson, 1971	DAS	Prison inmates with history of abuse (N=118)	vs.	No history (N=118)	21	5.5	36
Cavior et al., 1967	He	Prison inmates with history of abuse (N=160)	vs.	No history (N=160)	40	5.4	57

[a]Reprinted from Zager and Megargee (1981).
[b]The scale items were published by Button (1956).

Skeeters & Auvenshine, 1971), ARos (Rosenberg, 1972) and ICAS (Atsaides, Nueringer & Davis, 1977), along with two drug abuse scales that will be discussed later, DaS (Panton & Brisson, 1971) and He (Cavior, Kurtzberg & Lipton, 1967).

It can be seen from Table 1.2 that hospitalized male alcoholic patients with mean ages over 40 served in the criterion groups for most of the alcohol scales. The contrast groups were typically normals or psychiatric patients without significant drinking problems. The criterion groups and the settings used in deriving these scales thus differ from those found in preemployment screening in several important respects.

As part of a larger study evaluating the validity of these scales for detecting alcohol and drug abuse among a sample of 1048 youthful criminal offenders, Zager and Megargee (1981) intercorrelated and factor analyzed five of these alcohol scales (Ah, ARos [also known as CAK], MAC, Al, and ICAS) and the two drug scales (DaS and He). The results are presented in Table 1.3. Considering the fact that all of these scales were derived to assess substance abuse, the lack of convergence among them was rather surprising.

Zager and Megargee (1981) described their results as follows:

Hoyt and Sedlacek's (1958) Alcoholism (Ah) Scale and Rosenberg's Composite Alcoholism Key (CAK) correlated positively ($r = .70$) with one another but negatively or negligibly with the remaining alcoholism scales, whereas the scales developed by MacAndrew (1965), Hampton (1953) and Atsaides et al. (1977) (MAC, AL and ICAS) had moderate positive correlations ranging from .33 to .44 with one another. The two drug abuse scales, Panton and Brisson's DaS and Cavior et al.'s He, correlated positively with one another ($r = .51$) and had zero-order to moderate correlations ranging from $-.03$ to .38 with the five alcoholism scales.

As might be expected from the correlational data, the factor analysis yielded three factors. Ah and the CAK had their principal loadings on the first factor, which accounted for 46% of the variance, while MAC, Al and ICAS defined the second factor, which accounted for 37% of the variance. The two drug abuse scales, DaS

TABLE 1.3
Intercorrelations of Seven Alcohol and Drug Abuse Scales*

Scales	Ah	CAK	MAC	Al	ICAS	DaS	He
Ah	--	.70	-.17	-.53	-.22	-.01	-.01
CAK	.70	--	.11	-.08	.08	.19	.21
MAC	-.17	.11	--	.33	.43	-.03	.33
Al	-.53	-.08	.33	--	.44	.27	.27
ICAS	-.22	.08	.43	.44	--	.06	.38
DaS	-.01	.19	-.03	.27	.06	--	.51
He	-.01	.21	.33	.27	.38	.51	--

*Reprinted from Zager and Megargee, 1981.

and He, defined the third factor, which accounted for the remaining 17% of the variance.

> Although it was not unexpected that the drug abuse scales would cluster separately from the alcohol scales, a finding which is consistent with their discriminant validity, the subdivision of the alcohol abuse scales into two negatively correlated subgroups had not been anticipated. This subdivision was not readily attributable to consistent differences in methods of scale derivation. Instead, it appeared due to differences in the samples used in the derivation and the vagaries of empirical item analyses. Inspections of the items revealed that some are common to different scales but are scored in the opposite direction. (p. 536)

Whether or not Zager and Megargee's (1981) explanation of the possible reasons for the differences among the scales was correct, it is clear that although these measures were all derived from the same inventory, they are not interchangable and must be evaluated individually. The alcohol scales will be discussed in this section and the drug abuse scales evaluated in the next.

Hampton's (1953) Al scale.   Hampton's Al scale was the first alcoholism scale to be published. (Holmes' Am scale was also derived in 1953, but did not appear in the literature until it was published by Button in 1956.) Miller (1976) noted, "Hampton (1953) used a highly selected criterion group to develop his alcoholism (Al) scale, requiring membership in AA, hospitalization or imprisonment, and diagnosis as alcoholic. Eighty four such alcoholics were contrasted with an equal number of nonalcoholics to produce a 125-item scale. On cross validation, with 100 alcoholics and 150 nonalcoholics, the test produced significant mean differences (p. 651).

Vega (1971) reported that the Al scale significantly differentiated alcoholics from control samples consisting of nonalcoholic psychiatric patients and normals, but this finding runs counter to the experience of a number of investigators who failed to obtain significant differences between alcoholic and nonalcoholic psychiatric patients (MacAndrew & Geertsma, 1963; Rich & Davis, 1969; Rotman & Vestre, 1964; Uecker, Kish & Ball, 1969). Apfeldorf and Hunley (1976) found no difference on Al between domiciliary patients with drinking problems and those with disciplinary problems, but reported the alcoholics did score higher than the problem-free patients. Among youthful offenders in a Federal Correctional Institution, Zager and Megargee (1981) found no convergent validity for the Al scale among whites, but reported that among the black inmates the heavy alcohol abusers scored higher than the samples of moderate alcohol abusers, heavy and moderate drug abusers, and nonsignificant substance users. Conley and Kammeier (1980) used Al in an attempt to differentiate admitted alcoholics from other types of psychiatric patients and normals. They reported it correctly identified 57% of the men and 55% of the women, rates poorer than those reported for the other scales evaluated. Reanalyzing data originally reported by

Holmes, Dungan and McLaughlin (1982), Hays and Stacy (1983b) reported Al had statistically significant but low relationships to alcoholism (Tau = .12, *p* < .05); in this study, Al did poorer than Am, MAC, and ARos.

Because Al was more successful at discriminating alcoholics from normals than from psychiatric patients, MacAndrew and Geertsma (1963) charged that Al assessed general maladjustment rather than alcoholic tendencies per se. This position was supported by Rosenberg's (1972) finding that Al correlated highly (*r* = .89) with Welsh's factor A scale, long accepted as a measure of general maladjustment, and reviewers such as Apfeldorf (1978), Butcher and Owen (1978), and Miller (1976) have reiterated this conclusion. Clopton (1978) disagreed, citing Al's lack of correlation with Am and Ah, also damned as measures of general maladjustment. Zager and Megargee (1981) sided with Clopton after finding their heavy-drug-using group, whom they presumed to have the greatest degree of maladjustment, obtained the lowest Al scores in their investigation. Measure of general maladjustment or not, it appears clear from the literature that the Al scale is one of the MMPI's least satisfactory or useful measures of alcoholic tendencies and that it would probably not be helpful in screening.

Holmes (1953) Am scale.   Although Holmes' criterion groups were less rigorously selected than Hampton's, the Am scale has generally achieved better results. Holmes contrasted the MMPI responses of 22 alcoholics committed to a state institution with those of the Minnesota normative sample on which the MMPI was standardized. On cross-validation the 59-item scale successfully discriminated alcoholics from normals. Subsequently, significant differences between alcoholics and various nonalcoholic groups were reported by Apfeldorf and Hunley (1976); Atsaides et al. (1977); Conley and Kammeier (1980); Hays and Stacy, (1983a); MacAndrew and Geertsma (1963); Rich and Davis (1969); Uecker et al. (1969); and Vega (1971). Rhodes and Chang (1978) reported Am significantly discriminated alcoholics from neurotics but not from heroin addicts. Hays and Stacy (1983a) reported modest but significant correlations with college students' self-reported drinking practices.

Nevertheless, Am is not highly regarded. Rotman and Vestre (1964) failed to find significant differences, and those reported by Holmes et al. (1982) (re-analyzed by Hays & Stacy, 1982b) and MacAndrew and Geertsma (1963) although significant statistically, were of such small magnitude that their practical usefulness was doubtful. Moreover, when MacAndrew and Geertsma, attempting to make the Am scale more subtle, removed the MMPI items bearing an obvious and direct relation to drinking problems, the point-biserial correlation with the diagnosis shrank from .34 to .22. They concluded that Am, like Al, assesses only maladjustment. Butcher and Owen (1978) agreed, but Rosenberg (1972), citing a minimal correlation with the Welsh A scale, disagreed. Studying its internal consistency, Hays and Stacy (1983a) recently concluded, ''. . . Am had essentially no homogeneity (p. 285).'' In terms of potential value for employment screening, although the evidence for the convergent validity of the Am scale is stronger than that for Al, it has been overshadowed by other scales with stronger support that would probably prove more valuable.

Hoyt and Sedlacek's (1958) Ah scale.   Hoyt and Sedlacek (1958) derived their 58-item Ah scale by contrasting the responses of 177 inpatient alcoholics with those of 710 other patients as well as 258 normals. Although MacAndrew and Geertsma (1963) found a small but significant correlation (.33) between Ah and the criterion measure and Uecker et al. (1969) reported significant mean differences between the Ah scores of male alcoholics and psychiatric patients, a number of other investigators have been unable to obtain statistically significant results (Apfeldorf & Hunley, 1976; Johnson & Cooke, 1973; Holmes et al. 1982 [reanalyzed by Hays & Stacy, 1983b]; Rich & Davis, 1969; Rotman & Vestre, 1964; Vega, 1971; Zager & Megargee, 1981). Rhodes and Chang (1978) found Ah significantly differentiated alcoholics from neurotics (with a false positive rate of 44%) but not from heroin addicts.

MacAndrew and Geertsma (1963) included Ah among the three scales they suggested assessed general maladjustment, but Rosenberg (1972) failed to find a significant correlation with Welsh's A scale and Johnson and Cooke (1973) reported significant negative correlations with such MMPI measures of maladjustment as scales F, D, Pa, Pt, Sc, and Si. Zager and Megargee also (1981) reported significant racial bias, with whites scoring significantly lower than blacks. All in all, Ah does not appear to be a promising screening device.

MacAndrew's (1965) MAC scale.   The MacAndrew (1965) alcoholism scale is by far the best regarded and most thoroughly studied of the special MMPI substance abuse scales. Whereas previous investigators had begun by contrasting the MMPI responses of alcoholics with those of normals in an effort to identify alcoholics, MacAndrew's technique was to compare the responses of outpatient alcoholics with those of other psychiatric outpatients to shed light on the question of whether alcoholics constitute a unique syndrome or are simply neurotics who drink excessively (MacAndrew, 1979).

Miller (1976) described MacAndrew's procedure:

Recognizing that previous scales had been developed only to distinguish alcoholics from normals, MacAndrew (1965) offered yet another MMPI-derived instrument. By contrasting his 300 alcoholic and 300 psychiatric outpatients, he found 51 items which discriminated the two groups ($p < .01$). MacAndrew decided to exclude the two most discriminating items from his scale because of their obvious relation to alcohol intake. These two items are: "I have used alcohol excessively" and "I have used alcohol moderately (or not at all)." The final 49-item scale was cross-validated on a comparable sample and generated a record-breaking level of significance for mean differences ($p < .000000001$). Correct assignment was 81.5%, which was increased to 84% if the two alcohol-related items were included. Mac-

Andrew maintained that these items should be deleted, however, arguing that the same increment in discrimination would be more than offset by the potential validity shrinkage if subjects should falsify them. The MacAndrew scale (MAC) thus contains 49 items. In general these items indicate that alcoholics typically report themselves to be outgoing and social, to have few problems with concentration, sex, or self-image, to have had school problems, to have religious beliefs, and to experience bodily effects of excessive alcohol intake. (p. 651)

Three comprehensive reviews of the validational literature on the MAC have recently appeared (Apfeldorf, 1978; MacAndrew, 1981; Owen & Butcher, 1979); the present reviewer will simply summarize their overall conclusions, adding the details of studies published subsequently.

Most of the early studies evaluated the concurrent validity of the MAC by comparing the scores of known alcoholics (typically middle-aged, white, male, inpatients) with contrast groups consisting of other psychiatric patients or, occasionally, normals. In most studies the mean scores of the two groups were compared, and in some the number of subjects correctly classified using Mac-Andrew's recommended cutting score of 24 or greater was also reported. Owen and Butcher's (1979) review reported the true and false positive rates as well as the overall number correctly identified.

In his review, MacAndrew (1981) summarized the results obtained with 28 samples comprising 2045 alcoholic subjects with an average age of 42.74. In these studies the overall mean MAC score was 28.84 and the overall detection rate 85.9%. In the individual studies he reviewed, the MAC scale means ranged from 26.8 to 30.9 and the overall hit rates from 79.0% to 97.5%. In the studies reviewed by Owen and Butcher (1979), most of which were also included in MacAndrew's review, the overall hit rates ranged from 55% to 95%; the false negative rates ranged from 7.0% to 10.0% with a median of 8.5%, and the false positive rate from 10.0% to 37.1% with a median of 18%. Owen and Butcher (1979) noted that there was reason to question the validity of the criterion samples used in the studies reporting high false positive rates. For example, in the study reporting a false positive rate of 37.1% (Whisler & Cantor, 1966), the "normals" consisted of domiciliary residents who had not been screened for possible drinking problems. It is possible, therefore, that some of the apparent false positives were, in fact, true positives.

Turning to the more recent studies not included in these reviews, Conley and Kammeier (1980) assessed the ability of the MAC to discriminate male and female alcoholic inpatients from nonalcoholic psychiatric patients and normals. They also compared the discriminating efficiency of the MAC with that of several other scales (Al, Am, Ah, ALF and ARos). Among men, they reported the hit rate for the MAC was better than those for Al, Am and Ah, but not as good as for ALF or ARos. Among women, the MAC scale was superior to all the others. The best discrimination of both the male and female alcoholic patients in this study was provided by seven face-valid MMPI items that dealt obviously with drinking problems. This finding supports the general notion that direct measures of drinking behavior or drug abuse would provide the most accurate identification of people with such problems if veridical answers could be obtained.

Clopton, Weiner and Davis (1980) also compared alcoholic and nonalcoholic psychiatric patients in a state hospital. These investigators reduced their overall population to 112 matched pairs of alcoholic and psychiatric patients, then randomly divided the pairs into two 56-pair subsamples. They used the first subsample to derive a discriminant function optimally combining the 13 regular MMPI scales and cross-validated this equation on the second subsample. Not surprisingly, the resulting discriminant function outperformed the MAC on the subsample from which it had been derived, but it failed to do as well on the cross-validation. The overall hit rate for the MAC was 68% on the first sample and 66% on the second. The major problem with Clopton et al.'s study was that the MAC apparently had false positive rates of 41% and 50% in the two nonalcoholic samples, even when the unusually high cutting score of 27 was used. This false positive rate is considerably higher than any others in the literature and would be disastrous in large-scale screening.

Apfeldorf and Hunley (1981) set out to determine whether the MAC scale reflects excessive drinking per se or simply identifies diagnosed alcoholics. They used samples of VA domiciliary patients who had diagnoses of (a) alcoholism, (b) psychiatric disorder (typically schizophrenia), or (c) normal. They subdivided each diagnostic category into those patients who were currently drinking to excess and those who were not. The highest MAC scores were obtained by those diagnosed as alcoholics, whether or not they were still drinking to excess. Moreover, the scale did not distinguish the excessive drinkers among the psychiatric patients or normals. The authors concluded the MAC scale is useful in identifying men who have been diagnosed as alcoholics, but not those who are currently drinking excessively.

The final recent study is also more negative than those included in the comprehensive reviews. Based on indepth interviews obtained as part of a larger longitudinal study, Zager and Megargee (1981) classified 1048 black and white youthful offenders at a Federal Correctional Institution into five groups: Heavy Alcohol Users, Moderate Alcohol Users, Heavy Drug Users, Moderate Drug Users, and Nonsignificant Substance Users. They then compared the mean scores of these five groups on a number of MMPI drug and alcohol abuse scales. There were no significant differences among the MAC scores of the five groups in either the white or the black sample. This study is disquieting because it is one of the few to use younger subjects who were not in alcoholic treatment programs.

All of the groups in Zager and Megargee's study had mean MAC scores well into the clinical range (25 or higher). Perhaps this population's criminality wiped out the intergroup differences, for there is considerable evidence that criminals and drug abusers, as well as alcoholics, obtain elevated MAC scores. Whatever the explanation, Zager and Megargee's (1981) results underscore the need to test even a scale as thoroughly studied as the MAC before applying it to a new population.

This leads us to our next major finding in the MAC literature. It is clear that the MAC is not a scale that only identifies alcoholics; a number of studies have reported that drug abusers and other socially deviant people such as juvenile delinquents and adult criminals also obtain elevated MAC scores (MacAndrew 1981). Summarizing the empirical findings with his scale, MacAndrew concluded:

> . . . (1) . . . the MAC scale taps a fundamental bipolar dimension of character; (2) . . . the character orientation which is indexed by high MAC scale scores— while not specific to alcoholism, to substance abuse, nor even to addiction in its broadest rendering—is present either as a tendency or "full-blown" in a relatively stable majority of aproximately 85% of the members of diverse samples of independently verified alcoholics; (3) . . . this character orientation is also present as a tendency or "full-blown" in a similarly stable majority of approximately 85% of the members of the diverse samples of independently verified drug abusers; (4) . . . the presence of this character orientation in such ones predates the onset of the sorts of substance usage and/or of substance usage-related comportment which leads to a diagnosis of "alcoholism" and/or "drug abuse/addiction"; (5) . . . a stable minority of independently identified alcoholics give every appearance of being "neurotics-who-also-drink-too-much. . . ." (p. 66)

Noting that he had developed the MAC "on and for men", and limiting his generalizations accordingly, MacAndrew went on to differentiate two types of alcoholics; bold, assertive, "primary" alcoholics who obtain high scores on the MAC and more passive, neurotic, "secondary" alcoholics who do not score high on the scale. In short, he maintains that instead of tapping alcoholism or problem drinking per se, the MAC scale may assess a characterological deficit, a rather psychopathic orientation, that is common to many alcoholics, drug abusers, and criminals.

Since all of these groups are rather undesirable and share a propensity for causing problems, this could make the MAC scale of even greater potential value in screening than if it merely measured drinking behavior. Certainly, of the scales discussed thus far, the MAC appears to have the greatest potential, and a longitudinal test of its predictive validity would appear warranted. Particularly important in an employment context is the fact that, unlike many of the MMPI clinical scales, the MAC thus far has been demonstrably free of racial or ethnic bias (Page & Rozlee, 1982; Zager & Megargee, 1981).

Rich and Davis' (1969) ARev scale.   Rich and Davis compared item lists for the Al, Am and Ah scales and combined 40 of the 42 items common to at least two of these three scales into a new scale, ARev (Miller, 1976). The MMPIs of samples of 60 male and 60 female alcoholics, along with equal-sized samples of psychiatric patients and normals (including a particularly inappropriate subsample of college student volunteers) were scored for this new ARev scale, as well as for Al, Am, Ah, and MAC, and the concurrent validities of these five scales were compared. The MAC scale was the best at differentiating the 60 female alcoholics from the 60 female psychiatric patients, but in all the other comparisons ARev proved superior.

Miller (1976) criticized Rich and Davis' investigation for a failing common to many such studies, namely using equal numbers of subjects in the criterion and contrast groups: "The base rate of alcoholism in this research sample should be noted, though. For both comparisons (alcoholic versus normal and alcoholic versus psychiatric control), the expected value was .50, whereas in any standard normal or psychiatric sample, the base rate of alcoholism is much lower. This elevated base rate probably provides exaggerated estimates of the power of these tests to identify alcoholics within a general clinical setting" (p. 653). Miller's point is well taken, and the complications of the base-rate problem for screening will be explored in the concluding section of this chapter.

Little has been done with ARev since its derivation. If an investigator was to administer the MMPI in an attempt to determine its usefulness in screening, it would be worth scoring it for ARev as well as for MAC to test the scale's usefulness further.

Finney, Smith, Skeeters and Auvenshine's (1971) ALF Scale.   Finney et al. (1971) manufactured a second combined scale, ALF, this one combining items from four previously described scales (AL, Am, Ah, and MAC) as well as Haertzen, Hill and Monroe's (1968) AAF scale designed for differentiating alcoholics from drug addicts. Little research has been reported on the 85-item ALF scale. In a recent study (Conley & Kammeier, 1980) it compared favorably with the MAC scale, differentiating alcoholics from normals and psychiatric patients somewhat better than Al, Am, or Ah, but not as well as yet another combined scale, ARos.

Rosenberg's (1972) ARos scale.   Rosenberg (1972) attempted to derive a combined alcoholism scale that would not be influenced by overall maladjustment. Using a sample of 111 male veterans in an alcoholic treatment unit and a comparison group of 56 psychiatric patients originally tested by Uecker (1970), Rosenberg scored the protocols for the Ah, Am, Al, and MAC scales as well Welsh's Factor A scale. Finding that Al correlated $+.89$ with Welsh's A scale, he eliminated it from further consideration, reasoning it merely reflected general adjustment. He noted the remaining three scales, Ah, Am, and MAC had low intercorrelations with one another; deducing from this that each tapped somewhat different sources of variance, he selected the six items common to all three scales and the 21 items common to two of the three for his "Combined Alcoholism Key" (CAK, more often referred to in the literature as ARos). He found this scale discriminated the psychiatric patients from the hospitalized alcoholics.

Conley and Kammeier (1980) compared ARos with Al, Am, Ah, MAC, and ALF in its ability to discriminate 903 male alcoholics from 153 male psychiatric patients as well as 324 female alcoholics from 240 female psychiatric patients. They found that ARos correctly identified 70.5% of the men and 64.8% of the women. This made ARos the most successful of the scales tested in discriminating among the male patients, but less successful than MAC among the women. Holmes et al.'s (1982) data (reanalyzed by Hays & Stacy, 1983b) showed ARos to be one of the two best discriminating scales, equaling Am and exceeding Al, Ah, and MAC. However the absolute level of accuracy was too low to be useful.

Zager and Megargee (1981) found that their heavy alcohol users had the highest scores on ARos, followed closely by heavy drug users. Among their white subjects, the scores of these two "heavy" groups were significantly higher than those of the moderate alcohol, moderate drug, and nonsignificant users; in the black sample, however, the differences only approached statistical significance ($p = .07$). Moreover, the races differed significantly, with each of the black samples scoring significantly lower than their white counterparts.

Hoffman, Loper and Kammeier (1974) reported that ARos was one of only two scales (MAC being the other) that significantly differentiated prealcoholic University of Minnesota freshmen from their classmates who did not subsequently develop drinking problems. It would thus appear that the ARos scale should be one of those included in any study investigating the feasibility of using MMPI as a screening device.

Atsaides, Nueringer and Davis' (1977) ICAS Scale.   The last and also the least scale (insofar as the number of items is concerned) is Atsaides et al.'s eight-item Institutionalized Chronic Alcoholic Scale (ICAS). Atsaides et al. (1977) maintained (on the basis of Whisler and Cantor's (1966) study of domiciliary patients) that the MAC scale was inadequate. We have already noted the deficiencies in the contrast group used in that study. Rhodes and Chang (1978) also criticized Atsaides et al. for raising MacAndrew's recommended cutting score from 24 to 28, and Clopton (1978) in his review rebuked them for ignoring the many studies in the literature supporting the usefulness of the MAC scale.

Atsaides et al. (1977) selected 70 42 year old inpatient alcoholics and a contrast group of 70 41 year old inpatient neurotics. These two samples were divided in half and the responses of each subsample were item analyzed. Only eight items were statistically significant ($p < .05$) in both analyses and they were selected for the ICAS scale. Atsaides et al. then scored the total sample of 140 MMPIs on the new scale to establish the optimal cutting score. Next, they compared the hit rate using this optimal score with the number of correct classifications obtained using the published cutting scores for the Am, Ah, and MAC scales. Not surprisingly, the ICAS outperformed the others, correctly classifying 86% of the alcoholics and 84% of the neurotics. The surprising aspect is that subsequent reviewers (cf. Clopton, 1978) have failed to point out that this was a totally inappropriate comparison because the new scale was being applied back to the original derivation samples, thereby enjoying a considerable "home court" advantage.

A better estimate of the comparative efficiency of the ICAS was provided by Rhodes and Chang (1978), who applied the scale, along with MAC, Ah, and Am, to the MMPIs of 155 male VA inpatients, 75 alcoholics, 50 neurotics and 30 heroin addicts. The ICAS correctly identified 84% of the alcoholics and 68% of the neurotics, but only 40% of the addicts. The MAC and Am scales were somewhat more accurate.

Relatively little research has yet been published using the ICAS. Although it was derived on an older population, Zager and Megargee (1981) reported that among their white, youthful offenders the heavy-alcohol group scored significantly higher than each and every one of the other five groups, including the heavy drug users. Similar, but somewhat less clearcut, mean differences were obtained among their black subjects. The good news was that application of the recommended cutting score correctly identified 82% of the heavy alcohol users in the white sample, and 87% among the black. The bad news was that this cutting score resulted in false positive rates of 46% and 54% among the white and black nonsignificant users respectively. Increasing the cutting score to reduce the number of false positives would, of course, also decrease the number of true positives as well.

Summary and Conclusions

Over three decades ago, after reviewing all the available empirical studies that had attempted to differentiate the personality traits of alcoholics from those of nonalcoholics, Sutherland, Schroeder, and Tordella (1950) concluded, "No satisfactory evidence has been discovered that justifies a conclusion that persons of one type are more likely to become alcoholics than persons of another type" (p. 559). Over the years others have attempted to delineate a "prealcoholic personality type" with equal lack of success (Lang, 1983). As Owen and Butcher (1979) have noted, "Any attempts to understand personality factors in addictive behavior that fail to take into account the situational context in which the individual is immersed, and the environmental stressors acting upon them (sic) are doomed to incomplete results" (p. 84).

Nevertheless, the literature on the MMPI has shown that certain clinical scales and some of the specialized scales for the assessment of alcoholism are reliably associated with chronic alcoholism. This association is far from perfect. There is no MMPI pattern or scale that is uniquely or exclusively associated with alcoholism. The literature indicates that there are various types of alcoholics, only some of whom may be detectable by the MMPI. Moreover, the MMPI patterns most closely associated with problem drinking, as well as high scores on the scales devised to identify problem drinkers, are also found among other deviant groups such as drug abusers and criminals. If employers are interested in identifying these other types of social deviants as well as problem drinkers, this lack of discriminant validity is less worrisome.

Of greater concern is the age of most of the alcoholics studied. Most samples were considerably older than the young adults who would be assessed in entry level preemployment screening. Moreover, most were acknowledged chronic alcoholics who were taking the MMPI in inpatient settings. Their emotional condition and their approach to the test would obviously differ greatly from applicants for employment, who would be motivated to present themselves as favorably as possible. Before the MMPI could actually be used in identifying job applicants who have alcohol-related problems or are likely to develop them, longitudinal empirical studies determining its feasibility for this purpose will be needed.

THE MMPI AND THE USE OF ILLICIT DRUGS

Performance of Drug-Abusing Samples on the Regular MMPI Scales

A number of studies have examined the performance of various samples of drug users and abusers on the regular clinical scales of the MMPI.[2] Some investigators

[2]In the last decade a substantial and varied literature has accumulated on the characteristics of various types of drug-using groups tested in a broad array of settings. Whereas there have been several excellent reviews of the MMPI literature on alcoholism, this is not true of the MMPI drug abuse literature, so the reader is forced to go directly to the primary sources. In order to avoid bogging down the text with a seemingly endless list of citations, the primary sources used in this section will be listed alphabetically in this footnote: Berzins, Ross and English, 1974; Berzins, Ross, and Monroe, 1971; Black, 1975; Black and Heald, 1975; Brill, Crumpton and Grayson, 1971; Brook, Szandorowska and Whitehead, 1976; Burke and Eichberg, 1972; Collins, 1979; Fitzgibbons, Berry and Shearn, 1973; Gendreau, Andrews and Wormith, 1977; Gendreau and Gendreau, 1970; Greaves, 1971; Heller and Mordkoff, 1972; Henriques, Arsenian, Cutter and Samuraweeka, 1972; Holland, 1977; Jarvis, Sumnegar, and Traweek, 1975; Keller and Redfinger, 1973; Kojak and Canby, 1975; Kwant, Rice and Hays, 1976; Lachar, Gdowski and Keegan, 1979; Lerner & Wesson, 1973; McAree, Steffenhagen and Zheutlin, 1969 & 1972; McGuire and Megargee, 1974; MacLachlan, 1975a; Overall, 1973; Panton and Behre, 1973; Patalano, 1980a, 1980b; Penk, Fudge, Robinowitz and Newman, 1979; Penk, Roberts, Robinowitz, Dolan and Atkins, 1982; Penk and Robinowitz, 1976; Penk, Woodward, Robinowitz and Hess, 1978; Penk, Woodward, Robinowitz and Parr, 1980; Penk, Robinowitz, Roberts, Dolan and Atkins, 1981; Pittel, 1971; Ross and Berzins, 1974; Sheppard, Ricca, Fracchia and Merlis, 1973; Smart & Fejer, 1969; Spiegel, Hadley and Hadley, 1970; Steffenhagen, Schmidt, and McAree, 1971; Stein and Rozynko, 1974; Sutker, 1971; Sutker and Allain, 1973; Trevithick and Hosch, 1978; Zager and Megargee, 1981; Zuckerman, Sola, Masterson and Angelonie, 1975.

have attempted to test the hypothesis that different personality types are associated with each drug and, have, therefore, selected samples according to their preferred substance. Others have used heterogeneous samples. In this section we examine the mean MMPI profiles associated with three broad groupings: heroin abusers, polydrug abusers, and other drug abusers.

Heroin users. The mean MMPI profiles of 20 samples of heroin users totaling 2,986 subjects are presented in Table 1.4. Most of the subjects are male, and their mean ages are considerably younger than the alcoholics whose profiles were included in Table 1.1. Several samples include blacks and Hispanics as well as whites.

It can be seen from Table 4 that the average MMPI profiles of heroin users differ in certain important respects from those of alcoholics. Their mean elevations are considerably higher, with more scales exceeding the T-score of 70, which is generally considered the clinically significant level. Scales 8 (Schizophrenia) and 9 (Mania) are more prominent, suggesting the use of psychotic defenses such as withdrawal and denial. The profiles indicate more alienation and psychopathology than was found among the problem drinkers.

One issue addressed by several investigations was whether one obtained different MMPI profiles from patients who were taking the test voluntarily as opposed to involuntarily. (It was thought that this distinction might underlie some of the differences obtained between addicts seeking treatment and addicts who were incarcerated.) In the best-controlled test of this hypothesis, Penk and Robinowitz (1976) found that VA patients voluntarily seeking treatment obtained substantially higher scores on several MMPI scales including Pd, Pt, Sc, and Ma than did VA patients being treated involuntarily. Assuming that voluntariness was the key issue accounting for the differences in these MMPI profiles, the implications are disturbing for those who would use the MMPI as a screening device. The results suggest that much more benign MMPI profiles are found when the test is administered to people who may be motivated to minimize their psychopathology.

Also noteworthy is Kojak and Canby's (1975) study of U.S. servicemen in Thailand whose heroin use was discovered through urinalysis screening. Although their three-point code is similar to that of the other heroin-using groups, the average elevation found among these servicemen was considerably lower with no scales approaching a mean T-score of 70. In fact, Kojak and Canby found these profiles did not differ significantly from those of 50 randomly chosen servicemen with negative urinalyses. This is a further indication that the personality test data obtained on drug abusers in clinical settings may differ considerably from the patterns found among recreational users in the community.

Polydrug samples. Table 1.5 presents the mean profiles for 33 samples of patients who used a wide variety of drugs. Compared with the previous tables,

TABLE 1.4
Mean MMPI Profiles and Three Point Codes of Twenty Samples of Heroin Users

Study	Sample	N	Sex	Race
1. Berzins, Ross, English, & Haley, 1974	Addicts in USPHS Hospital*	750 750	M W	50%W; 50%B 50%W; 50%B
2. Kojak & Canby, 1975	US Servicemen in Thailand	25	M	--
3. Kwant, Rice & Hays, 1976	Prisoners in Methadone Program	76 21	M F	56%W 25%B 20%Mexican
4. Penk & Robinowitz, 1976	VA pts volunteering for treatmt VA pts not volunteering for treatment	34 34	M F	not reported
5. Penk, Woodward & Hess, 1978	VA pts volunteering for treatmt VA pts volunteering for treatmt	120 252	M M	W B
6. Penk, Fudge, Robinowitz and Newman, 1979	VA first admissions	65	M	White
7. Penk, Robinowitz, Roberts, Dolan & Atkins, 1981	First admission VA pts; volunteering for treatment	41 161 268	M M M	Hispanic White Black
8. Penk, Woodward, Robinowitz & Parr, 1980	VA first admissions	132	M	
9. Sheppard, Ricca, Fracchia & Merlis, 1973	State Hospital voluntary Commitments	42	M	--
10. Sutker, 1971	Prisoners	40	M	
11. Sutker & Allain, 1973	Prisoners "Street Addicts" seeking treatments	35 82	M M	-- --
12. Zuckerman, Sola, Masterson & Angelonie, 1975	Pts who stayed in treatment Pts who quit treatment	28 30	M M	57%W; 44%B 60%W; 40%B

*Overall means calculated by present investigator.

many more women are included among these 3255 subjects and the average ages are quite young with many groups being in their teens.

The most striking aspect of these mean profiles is the extraordinarily elevated scores on scales 4, 8, and 9. As a general rule, mean MMPI profiles are rather benign and insipid, as many of the extreme deviations found in individual profiles are lost in the process of averaging. Not so with these means. To yield mean T-scores exceeding 75 and even 80, the individual profiles comprising these polydrug-using samples must be consistently elevated. The most deviant profiles are found among the youngest samples, perhaps stemming in part from the application of adult rather than adolescent norms.

Given the heterogeneity of these 33 samples and the broad array of settings in which they were evaluated, it is not surprising that the profiles and their associated three-point codes are more heterogeneous than those found among the heroin addicts. There is little evidence of any unitary addiction-prone personality

Mean Age	VALIDITY SCALES						CLINICAL SCALES							Three Point Code
	L	F	K	Hs	D	Hy	Pd	Mf	Pa	Pt	Sc	Ma	Si	
--	--	60	55	64	86	64	75	59	62	62	65	60	68	2"4'8-
--	--	64	50	61	64	63	75	52	61	61	66	65	58	4'79-
18-25	49	59	50	57	61	58	64	57	61	60	62	63	50	426-
25.8	48	67	49	68	74	64	76	59	61	69	72	69	59	428'
27.9	47	64	47	60	67	63	74	49	63	63	65	68	57	4'28-
21.9	47	76	45	72	77	69	81	63	71	74	85	80	56	849"
20.2	52	59	54	55	58	57	69	58	57	60	62	70	55	9T48-
28.2	46	72	48	70	76	67	79	62	66	73	77	72	59	482'
30.9	49	68	50	69	71	64	74	60	64	68	73	69	54	482'
23	50	69	51	49	52	48	68	55	59	64	64	70	48	9'478-
31.5	51	66	50	69	76	64	73	55	62	70	71	66	55	248'
27.8	47	66	48	67	75	66	77	61	63	70	71	70	57	428'
31.2	49	64	50	68	70	64	74	60	61	67	70	70	54	4298'
ca.25	48	65	49	50	70	64	75	61	63	68	72	70	55	4829'
--	50	49	50	61	72	59	77	60	63	68	73	70	57	482'
27	47	62	49	64	75	65	81	58	62	69	69	68	55	4"2'78-
27	49	62	50	53	64	55	76	58	59	59	62	68	50	4' 92-
27	48	63	50	67	73	65	79	58	61	69	68	69	55	42' 79-
22.4	--	69	47	60	71	62	76	64	64	66	72	72	55	489'
23.8	--	73	46	64	71	63	78	64	70	74	80	76	57	8"49'

type, and, as we shall see when we discuss typological studies, most investigators found considerable diversity among the individual profiles that were averaged.

Profiles associated with specific drug preferences: Amphetamines, LSD, Marijuana. In searching for personality types associated with specific substances, some investigators have tested groups characterized by particular drug preferences. (See Table 1.6.) Some, for example, have sought to test the notion that amphetamine users are depressed and need stimulation, whereas barbiturate and heroin users are anxious and require sedation. These hypotheses have generally not been supported (Gendreau,Andrews,& Wormith 1977; Henriques, Arsenian, Cutter & Samuraweeka, 1972; Pittel, 1971). Instead, it appears that once a person moves beyond alcohol and marijuana into the use of harder drugs, specialization seems less common. People tend to use what is available, although

TABLE 1.5
Mean MMPI and Three Point Codes for Polydrug Samples

Study	Sample	N	Sex	Race
1. Berzins, Ross & Monroe, 1971	Civily committed addicts	200	M	57%W; 43%B
	Voluntarily committed addicts	204	M	53%W; 47%B
	Addicts on probation	210	M	57%W; 43%B
	Addicts in prison	213	M	23%W; 77%B
2. Black & Heald, 1975	Servicemen in treatment prgm	50	M	
3. Burke & Eichenberg, 1972	Inpatient adolescent drug users	53	M	
	Inpatient adolescent drug users	34	F	
	Outpatient adolescent drug users	34	M	
	Outpatient adolescent drug users	36	F	
4. Gendreau, Andrews & Wormith, 1977	Canadian Prisoners (Mostly burglary)	23	M	
5. Hill, Haertzen & Davis, 1962	Addicts in State Hospital 40% voluntary; 60% sentenced	192	M	
6. Holland, 1977	Prisoners: Low Alcohol/High Drug	43	M	
	Prisoners: High Alcohol/Low Drug	45	M	
	Prisoners: High Alcohol/High Drug	61	M	
7. Keegan & Lachar, 1979	Inpts who stayed in treatment	104	M&F	88%W; 12%B
	Inpts who quit treatment	70	M&F	78%W; 21%B
8. McGuire & Megargee, 1974	Federal Prisoners Heavy Multiple Drug Users	24	M	79%W; 21%B
9. Panton & Behre, 1973	State Prisoner Addicts	32	M	50%W; 50%B
10. Patalano, 1980, 1981	Abusers in residential treatment	80	F	50%W; 50%B
11. Penk, Roberts et al., 1982	VA patients seeking treatment	494	M	W
	for use of multiple nonopiate	159	M	B
12. Penk & Robinowitz, 1976	VA patients admitted voluntarily	34	M	
	VA patients admitted involuntarily	34	M	
13. Penk, Woodward, Robinowitz & Parr, 1980	VA inpatients, first admission	122	M	
14. Ross & Berzins, 1974	Committed addicts		F	
	Voluntary hospitalized addicts	395	F	
	Federal prisoners		F	
	Probationers		F	
15. Schoolar, White & Cohen, 1972	Pts seeking treatmnt at drug clin	53	M	
	Pts seeking treatmnt at drug clin	27	F	
16. Stein & Rozynuko, 1974	Voluntary admission to state hosp 91% used heroin on daily basis 35% admitted present addiction 70% used other drugs	201	M	67%W 17%B 12%Chicano
17. Zuckerman, Sola, Masteron & Angelonie, 1975	Pts who stayed in treatment	14	F	71%W; 29%B
	Pts who quit treatment	14	F	93%W; 7%B

Mean Age	VALIDITY SCALES			CLINICAL SCALES										Three Point Code
	L	F	K	Hs	D	Hy	Pd	Mf	Pa	Pt	Sc	Ma	Si	
ca30	--	63	56	65	72	67	73	61	65	69	72	64	53	428'
"	--	64	55	66	76	66	77	61	64	69	71	66	54	428'
"	--	64	53	62	72	63	78	60	64	66	71	65	55	428'
"	--	63	54	63	68	62	75	62	62	64	69	67	53	4'82-
20.7	52	68	53	63	64	63	72	64	66	68	75	72	52	849'
19.7	47	83	48	65	81	70	82	75	75	82	96	74	64	8*47"
18.7	46	83	48	62	71	69	81	48	76	71	87	71	64	84"6'
17.2	45	76	51	59	66	65	79	74	67	72	86	74	55	48'69-
17.0	45	74	47	54	65	63	77	46	69	68	77	69	61	48'69-
--	47	72	46	55	63	56	76	57	66	67	71	70	57	4'89-
37.4	50	58	53	61	68	60	74	58	57	60	60	62	--	4'29-
	54	56	57	54	59	58	70	58	59	57	58	58	53	4'-26/
26.5	52	60	54	59	62	59	71	58	60	60	61	60	54	4'28-
	52	62	53	54	60	57	72	60	60	62	62	65	53	4'978-
25.8	46	68	46	66	72	67	74	--	64	68	73	68	56	482'
25	45	74	44	70	77	69	81	--	70	72	81	74	57	84"2'
22	51	62	55	56	62	63	76	65	61	62	66	69	48	4'98-
--	--	--	--	61	63	61	76	64	59	60	63	67	47	4'95-
--	48	68	48	61	69	62	78	65	65	69	76	72	57	489'
	46	70	45	58	65	58	78	49	68	65	73	71	63	489'
28	48	73	49	69	77	68	79	64	69	74	81	72	58	8"42'
27	50	75	49	70	73	66	75	61	68	72	80	74	56	8"49'
21.7	47	72	48	68	74	69	83	69	68	76	84	76	55	84"79'
20.0	53	64	58	61	64	61	71	59	59	63	70	66	53	482'
25	50	68	49	66	71	65	75	62	64	70	74	68	56	482'
27.8	--	60	56	60	65	64	71	53	63	61	65	62	54	4'28-
35.3	--	62	49	64	68	65	72	53	64	62	65	64	60	4'2'38
29.4	--	62	49	59	62	59	73	56	65	59	64	64	60	4'689-
30.2	--	63	49	60	66	61	76	54	65	63	67	65	60	4'82-
19.2	48	74	51	64	73	67	80	68	69	76	85	73	59	84"7'
19.2	47	67	49	61	66	65	79	49	65	67	72	69	57	48'9-
25.5	47	72	47	50	82	64	68	64	65	49	54	--	--	
20.1	--	72	47	63	71	66	83	50	73	70	80	74	57	48"9'
i7.7	--	88	35	73	73	71	81	54	83	76	90	80	65	8*64"

TABLE 1.6
Mean MMPI Profiles and Three Point Codes for Eleven Samples with Other Drug Preference

| Preferred Drug | SUBJECTS | | | | |
	Study	Sample	N	Sex	Race
	Brook, Szandorowska & Whitehead, 1976	Chronic users at residential treatment center	86 31	M F	W
Amphet- amines	Gendreau, Andrews & Wormith, 1977	"Light"-using Canadian prisoners	21	M	W
		"Heavy"-using Canadian prisoners	34	M	W
	Penk, Fudge, Robin- owitz & Newman, 1979	Daily-using first admission VA inpatients	45	M	W
Barbit- urates	Penk, Fudge, Robin- owitz & Newman, 1979	Daily-using first admission VA inpatients	34	M	W
	Keller & Redfinger, 1973	Average use: 90 times Range: 5 to 490 times	60	M&F	
L.S.D.	Zuckerman, Sola, Masterson & Angel- onie, 1975	"Soft" drug pts who stayed in treatment	27	M	96%W; 4%B
		"Soft" drug pts who quit treatment	32	M	84%W; 16%B
Mari- juana	McGuire & Megargee, 1974	Federal prisoners used occasionally	24	M	79%W; 21%B
		Federal prisoners used regularly	24	M	79%W; 21%B

those who are physiologically dependent will seek those substances that will best satisfy their particular dependency.

Marijuana is, of course, the major exception to most of these generalizations regarding illicit drugs.[3] Because it has achieved considerable social acceptance in many elements of society, especially among younger adults, its use is not associated with the same degree of social deviance as other illicit drugs and, not surprisingly, the tested personality characteristics of those who have experimented with marijuana or use it with some degree of regularity are consistently found to be more favorable than those of people who use other illicit substances (Brill, Crumpton & Grayson, 1971; Greene & Haymes, 1973; Hogan, Mankin, Conway & Fox, 1970; Kurtines, Hogan & Weiss, 1975; McAree, Steffenhagen & Zheutlin, 1969; 1972; McGuire & Megargee, 1974; Steffenhagen, Schmidt & McAree, 1971). Indeed some studies among college students and other young adults have shown the marijuana users as a group to be better adjusted in certain respects than their peers who absolutely refrain from any use of marijuana.

[3]Cocaine might be another exception since it has for decades enjoyed an "uptown" image. However, in contrast to the users of others less prestigious illicit substances, cocaine-users have not yet contributed greatly to the MMPI literature.

	VALIDITY SCALES			CLINICAL SCALES										
Mean Age	L	F	K	Hs	D	Hy	Pd	Mf	Pa	Pt	Sc	Ma	Si	Point Three Code
Range	47	79	46	71	83	70	83	--	72	83	92	74	64	8*247''
15-26	45	60	43	66	75	70	87		77	78	92	75	67	8*4''7
---	48	67	47	56	59	59	70	60	62	61	71	70	53	849'
---	47	74	47	63	66	62	75	57	63	69	77	76	55	894'
23	48	74	46	55	65	55	77	61	68	74	75	67	57	487'
23	51	71	46	57	62	55	68	60	63	68	75	68	58	8'49-
---	--	--	--	57	60	62	70	75/89	62	63	71	69	63	584'
19.6	--	69	46	62	74	63	80	69	66	74	76	69	63	4''827'
19.4	--	81	45	65	83	66	83	64	77	82	91	74	64	8*24''
22	50	56	54	54	57	57	69	55	57	59	57	69	49	49-7/
22	54	55	58	57	59	60	64	63	58	58	56	58	61	450-

Profile heterogeneity.   As was the case with alcoholics, the MMPI profiles of individual drug abusers deviate markedly from their groups' mean profiles. Although Patalano (1980b) found that 80% of the polydrug abusers he studied fell into seven two-point codes, Black (1975) reported considerable variability among the profiles of Army personnel identified as heroin addicts. Penk, Woodward, Robinowitz and Parr (1980) found that the MMPI profiles of their heroin users scattered over 17 different two-point codes and their polydrug users over 18, while Zuckerman, Sola, Masterson and Angelonie (1975) reported their subjects fell into all 24 of the code types delineated by Gilberstadt and Duker (1965).

The diversity is even more apparent when we examine the most common code types in the various studies. In Patalano's sample the two most frequent codes were 48/84 and 49/94, each accounting for 20% of the total. Penk et al. (1980), however, found the 824 code type to be most common among their subjects (16%), while Zuckerman et al.'s (1975) favorites were 24/42 and 49/94 (14% each). Penk et al. (1980) concluded, ". . . the extraordinary variety, of personality types found for both heroin and polydrug abusers was interpreted as unequivocally refuting the notion that one personality type is addiction prone" (p. 299).

As one would expect, researchers have cluster-analyzed the MMPI profiles of drug abusers to differentiate homogeneous subtypes. Some have isolated two (Berzins, Ross & English, 1974; Heller & Mordkoff, 1972) or three (Collins, 1979; Rothaizer, 1980) types, but others have differentiated as many as 10 (Stein & Rozynko, 1974). Moreover, it is not unusual to find more than half the profiles do not fall into any cluster at all (Berzins et al., 1974; Rothaizer, 1980). As Penk et al. (1982) pointed out, these findings are discouraging for those who would seek a unitary personality profile uniquely associated with illicit drug abuse or addiction.

MMPI Drug Abuse Scales

As we have noted, a number of alcohol abuse scales have been derived for the MMPI, some of which also identify people who abuse illicit psychoactive substances. In addition to these alcohol scales, two scales have been specifically derived to identify drug abusers, Panton and Brisson's (1971) Drug Abuse scale (DaS) and Cavior, Kurtzberg and Lipton's (1967) Heroin (He) scale. Each will be examined in turn.

Panton and Brisson's (1971) Drug Abuse (DaS) Scale.   Panton and Brisson (1971) compared 118 North Carolina prison inmates with a history of drug abuse with 118 other prisoners with no such history. They found the two groups differed on a number of social and demographic characteristics as well as in their responses to psychological tests. Using empirical item analysis techniques they derived a 36-item scale to identify drug users. Applied back to the derivation sample, a cutting score of 16 correctly identified 75% of the drug users and 81% of the nonusers.

Muschewske (1972) applied the DaS to a sample of Kansas State prisoners; increasing the cutting score to 18, he reported that 68% of the overall cross-validation sample was correctly classified.

In the most comprehensive validation study of this scale to date, Zager and Megargee (1981) tested the DaS on their five samples of youthful federal prisoners; Heavy Drug Users (HDU); Moderate Drug Users (MDU); Heavy Alcohol Users (HAL), Moderate Alcohol Users (MAL) and Nonsignificant Substance Highly Users (NSU). Highly significant differences were found among these five groups in both the white and the black samples. Among the whites, the two drug-using groups obtained mean scores significantly higher than those of the other three groups, thereby demonstrating discriminant as well as convergent validity. Using the suggested cutting score of 16, 81% of the HDU and 71% of the MDU groups were correctly identified, with a false positive rate of 39% among the NSU groups.

Highly significant differences were also obtained among the black groups and, as in the white sample, the HDU group attained the highest scores. However, unlike the white sample, the black HDU group was not significantly higher than the other black drug and alcohol-using groups, although it did exceed the NSU group reliably. Using the recommended cutting score of 16, 66% of the HDU group was identified, but only 32% of the MDU group; the false positive rate among NSU subjects was 30%. Finally, significant racial differences were observed, with the whites scoring higher than the blacks at similiar levels of substance usage.

The DaS scale, derived on state prisoners, thus showed good convergent and fair discriminant validity when applied to federal offenders. It remains to be seen how well it can discriminate among substance abusers outside correctional settings. Based on the data collected thus far, it should be included among those scales used in any empirical test of screening effectiveness.

Cavior, Kurtzberg and Lipton's (1967) Heroin (He) Scale.   Cavior et al. (1967) compared the MMPI protocols of 160 prisoners with histories of heroin use with those of 160 with no such histories to derive their 40-item Heroin scale. One problem with evaluating this scale is the specificity of the criterion. If, for example, individuals abusing drugs other than heroin should score high on the scale, should they be counted as a true or false positives? Does it depend on how closely allied the drug is to heroin? As we test abusers of alcohol, marijuana, barbiturates, methadone, and heroin, where do we cross the line from an incorrect to a correct classification?

Sutker (1971) compared the He scores of 40 heroin addicts with those of a matched sample of 40 nonaddicted prisoners and obtained data supporting the scale's validity. Similarly Sheppard, Ricca, Fracchia, Rosenberg, and Merlis (1972) found higher scores among male heroin addicts admitted to a state hospital than among male alcoholics admitted to a state hospital or male veterans admitted to an alcoholic treatment unit. Kwant, Rice and Hays (1976) compared the He scores of male and female heroin addicts to those of vocational rehabilitation clients. Finding that He correlated +.41 with group membership, they concluded, "The success of the He scale in discriminating addicts from nonaddicts has been demonstrated" (p. 552). Unfortunately they also demonstrated racial bias, with black subjects scoring lower than the whites and Mexican-Americans.

Burke and Marcus (1977) compared the MAC and He scales' abilities to discriminate among black and white alcoholics, drug abusers, and general medical patients. They ascertained that 10 of the 13 patients (77%) with diagnoses of drug abuse scored at or above the cutting score of 36, while 57 of 72 patients (79%) with no such histories were correctly classified by scoring below 36. Although He successfully discriminated these patients, the investigators concluded that it was not powerful enough to be used as a general screening device.

Zager and Megargee (1981) evaluated the He scale by subdividing their Heavy Drug Use group into those who were strongly involved in heroin (HNARC) and those who were more oriented toward other drugs (MNARC). Significant overall mean differences were obtained in both white and black samples, with the HNARC having the highest scores, although these scores were not significantly higher than those attained by the MNARC group. The investigators concluded that if He was regarded as strictly a heroin scale it lacked discriminant validity, but that it was useful as a more generalized measure of substance abuse, including alcohol. They also noted significant racial differences in favor of blacks.

Summary and Conclusions

The MMPI drug abuse literature resembles the alcohol reports in certain salient respects and differs in others. Like alcoholics, drug abusers as a group have elevated MMPI profiles with elevations on Scale 4 being a common, although hardly universal, feature. As with alcoholics, considerable diversity underlies these mean profiles with virtually every conceivable two-point code being represented.

The drug-abusing samples studied were, for the most part, considerably younger than the alcoholics and much closer in age to the young adults who would be screened for most entry-level positions. This means that the cause–effect issue is less important among the drug-using subjects than it is among the alcoholics. Whether serious personality problems lead to drug abuse or drug abuse leads to personality problems is immaterial if the problems are reflected in the MMPI profiles at the time of screening.

The drug literature highlighted the problems of motivation and set more clearly than the alcohol literature because not all samples participated freely and voluntarily. Those samples that were not seeking treatment typically had much more normal profiles. Were their problems simply less serious, which is why they were not motivated to seek therapy? Or were they presenting themselves in an overly favorable light, that is, faking good? Both factors may have been at work, but in either case it suggests the MMPI profiles of drug-abusing subjects who are not actively seeking treatment are apt to be rather benign. Since these are the types of substance abusers who are most likely to be taking the MMPI in preemployment screening, these data imply that we might expect a higher false negative rate in the screening situation. Empirical research is required to test this hypothesis.

Possession of marijuana is illegal, so that any use whatsoever may pose a problem for some employers, such as law enforcement agencies. However, recreational use of marijuana is so widely accepted among young adults in this country that it can hardly be considered socially deviant in this population. Most subjects who occasionally use moderate amounts of marijuana and/or alcohol are not suffering from detectable psychopathology and cannot be effectively identified by means of personality tests such as the MMPI.

CONCLUSIONS AND RECOMMENDATIONS

Law enforcement agencies, professional sports teams, the military, and many private employers would welcome a psychological assessment technique that could accurately and inexpensively identify people with current or potential substance abuse problems. Is the MMPI such an instrument?

The literature we have reviewed indicates that distinctively elevated MMPI profiles and high scores on certain substance abuse scales have been repeatedly obtained among many samples of diagnosed alcoholics and drug abusers. However, there are some important reservations about the relevance of this literature to screening. First, although the ages of the heroin addicts and polydrug abusing samples were similar to the ages of the men and women who would be seeking employment, the alcoholics were considerably older. Moreover, longitudinal studies indicated that the MMPI profiles of prealcoholic college freshmen were considerably more benign than the profiles obtained later after they had developed serious drinking problems.

Second, most of the distinctively elevated MMPI profiles were found among subjects who were actively seeking treatment and readily acknowledged their drinking and/or drug-abuse problems. Unlike job applicants, who are motivated to make a favorable impression, it can be assumed that most of these patients were taking the MMPI at a low point in their lives, a time when their substance-abuse problems had become overwhelming and were causing them great difficulties and distress. In such circumstances, they would be more likely to emphasize than minimize their problems while taking the MMPI.

Third, there are no MMPI profile patterns or scales uniquely associated with alcohol or drug abuse. At best, a deviant MMPI pattern or score can place one in a pool of people who, as a group, have an excessive rate of substance-abuse problems. However, some people with these test characteristics will never develop any difficulties.

Fourth, is the perennial "base rate" problem (Meehl & Rosen, 1955; Megargee, 1976). Most of the studies investigating the "hit rates" of scales such as the MAC or DaS used samples containing many more alcoholics or drug abusers than one would find in the general population. Often the incidence or "base rate" of substance abuse in these studies was 50%, so that any test improving on the hit rate obtainable by flipping a coin could make a statistically significant contribution to accurate selection.

The rate of accuracy is much less when tests are applied to populations with a low incidence or base rate of problem behavior such as those that would be sampled in preemployment screening. A few simple calculations will quickly demonstrate why. Since the MacAndrew's alcoholism scale is the best studied and most respected of the measures we have reviewed, we will demonstrate its application to a young population in which the incidence of alcohol abuse has been well documented, the Army. Burt and Biegel's (1980) survey indicated that 11% of the E-1 through E-5 Army personnel surveyed could be classified as "alcohol dependent" and that 11% also reported serious adverse consequences from alcohol abuse. Let us then use 11% as the base rate for serious alcohol problems in the U.S. Army, and project the number and kinds of errors that might be made if the MacAndrew Alcoholism Scale was applied to 100,000 prospective inductees in an effort to identify those most likely to develop drinking problems in the service.

Of the 100,000 prospective recruits, on the basis of the DOD survey we would expect 11,000 (11%) to develop serious alcohol problems. If the MAC predicts alcohol abuse among Army recruits as well as it postdicts alcoholism among hospitalized alcoholics (which is, of course, unlikely) we would expect a false negative rate of 8.5% and a false positive rate of 18% based on the median values obtained in the studies surveyed by Owen and Butcher (1979). If these rates held up among enlistees, in this hypothetical example the MacAndrew would detect 10,065 (91.5%) of the 11,000 alcoholics, and miss 935 false negative alcoholics (8.5%), an excellent hit rate. (See Table 1.7).

Turning to the 89,000 who would not develop alcohol-related problems, we would expect the scale to classify correctly 72,980 (82%) but to misclassify as false positives 16,020 (18%). False positives would thus be 17 times as frequent as false negatives, and the consequences would be that over 26,000 applicants would be labeled potential alcoholics, less than 39% of whom would actually develop drinking problems. Higher false positive rates such as those of ca.50% associated with the ICAS (Zager & Megargee, 1981) would make for even greater problems.

TABLE 1.7
Hypothetical Application of the MacAndrew Alcoholism Scale
to Army Screening

		ACTUAL BEHAVIOR		
		ALCOHOL PROBLEM	NO ALCOHOL PROBLEM	TOTAL
	ALCOHOL PROBLEM	10,065 (true positives)	16,020 (false positives)	26,085
PREDICTED BEHAVIOR	NO ALCOHOL PROBLEM	935 (false negatives)	72,980 (true negatives)	73,915
	TOTAL	11,000	89,000	100,000

Hits = 83,045
Misses = 16,955

In some situations, externally imposed selection ratios can offset the base-rate problem. When the number of applicants greatly exceeds the number of available positions, many qualified applicants will have to be rejected in any case and the employer can afford to be highly selective. The NASA team charged with selecting the original Mercury astronauts had over 1000 applicants for seven positions. They did not have to worry about false positives since over 99% of the applicants would be rejected in any case. On the other hand, if the Army had to fill 95,000 positions with only 100,000 applicants, it certainly would not reject 26,085 on the basis of their scoring over 23 on the MacAndrews alcoholism scale.

Although more than 6,000 studies have been published on the MMPI, the question of its usefulness as a screening device for the detection of those with potential substance abuse problems in nonclinical settings has not been adequately addressed. Longitudinal studies, in which the MMPI is administered to job applicants who are then followed over time, are needed to establish its predictive validity, derive and cross-validate scales, discriminant functions and cutting scores, establish base rates, and, ultimately, determine cost-effectiveness. Preliminary indications that the MMPI might not be adequate for the screening function would be finding; (a) an unacceptably high rate of positive dissimulation ("faking good") among applicants for employment in a particular setting; or (b) determining the MMPI can not discriminate (postdict) those who have already developed substance abuse problems in that employment setting; or (c) determining that MMPI scales or indices discriminated against members of minority groups in that setting.

In contrast, with these negative indicators, positively establishing the MMPI's predictive validity in preemployment screening will require large-scale longitudinal studies.[4] Rather than collecting more post hoc profiles of patients already diagnosed as alcoholics or drug abusers, cross-validated longitudinal studies on nonclinical populations must be undertaken by those interested in using the MMPI as a screening instrument.

REFERENCES

Apfeldorf, M. (1978). Alcoholism scales of the MMPI: Contributions and future directions. *International Journal of the Addictions, 13,* 17–53.

Apfeldorf, M., & Hunley, P. J. (1976). Exclusion of subjects with F scores at or above 16 in MMPI research on alcoholism. *Journal of Clinical Psychology, 32,* 498–500.

Apfeldorf, M., & Hunley, P. J. (1981). The MacAndrew scale: A measure of the diagnosis of alcoholism. *Journal of Studies on Alcohol, 42,* 80–86.

Atsaides, J. P., Nueringer, C., & Davis, K. L. (1977). Development of an institutional chronic alcoholic scale. *Journal of Consulting and Clinical Psychology, 45,* 609–611.

Bean, K. L., & Karasievich, G. O. (1975). Psychological test results at three stages of inpatient alcoholism treatment. *Journal of Studies in Alcohol, 36,* 838–852.

[4]A detailed design for such a study can be found in Megargee (1982).

Berzins, J. I., Ross, W. F., & English, G. E. (1974). Subgroups among opiates addicts: A typological investigation. *Journal of Abnormal Psychology, 83,* 65–73.

Berzins, J. I., Ross, W. F., & Monroe, J. J. (1971). A multivariate study of the personality characteristics of hospitalized narcotic addicts on the MMPI. *Journal of Clinical Psychology, 27,* 174–181.

Black, F. W. (1975). Personality characteristics of Vietnam veterans identified as heroin abusers. *American Journal of Psychiatry, 132,* 748–749.

Black, F. W. & Heald, A. (1975). MMPI characteristics of alcohol and illicit drug-abusers enrolled in a rehabilitation program. *Journal of Clinical Psychology, 31,* 572–575.

Brill, N., Crumpton, E., & Grayson, H. (1971). Personality factors in marijuana use. *Archives of General Psychology, 24,* 163–165.

Brook, R., Szandorowska, R., & Whitehead, P. C. (1976). Psychosocial dysfunctions as precursors to amphetamine abuse among adolescents. *Addictive Diseases: An International Journal, 2,* 465–478.

Burke, E. L., & Eichberg, R. J. (1972). Personality characteristics of adolescent users of dangerous drugs as indicated by the MMPI. *Journal of Nervous and Mental Disease, 154,* 291–298.

Burke, H. R. & Marcus, R. (1977). MacAndrew alcoholism scale: Alcoholism and drug addictiveness. *Journal of Psychology, 96,* 141–148.

Burt, M. R. (1982). Prevalence and consequences of alcohol use among U.S. Military personnal, 1980. *Journal of Studies on Alcohol, 43,* 1097–1107.

Burt, M. R., & Biegel, M. M. (1980). *World wide survey of non-medical drug use and alcohol use among military personnel: 1980.* Defense Technical Information Center, Alexandria, VA 22314.

Butcher, J. N., & Owen, P. L. (1978). Objective personality inventories. In B. B. Wolman (Ed.), *Clinical diagnosis of mental disorders: A handbook.* (pp. 475). New York: Plenum, 1978.

Butcher, J. N., & Pancheri, P. (1976). *A handbook of cross-national MMPI research.* Minneapolis: University of Minnesota.

Button, A. D. (1956). A study of alcoholics with the Minnesota Multiphasic Personality Inventory. *Quarterly Journal of Studies on Alcohol, 17,* 263–281.

Cavior, H., Kurtzberg, R. L., & Lipton, D. S. (1967). The development and validation of a heroin addiction scale for the MMPI. *International Journal of the Addictions, 2,* 129–137.

Clopton, J. R. (1978). Alcoholism and the MMPI: A review. *Journal of Studies on Alcohol, 39,* 1540–1558.

Clopton, J. R., Weiner, R. H., & Davis, H. G. (1980). Use of the MMPI in identification of alcoholic psychiatric patients. *Journal of Consulting and Clinical Psychology, 48,* 416–417.

Collins, H. A. (1979). Personalities of addicts. *Psychological Reports, 44,* 603–608.

Conley, J. J. (1981). An MMPI typology of male alcoholics: Admission, discharge, and outcome comparisons. *Journal of Personality Assessment, 45,* 33–39.

Conley, J. J., & Kammeier, M. L. (1980). MMPI item responses of alcoholics in treatment: Comparisons with normals and psychiatric patients. *Journal of Consulting and Clinical Psychology, 48,* 668–669.

Curlee, J. E. (1970). A comparison of male and female patients at an alcoholism treatment center. *Journal of Psychology, 74,* 239–247.

Dahlstrom, W. G., Welsh, G. S., & Dahlstrom, L. E. (1972). *An MMPI handbook (2nd ed.) Vol. 1: Clinical interpretation.* Minneapolis: University of Minnesota.

Donovan, D. M., Chaney, E. F., & O'Leary, M. R. (1978). Alcoholic subtypes: Relationship to drinking styles, benefits and consequences. *Journal of Nervous and Mental Disease, 166,* 553–561.

English, G. E., & Curtin, M. E. (1975). Personality differences in patients at three alcoholism treatment agencies. *Journal of Studies on Alcohol, 36,* 52–61.

Eshbaugh, D. M., Hoyt, C., & Tosi, D. J. (1978). Some personality patterns and dimensions of male alcoholics: A multivariate description. *Journal of Personality Assessment, 42,* 409–417.

Finney, J., Smith, D., Skeeters, D., & Auvenshine, C. (1971). MMPI alcoholism scales, factor structure, and content analysis. *Quarterly Journal of Studies on Alcohol, 32,* 1055–1060.

Fitzgibbons, D. J., Berry, D. F., & Shearn, C. R. (1973). MMPI and diagnosis among hospitalized drug abusers. *Journal of Community Psychology, 130,* 1379–1380.

Gendreau, P., Andrews, D. A., & Wormith, J. S. (1977). Personality characteristics of incarcerated speed abusers. *Canadian Journal of Behavioral Science, 9,* 341–347.

Gendreau, P., & Gendreau, L. (1970). The "addiction-prone" personality: A study of Canadian heroin addicts. *Canadian Journal of Behavioral Science, 2,* 18–25.

Gerstein, D. R. (1981). Alcohol use and consequences. In M. H. Moore & D. R. Gerstein (Eds.), *Alcohol and public policy: Beyond the shadow of prohibition.* (pp. 182–224). Washington, D.C.: National Academy Press.

Gilbertstadt, H., & Duker, J. (1965). *A handbook for clinical and actuarial MMPI interpretation.* Philadelphia: Sanders.

Goldberg, L. R. (1974). Objective diagnostic tests and measures. In M. R. Rosenzweig & L. W. Porter (Eds.), *Annual review of psychology,* Vol. 25. Palo Alto, CA: Annual Reviews, Inc.

Goldstein, S. G., & Linden, J. D. (1969). Multivariate classification of alcoholics by means of the MMPI. *Journal of Abnormal Psychology, 74,* 661–699.

Goss, A., & Morosko, T. (1969). Alcoholism and clinical symptoms. *Journal of Abnormal Psychology, 74,* 682–684.

Graham, J. R. (March 1978). MMPI characteristics of alcoholics, drug abusers, and pathological gamblers. *Paper presented at the 13th Annual MMPI Symposium,* Mexico. (Cited by Owen & Butcher, 1979).

Greaves, G. (1971). MMPI correlates of chronic drug abuse in hospitalized adolescents. *Psychological Reports, 29,* 1222.

Greene, L. L., & Haymes, M. (1973). Value orientation and psycho-social adjustment at various levels of marijuana use. *Journal of Youth and Adolescence, 2,* 213–231.

Haertzen, C. A., Hill, H. E., & Monroe, J. J. (1968). MMPI scales for differentiating and predicting relapse in alcoholics, opiate addicts and criminals. *International Journal of Addiction, 3,* 91–106.

Hampton, P. J. (1953). A psychometric study of drinkers: The development of a personality questionnaire for drinkers. *Genetic Psychology Monograph, 48,* 55–115.

Hays, R., & Stacy, A. (1983a). A study of the reliability and validity of the Holmes Alcoholism scale. *Journal of Clinical Psychology, 39,* 284–286.

Hays, R. & Stacy, A. (1983b). Validity of five MMPI alcoholism scales: A critique and reanalysis. *Journal of Clinical Psychology,**39,* 459–460.

Heller, M. E., & Mordkoff, A. M. (1972). Personality attributes of the young, nonaddicted drug abuser. *International Journal of the Addictions, 7,* 65–72.

Henriques, E., Arsenian, J., Cutter, H., & Samuraweeka, A. B. (1972). Personality characteristics and drug of choice. *International Journal of the Addictions, 7,* 73–76.

Hewitt, C. C. (1943). A personality study of alcohol addiction. *Quarterly Journal of Studies on Alcohol, 4,* 368–386.

Hill, H. E., Haertzen, A., & Davis, H. (1962). An MMPI factor analytic study of alcoholics, narcotic addicts and criminals. *Quarterly Journal of Studies on Alcohol, 23,* 411–431.

Hodo, G. L., & Fowler, R. D. (1976). Frequency of MMPI two-point codes in a large alcoholic sample. *Journal of Clinical Psychology, 32,* 487–489.

Hoffman, H. (1976). Personality measurement for the evaluation and prediction of alcoholism. In R. E. Tarter & A. A. Sugerman, (Eds.), *Alcoholism: Interdisciplinary approaches to an enduring problem.* Reading, MA: Addison-Wesley.

Hoffman, H., Loper, R. G., & Kammeier, M. L. (1974). Identifying future alcoholics with MMPI alcoholism scales. *Quarterly Journal of Studies on Alcohol, 35,* 490–498.

Hogan, R., Mankin, D., Conway, J., & Fox, S. (1970). Personality correlates of undergraduate marijuana use. *Journal of Consulting and Clinical Psychology, 35,* 58–63.

Holland, T. R. (1977). Multivariate analysis of personality correlates of alcohol and drug abuse in a prison population. *Journal of Abnormal Psychology, 86,* 644–650.

Holland, T. R., Levi, M. & Watson, C. (1981). MMPI basic scales vs. two-point codes in the discrimination of psychopathological groups. *Journal of Clinical Psychology, 37,* 394–396.

Holmes, C. B., Dungan, D. S., & McLaughlin, T. P. (1982). Validity of five MMPI alcoholism scales. *Journal of Clinical Psychology, 38,* 661–664.

Holmes, W. V. (1953). *The development of an empirical MMPI scale for alcoholism.* Unpublished master's thesis, San Jose State College, San Jose, California.

Horn, J. L., & Wanberg, K. W. (1969). Symptom patterns related to excessive use of alcohol. *Quarterly Journal of Studies on Alcohol, 30,* 35–58.

Hoyt, D. P., & Sedlacek, G. M. (1958). Differentiating alcoholics from normals and abnormals with the MMPI. *Journal of Clinical Psychology, 14,* 59–74.

Huber, N. A. & Danahy, S. (1975). Use of the MMPI in predicting completion and evaluating changes in a long-term alcoholism treatment program. *Journal of Studies on Alcohol, 36,* 1230–1237.

Jarvis, L. G., Sumnegar, R. R., & Traweek, A. R. (1975). An MMPI comparison of U.S.A.F. groups identified as drug users. *Psychological Reports, 37,* 1339–1345.

Johnson, N., & Cooke, G. (1973). Relationship of MMPI alcoholism, prison escape, hostility control, and recidivism scales to clinical judgments. *Journal of Clinical Psychology, 29,* 32–34.

Kammeier, M. L., Hoffman, H., & Loper, R. G. (1973). Personality characteristics of alcoholics as college freshmen and at time of treatment. *Quarterly Journal of Studies on Alcohol, 34,* 390–399.

Keegan, J. F., & Lachar, D. (1979). The MMPI as a predictor of early termination from polydrug abuse treatment. *Journal of Personality Assessment, 43,* 379–384.

Keller, J. & Redfinger, D. I. (1973). Comparison between the personalities of LSD users and nonusers as measured by the Minnesota Multiphasic Personality Inventory. *Journal of Nervous and Mental Disease, 156,* 271–277.

Khavari, K., & Farber, P. D. (1978). A profile instrument for the quantification and assessment of alcohol consumption: The Khavari Alcohol Test. *Journal of Studies on Alcohol, 39,* 1525–1529.

King, G. D. (1978). Review of the Minnesota Multiphasic Personality Inventory. In O. K. Buros (Ed.), *The eighth mental measurements yearbook,* Vol. 1. Highland Park, NJ: Gryphon.

Kline, J. A., Rozynko, V. V., Flint, G., & Roberts, A. C. (1973). Personality characteristics of male native American alcoholic patients. *International Journal of the Addictions, 8,* 729–732.

Kojak, G. Jr., & Canby, J. P. (1975). Personality behavior patterns of heroin-dependent American servicemen in Thailand. *American Journal of Psychiatry, 132,* 246–250.

Krauthamer, C. (1979). The personality of alcoholic middle-class women: A comparative study with the MMPI. *Journal of Clinical Psychology, 35,* 442–448.

Kristianson, P. (1976). Classification of the MMPI profiles of two alcoholic groups. *Acta Psychiatrica Scandinavia, 54,* 359–380.

Kurtines, W., Hogan, R., & Weiss, D. (1975). Personality dynamics of heroin use. *Journal of Abnormal Psychology, 84,* 87–89.

Kwant, F., Rice, J. A., & Hays, J. R. (1976). Use of Heroin Addiction Scale to differentiate addicts from rehabilitation clients. *Psychological Reports, 38,* 547–553.

Lachar, D., Gdowski, C. L., & Keegan, J. F. (1979). MMPI profiles of men alcoholics, drug addicts and psychiatric patients. *Journal of Studies on Alcohol, 40,* 45–56.

Lang, A. R. (1983). Addictive personality: A viable construct? In P. K. Levison, D. R. Gerstein, & D. R. Maloff (Eds.), *Commonalities, substance abuse, and habitual behavior.* Lexington, MA., Lexington Books.

Laudeman, K. (1977). Personality, drinking patterns and problem drinking among young adult offenders. *Journal of Drug Education, 7,* 259–269.

Lerner, S. E., & Wesson, D. R. (1973). The Haight-Ashbury drug-using subculture and the MMPI psychopathic scale. *International Journal of Addictions, 8,* 401–402.

Loberg, T. (1981). MMPI-based personality subtypes of alcoholics. Relationships to drinking history, psychosomatics and neuropsychological deficits. *Journal of Studies on Alcohol, 42,* 766–782.

Loper, R. G., Kammeier, M. L., & Hoffman, H. (1973). MMPI characteristics of college freshman males who later became alcoholics. *Journal of Abnormal Psychology, 82,* 159–162.

MacAndrew, C. (1965). The differentiation of male alcoholic outpatients from nonalcoholic psychiatric patients by means of the MMPI. *Quarterly of Studies on Alcohol, 26,* 238–246.

MacAndrew, C. (1978). Women alcoholics' responses to Scale 4 of the MMPI. *Journal of Studies on Alcohol, 39,* 1841–1854.

MacAndrew, C. (1979). On the possibility of the psychometric detection of persons who are prone to the abuse of alcohol and other substances. *Addictive Behaviors, 4,* 11–20.

MacAndrew, C. (1981). What the MAC scale tells us about alcoholic men: An interpretive review. *Journal of Studies on Alcohol, 42,* 604–625.

MacAndrew, C., & Geertsma, R. H. (1963). A analysis of responses of alcoholics to scale 4 of the MMPI. *Quarterly Journal of Studies on Alcohol, 24,* 23–38.

Manson, M. P. (1949). *The Alcadd Test.* Beverly Hills, CA: Western Psychological Service.

McAree, C. P., Steffenhagen, R. A., & Zheutlin, L. S. (1969). Personality factors in college drug users. *International Journal of Social Psychiatry, 5,* 102–106.

McAree, C. P., Steffenhagen, R. A., & Zheutlin, L. S. (1972). Personality factors and patterns of drug usage in college students. *American Journal of Psychiatry, 128,* 890–893.

McGuire, J. S., & Megargee, E. I. (1974). Personality correlates of marijuana use among youthful offenders. *Journal of Consulting and Clinical Psychology, 42,* 124–133.

McLachlan, J. F. C. (1975a). An MMPI discriminant function to distinguish alcoholics from narcotic addicts: Effects of age, sex, and psychopathology. *Journal of Clinical Psychology, 31,* 163–165.

McLachlan, J. F. C. (1975b). Classification of alcoholics by an MMPI actuarial system. *Journal of Clinical Psychology, 31,* 145–147.

Meehl, P. E., & Rosen, A. (1975). Antecedent probability and the efficiency of psychometric signs, patterns or cutting scores. *Psychological Bulletin, 52,* 194–216.

Megargee, E. I. (1976). The prediction of dangerous behavior. *Criminal Justice and Behavior, 3,* 3–21.

Megargee, E. I. (1982). *Screening Army enlistees to identify individuals with potential substance abuse problems.* Committee on Substance Abuse and Habitual Behavior, National Research Council, Washington, D.C.

Miller, W. R. (1976). Alcoholism scales and objective assessment methods: A review. *Psychological Bulletin, 83,* 649–674.

Mogar, R. E., Wilson, W. M., & Helms, S. T. (1970). Personality subtypes of male and female alcoholic patients. *International Journal of the Addictions, 5,* 99–113.

Mulford, H. A., & Miller, D. E. (1960). Drinking in Iowa: IV. Preoccupation with alcohol and definitions of alcohol, heavy drinking and trouble due to drinking. *Quarterly Journal of Studies on Alcohol, 21,* 279–291.

Muschewske, R. (1972). A cross-validation of the MMPI Drug Abuse Scale. *Correctional Psychologist, 23,* 33–36.

Nathan, P. E. (1983). Failures in prevention: Why we can't prevent the devastating effect of alcoholism and drug abuse. *American Psychologist, 38,* 459–467.

Newsweek, Aug. 22, 1983. Taking drugs on the job, pp. 52–60.

O'Leary, M. R., Donovan, D., & Hayes, W. H. (1974). Relationships between locus of control and MMPI scales among alcoholics: A replication. *Journal of Clinical Psychology, 30,* 312–314.

Overall, J. E. (1973). MMPI personality patterns of alcoholics and narcotic addicts. *Quarterly Journal of Studies on Alcohol, 34,* 104–111.

Owen, P. L. (1979). Bibliography of MMPI research. In J. N. Butcher (Ed.), *New directions in MMPI research.* Minneapolis: University of Minnesota.

Owen, P. L. & Butcher, J. (1979). Personality factors in problem drinking: A review of the evidence and some suggested directions. In R. Pickens & L. Heston (Eds.), *Psychiatric factors in drug abuse*. New York: Grune & Stratton.

Page, R. D., & Bozlee, S. (1982). A cross-cultural MMPI comparison of alcoholics. *Psychological Reports, 50,* 639–646.

Panton, J. H., & Behre, C. (1973). Characteristics associated with drug addiction within a state prison population. *Journal of Community Psychology, 1,* 411–416.

Panton, J., & Brisson, R. (1971). Characteristics associated with drug abuse within a state prison population. *Corrective Psychiatry and Journal of Social Therapy, 17,* 3–33.

Patalano, F. (1980a). Comparison of MMPI scores of drug abusers and Mayo Clinic normative groups. *Journal of Clinical Psychology, 36,* 576–579.

Patalano, F. (1980b). MMPI two-point code-types frequencies of drug abusers in a therapeutic community. *Psychological Reports, 46,* 1019–1022.

Patterson, E. T., Charles, H. L., Woodward, W. A., Roberts, W. R. & Penk, W. R. (1981). Differences in measures of personality and family environment among Black and White alcoholics. *Journal of Consulting and Clinical Psychology, 49,* 1–9.

Penk, W. E., Charles, H. L., Patterson, E. T., Roberts, W. R., Dolan, M. P., & Brown, A. S. (1982). Chronological age differences in MMPI scores of male chronic alcoholics seeking treatment. *Journal of Consulting and Clinical Psychology, 50,* 332–324.

Penk, W. E., Fudge, J. W., Robinowitz, R., & Newman, R. S. (1979). Personality characteristics of compulsive heroin, amphetamines, and barbiturate users. *Journal of Consulting and Clinical Psychology, 47,* 583–585.

Penk, W. E., Roberts, W. R., Robinowitz, R., Dolan, M. P., & Atkins, H. G. (1982). MMPI differences of black and white polydrug abusers seeking treatment. *Journal of Consulting and Clinical Psychology, 50,* 463–466.

Penk, W. E., & Robinowitz, R. (1975). Personality differences of volunteer and nonvolunteer heroin and nonheroin drug users. *Journal of Abnormal Psychology, 85,* 91–100.

Penk, W. E., Robinowitz, R., Roberts, N. R., Dolan, M. P., & Atkins, H. G. (1981). MMPI differences of male Hispanic-Americans, black, and white heroin addicts. *Journal of Consulting and Clinical Psychology, 49,* 488–490.

Penk, W. E., Woodward, W. A., Robinowitz, R., & Hess, J. L. (1978). Differences in MMPI scores of black and white compulsive heroin users. *Journal of Abnormal Psychology, 87,* 505–513.

Penk, W. E., Woodward, W. A., Robinowitz, R., & Parr, W. C. (1980). An MMPI comparison of polydrug and heroin abusers. *Journal of Abnormal Psychology, 89,* 299–302.

Pittel, S. M. (1971). Psychological aspects of heroin and other drug dependence. *Journal of Psychedelic Drugs, 4,* 40–45.

Quayle, D. (1983). American productivity: The devastating effect of alcoholism and drug abuse. *American Psychologist, 38,* 454–458.

Rhodes, R. J. & Chang, A. (1978). A further look at the Institutionalized Chronic Alcoholic Scale. *Journal of Clinical Psychology, 34,* 779–780.

Rich, C. C., & Davis, H. G. (1969). Concurrent validity of MMPI alcoholism scales. *Journal of Clinical Psychology, 25,* 425–426.

Rohan, W. P. (1972). MMPI changes in hospitalized alcoholics: A second study. *Quarterly Journal of Studies on Alcohol, 33,* 65–76.

Rosenberg, N. (1972). MMPI alcoholism scales. *Journal of Clinical Psychology, 28,* 515–522.

Ross, W. F., & Berzins, J. I. (1974). Personality characteristics of female narcotic addicts on the MMPI. *Psychological Reports, 35,* 779–784.

Rothaizer, J. M. (1980). A typological study of substance abusers using the MMPI. *Journal of Clinical Psychology, 36,* 1019–1021.

Rotman, S. R., & Vestre, N. (1964). The use of the MMPI in identifying problem drinkers among psychiatric hospital admissions. *Journal of Clinical Psychology, 20,* 526–530.

Schoolar, J. C., White, E. H., & Cohen, C. P. (1972). Drug abusers and their clinic-patient counterparts: A comparison of personality dimensions. *Journal of Consulting and Clinical Psychology, 39*, 9–14.

Schroeder, E. I., & Piercy, D. C. (1979). A comparison of MMPI two-point codes in four alcoholism treatment facilities. *Journal of Clinical Psychology, 35*, 656–663.

Selzer, M. L. (1971). The Michigan Alcoholism Screening Test: The quest for a new diagnostic instrument. *American Journal of Psychiatry, 127*, 1653–1658.

Sheppard, C., Ricca, E., Fracchia, J., Rosenberg, N., & Merlis, S. (1972). Cross-validation of a heroin addiction scale from the MMPI. *Journal of Psychology, 81*, 263–268.

Sheppard, C., Ricca, E., Fracchia, J., & Merlis, S. (1973). Personality characteristics of urban and suburban heroin abusers: More data and another reply to Sutker and Allain. *Psychological Reports, 33*, 999–1008.

Skinner, H. A., Jackson, D. N., & Hoffman, H. (1974). Alcoholic personality types: Identification and correlates. *Journal of Abnormal Psychology, 83*, 658–666.

Smart, R. G., & Fejer, D. (1969). Illicit LSD users: Their social backgrounds, drug use and psychopathology. *Journal of Health and Social Behavior, 10*, 297–308.

Soskin, R. A. (1970). Personality and attitude change after two alcoholism treatment programs; Comparative contributions of Lysergide and human relations training. *Quarterly Journal of Studies in Alcohol, 31*, 920–921.

Spiegel, D., Hadley, P. A., & Hadley, R. G. (1970). Personality test patterns of rehabilitation center alcoholics, psychiatric inpatients, and normals. *Journal of Clinical Psychology, 26*, 366–371.

Steffenhagen, R. A., Schmidt, F. E., & McAree, C. P. (1971). Emotional stability and student drug abuse. *Journal of Drug Education, 1*, 347–357.

Stein, K. B., & Rozynko, V. (1974). Psychological and social variables and personality patterns of drug abusers. *International Journal of the Addictions, 9*, 431–446.

Stein, K. B., Rozynko, V., & Pugh, L. A. (1971). The heterogeneity of personality among alcoholics. *British Journal of Social and Clinical Psychology, 10*, 253–259.

Sutherland, E. H., Schroeder, H. G., & Tordella, C. J. (1950). Personality traits and the alcoholic: A critique of existing studies. *Quarterly Journal of Studies on Alcohol, 11*, 547–561.

Sutker, P. B. (1971). Personality differences and sociopathy in heroin addicts and nonaddict prisoners. *Journal of Abnormal Psychology, 78*, 247–251.

Sutker, P. B., & Allain, A. N. (1973). Incarcerated and street heroin addicts: A personality comparison. *Psychological Record, 32*, 243–246.

Trevithick, L., & Hosch, H. M. (1978). MMPI correlates of drug addiction based on drug of choice. *Journal of Consulting and Clinical Psychology, 46*, 180.

Uecker, A. E. (1970). Differentiating male alcoholics from other psychiatric inpatients. *Quarterly Journal of Studies on Alcoholism, 31*, 379–383.

Uecker, A. E., Kish, G. D., & Ball, M. E. (1969). Differentiation of alcoholism from general psychopathology by means of two MMPI scales. *Journal of Clinical Psychology, 25*, 287–289.

Vega, A. (1971). Cross-validation of four MMPI scales for alcoholism. *Quarterly Journal of Studies on Alcohol, 32*, 791–797.

Whitelock, P. R., Overall, J. E., & Patrick, J. H. (1971). Personality patterns and alcohol abuse in a state hospital population. *Journal of Abnormal Psychology, 78*, 9–16.

Whisler, R. H., & Cantor, J. M. (1966). The MacAndrew alcoholism scale: A cross-validation in a domiciliary setting. *Journal of Clinical Psychology, 22*, 311–312.

Zager, L. D., & Megargee, E. I. (1981). Seven MMPI alcohol and drug abuse scales: An empirical investigation of their interrelationships, convergent and discriminant validity, and degree of racial bias. *Journal of Personality and Social Psychology, 40*, 532–544.

Zelen, S. L., Fox, J., Gould, E., & Olson, R. W. (1966). Sex-contingent differences between male and female alcoholics. *Journal of Clinical Psychology, 22*, 160–165.

Zuckerman, M., Sola, S., Masterson, J. & Angelonie, N. V. (1975). MMPI patterns in drug abuse before and after treatment in therapeutic communities. *Journal of Consulting and Clinical Psychology, 43*, 286–296.

2 Chronic Maternal Stress and Its Assessment

Norma Deitch Feshbach
University of California, Los Angeles

INTRODUCTION

During the past decade a group at UCLA has been engaged in the construction and use of measures designed to assess chronic stress in mothers of young children. This chapter summarizes findings from a series of early studies that influenced our decision to develop these measures. The chapter also summarizes and reviews more recent research that has been carried out in connection with the development and use of the measures, as well as describes the measures themselves. Although the project is ongoing and we continue to be engaged in the refinement of the measures, the research presented reflects their promise.

In recent years, there has been a growing recognition of the chronic tensions and difficulties (or stress) experienced by mothers of young children. In repeated studies over the last decade, women have been found to rate their children's preschool years as the period of greatest personal distress, dissatisfaction, and unhappiness (Campbell, Converse, & Rogers, 1976). Findings from field surveys indicate that mothers of preschool children are a high-risk group for serious depression, psychological disorder, and psychosomatic illness (Feld, 1963; Laws, 1971; McLean, 1976; Richman, 1976).

Within the popular literature, a number of authors have focused on the stresses inherent in the motherhood role and their potential negative impact on women (Radl, 1973). Such possible stressors as the monotonous and repetitive nature of housework, the frustrations and irritations of childrearing, and the narrowed opportunities for self-actualization have received considerable publicity. While some attempts have been made to substantiate the assumption that these are significant sources of stress (e.g., Gavron, 1966; Oakley, 1974), relatively little is known concerning the wider range of potential problems associated with the period of early motherhood.

Yet the topic of maternal stress is a vital one to those who seek to understand maternal behavior and the intricacies of the mother–child relationship. With increasing frequency, observers and researchers of the American family have begun to propose that chronic stress may be a factor that not only affects the well-being of mothers, but also the quality of care offered the young child (Bernard, 1974; Feshbach, 1973a). To paraphrase Jessie Bernard in her treatise on mother-hood as we now structure it, high stress levels in motherhood are not good for women or children (Bernard, 1974). Unfortunately, distressed mothers may exhibit socialization practices that are not conducive to optimal levels of cognitive and personal development in their children. It has been suggested that the stress experienced by mothers may be an important contributing factor in various maternal behaviors such as autocratic control, physical intrusion, and even child abuse (Garbarino, 1975; Rosenberg & Repucci, 1983).

A series of cross-cultural studies carried out in the United States, England, and Israel—the historical antecedent for the research program on chronic maternal stress in mothers of young children (to be described in this chapter)—was related to such issues. This earlier program was oriented to one important component of maternal behavior that may be a reflection of maternal stress—the manner, especially the reinforcement style, in which a mother directs and teaches her child in myriad day-to-day interactions.

Cross-Cultural Studies in Maternal Teaching Styles

These early studies investigated teaching styles in young children and their mothers in different socioeconomic, ethnic, and cultural groups as a way of exploring the impact of critical socialization practices on child behaviors that have particular relevance for school learning (Feshbach, 1973a, 1973b; Feshbach, & Devor, 1969). In many of these initial studies a four year old child was required to teach a simple task to a three year old. In addition, each four year old was subsequently taught a similar but somewhat more complex task by his or her mother. In general, the findings obtained in each of these cultural settings yielded a consistent pattern—namely, middle-class mothers tended to use significantly less negative reinforcement (criticism and other punitive behaviors) than lower-class mothers while middle-class children used significantly more positive reinforcement (praise, reward) than their lower-class counterparts. The data on use of maternal reinforcement are presented in Table 2.1.

The findings from this initial series of studies on teaching styles were congruent with data reported by other investigations (Bee, Egeren, Streissguth, Nyman, & Leckie, 1969; Brophy, 1970; Hess, Shipman, Brophy, & Bear, 1968). The results consistently reflected socioeconomic differences in maternal teaching behaviors, with more punitive, nonrewarding practices associated with less economically privileged groups.

TABLE 2.1
Mean Frequencies of Reinforcements Administered
by Mothers of Four Year Olds

Culture	Middle-Class White	Middle-Class Black	Lower-Class White	Lower-Class Black
	Positive Reinforcement			
American	6.4	4.6	4.7	4.7
Israeli	6.7		4.3	
English	4.4		3.0	
	Negative Reinforcement			
American	1.4	1.8	2.2	5.4
Israeli	2.9		3.8	
English	1.5		2.0	

My interpretation of the link between reinforcement style and socioeconomic level was that the lower-class family, by reason of its impoverished economic status, is subject to more privation, illness, and in general, to more stressful events than is the middle-class family, and consequently is less tolerant and more critical of children's errors and deviant behaviors than the middle-class family (Feshbach, 1973a). I further proposed that frequent use of negative reinforcements by parents, while understandably reflecting environmental pressures and frustrations, entailed parent–child interactions that did not foster optimal learning and development. And, perhaps, the most unfortunate consequence of the sequence of negative socialization experiences in stressful households is the evidence of internalization by the child of these negative response modes.

The findings from two additional studies propelled us further in the direction of studying chronic maternal stress. The first was carried out in England with middle- and working-class mothers and their three year old children, using a more extended teaching situation and focusing on a broader array of observational measures (Phinney & Feshbach, 1980).

In this study five separate tasks were used: a puzzle assembly; the construction of a toy village; a sorting task; a simple color-matching game; construction of patterns with Cuisenaire rods. The results again revealed significant class differences in the use of negative statements. In addition, middle-class mothers used fewer imperatives, asked more questions, and were less apt to be physically intrusive. Again, we interpreted this pattern of negative intrusive behaviors as an indication of the greater stress experienced by the working-class mothers.

Another study, carried out with an American middle-class sample, demonstrated that maternal style is not restricted to economic level, but that other factors, such as variations in personality, or situational pressures, may be critical antecedents. In this study, the independent variable was the reading competence of the child (Feshbach, 1973a; Bercovici & Feshbach, 1973). Mothers of matched successful and problem readers were observed while instructing a problem reader, a successful reader, and their own child, on several cognitive tasks. Few mothers in either group held jobs outside the home, and mothers in both groups were economically advantaged.

Significant differences between the two groups were obtained: Mothers of the problem readers used more negative reinforcement, were more directive, more intrusive, and appeared to be less patient than the mothers of successful readers, both when instructing their own children and when instructing other children. In addition, the mothers of problem readers revealed more punitive attitudes on a child-rearing inventory than did the mothers of successful readers.

These findings, along with other behavioral information, suggested that these mothers felt very pressured. The mothers of problem readers were invariably late for their appointments, and they looked stressed and harrassed during the teaching situation. The observation of the stress-like behavior of the parents of problem readers further stimulated our interest in stress and appropriate methods of assessment. Informal conversations with the mothers did not suggest that they or their families had experienced an unusual amount of life changes or crises in the previous 2 years. Rather, the kinds of stressors that the mothers spontaneously mentioned were relatively minor but recurrent day-to-day frustrations and tribulations such as "the washing machine has broken down," "the repairman was late," and "the babysitter never appeared." Thus, it seemed that if we wanted to assess maternal stress, especially in mothers of young children, we should focus on the stressors that punctuated the lives of these mothers; the day-to-day chronic stressors. Preliminary piloting with a variety of extant measures on life changes supported our desire to focus on chronic, rather than acute, stress. However, aside from rather time-consuming interview procedures, there were no extant measures of chronic stress. We decided to develop our own procedure.

CHRONIC MATERNAL STRESS

The principal inventories of stress that were available such as the instruments by Holmes and Rahe (1967) and by Sarason, Johnson and Siegel (1978) were addressed to the assessment of life changes or acute stress. We felt that these instruments were not adequate for our purposes for a number of reasons. First, our observations suggested that the mothers in our studies were more influenced by the trials of daily pressures than by the distress or excitement ensuing from major life events. A second factor in our decision to assess chronic stress was the generic character of the acute stress measures. The stress of major life events was applicable to all who experienced them—male or female, middle-aged or adolescent. We sought a measure that would be specifically applicable to mothers, especially mothers of young children.

The decision to develop a measure of chronic stress addressed to a specific target group was also influenced by theoretical discussions that have suggested that the burdens of ongoing stress may be more a function of repetitive daily pressures than of acute but episodic life events (Lazarus, 1980; Pearlin & Lieberman, 1977). Thus, from a clinical and therapeutic perspective, the analysis of chronic sources may be essential to the understanding and treatment of personal stress. Consequently, the concept of chronic maternal stress falls within a transactional approach to stress rather than a stimulus or response definition. The emphasis is on the pressures and tension experienced by the mother of the young child as she strives to meet the demands imposed by her obligation and her environment while, at the same time, attempting to satisfy in some degree her personal needs.

Mothers of young children are, of course, subject to the pain and anxiety of major distressing events and to the excitement of very positive events. But the patterns of tensions that are most commonly ascribed to mothers as they cope with marital, household, and child-rearing demands do not fit the model suggested by discrete and widely separated experiences of extreme threat or of a major goal attainment. Rather, maternal stress would appear to be more intimately related to the notions of conflict and frustration suggested by the transactional approach, and to be chronic in nature.

We chose to focus our stress measure on the assessment of chronic stress experienced by mothers of young children because of the importance that is generally ascribed to the early years of mother–child interactions. It is this population of mothers that is the primary target of parent training programs; it is the children of these mothers who are the participants in Head Start and related early childhood programs; and it was this category of mothers who participated in the teaching style studies.

Having chosen to develop a specific rather than generic measure of stress, and a measure that was oriented toward chronic stress in mothers of young children, we felt it important first to ascertain from samples of mothers of young children the sources of chronic stress that should be assessed by our measures. By deriving items for the measure from maternal reports, the ecological validity of the chronic maternal stress instrument would be enhanced. Maternal reports would also provide a useful model for wording the items in the language and phraseology employed by mothers. Finally, it was important to interview mothers from different backgrounds and cultural settings so as to increase the probability that the sources of chronic stress to be assessed by the measure would apply to widely varying populations of mothers of young children.

SOURCES OF MATERNAL STRESS IN AN AMERICAN POPULATION

The purpose of the American Study (Jordon & Feshbach, 1979; Feshbach & Jordon, 1980) was to survey situations and sources of chronic stress affecting mothers with young children. Our interest was manifold: to describe the samples with regard to stress; to obtain items for a potential chronic stress inventory; and to look at the relationship between chronic stress and a number of demographic variables.

The participants were 60 middle-class Anglo-American women with at least one child between the ages of three and five. The mothers were recruited from day care centers, parks, and other child-related facilities in a suburban Los Angeles community. Included were equal numbers of married housewives, wives employed outside the home, and single mothers employed outside the home. Subjects were individually contacted and interviewed at the child-related facility by a trained female graduate student. Each mother was asked to "list 10 separate situations, or conditions, or relationships, or events that cause you to feel pressured, or upset."

The following strategy of content analysis was employed. From the total sample of 600 maternal responses, a random subset of 100 items was selected and presented to five male and female adults to judge. Psychologists, educators, and parents served as judges. Each judge was asked to "sort the items into categories based on their content." The category systems for all 10 judges were compared and, due to their high level of surface similarity, were combined into one comprehensive system.

This comprehensive system consisted of 10 major categories labeled Children, Men, Self, Relations to Others, Time, Housework, Finances, Disruptions, Society, and Work. The total sample of stress items for all mothers was then sorted into these categories by two independent coders. Interrater reliability, defined by agreements/agreements + disagreements, was 93%.

The percentage of mothers reporting sources of stress bearing on each of the 10 categories is presented in Table 2.2. The four most predominant areas of stress involve the caregiving relationship with child, relationship with husband, concerns with self, and social relations with friends and relatives. Stress related to Children appeared in 92% of the responses. Of the 147 items cited, six basic aspects of child-related stress appeared: children's faults; uncertainties of child-rearing decisions; apprehensions over child's health; concerns over child's personal and social development; difficulties in meeting "legitimate" needs of children; and adequate daycare or babysitting.

Four fifths of the mothers referred to difficulties with Men (husband or other males). Of the 76 items, three types of distress appeared: complaints about the husband's behavior; his interaction with the children; his personal and professional well-being. Self was noted by 70% of the women, and reflected in the 77 items were stress associated with: concerns about the overload of responsibilities and obligations for their own and their children's lives; lack of opportunities for personal fulfillment; perceived inadequacies such as lack of weight control and inefficient housekeeping skills; and loneliness.

The fourth category was Social Relations with Others, both relatives and friends. In regard to the extended family, the primary stressor was unsolicited advice and criticism, and secondly, concern over the health of and lack of time

TABLE 2.2
American Study

Categories*	M/E	M/NE	NM/E	Total
Children	90	95	90	92
Men	75	75	90	80
Self	70	70	70	70
Others	55	80	55	63
Time	75	40	55	58
Housework	70	40	60	57
Finances	50	35	75	53
Disruptions	15	40	35	30
Society	35	10	20	22
Work	65	--	85	75

Note: Percentage of women included in each category for three groups of women:Married and employed (M/E), Married and not employed (M/NE), not married and employed (NM/E). Percentages based on N=20 for each group, N=60 for all totals except work where N=40.

with aging parents. In regard to friends, stress was associated with either conflict-laden interactions or undesired separation.

The next five major categories dealt with the management of daily life: Time (cited by 58% of mothers); Housework (57%); Finances (53%); Disruptions (30%); and Society (22%). Women expressed a desire to have more time to accomplish necessary tasks, to devote to personal interests, to relax and read, and to play with children. Housework items included cleaning, cooking, shopping and other errands, as well as lack of help from other family members. Most responses in the Finances category referred to a general lack of money, but others mentioned a lack of money for specific items such as home upkeep or extras for the children. The category of Disruptions included those items that occur irregularly or infrequently, such as car trouble, breakdown of an appliance, and holiday preparations. Stress associated with the quality of contemporary society was reflected in concern about the role of government, women and religion, the economy, crime, the quality of the schools, the environment, and drug abuse.

The final category, Work, was specific to employed women. One aspect of occupational concern was working conditions, such as strained relations with coworkers or the boring or difficult nature of the work. A second aspect was conflict between work schedules and the demands of homelife, in particular, inability to spend more time with the children.

Marital and Employment Status

Qualitative analysis of the maternal responses indicated three basic sources that were specific to either marital or employment status. While single and married mothers frequently cited a lack of emotional satisfaction in their relationships with men, only single women referred to conflicts between their relationship with men and their relationship with their children. In addition, only single women mentioned arguments with ex-spouses.

While working presented unique stresses for employed women, lack of outside employment was associated with boredom and desires for self-actualization. Breakdowns of the relative frequencies with which each of the three groups cited the 10 categories are reflected in Table 2. Separate chi-square analyses were performed to assess variations in citation rates for each category. Although no significant differences were found for the three categories of Children, Men, and Self, significant differences did appear for the remaining seven categories.

Married housewives referred to difficulties in social relations with extended family and friends more frequently than the employed groups (80% vs. 55%), who more frequently cited difficulties with time, housework, and finances. In contrast, the single mothers expressed more difficulties with family finances. Housewives cited events in the home more and concerns about the wider society less than working wives.

In general, we were struck with the similarity in findings between the three groups of mothers. Although there were qualitative and some quantitative differences reflecting the unique concerns and pressures of work and single parenthood, the limited variation in stress sources is noteworthy. Overall, the responses of the housewives, the working mothers, and the single mothers were strikingly similar in form and content. The content analysis appeared to reveal an underlying structural pattern of basic stress sources associated with the roles these women held in common. Also of significance was the finding that our mothers' stress responses did not focus exclusively on their child-rearing related responsibilities. Although in the past, popular discussions of maternal stress have emphasized children and child care as the central sources of distress among women with young children, the self-reports of our mothers indicate that this perspective, while partially valid, overlooks many additional sources of stress. Of the maternal responses, two thirds focused on aspects of daily life only indirectly related to children.

SOURCES OF CHRONIC MATERNAL STRESS IN AN ISRAELI SAMPLE

Although very encouraged by the range of individual items and face validity of the chronic stress categories derived from the American sample, we decided to replicate the entire study before proceeding with the construction of a Chronic Stress Inventory. Since a major goal in producing a stress assessment was to facilitate the study of the role of stress in the socialization process, it seemed appropriate to broaden the cultural base of our item pool. The population and culture we selected for the replication was Israel, a country that previously had contributed a comparison population for our teaching styles project. A number of different objectives motivated our Israeli study. Again, we wanted to survey sources of chronic stress in different samples of mothers of young children. We were also interested in comparing and contrasting the findings from this population with the American samples. And finally, we hoped that the information gained by this procedure would reduce the cultural bias of the stress measure that was being developed.

The Israeli sample consisted of 54 married Jewish mothers living in the capital city of Jerusalem (Hoffman, Hoffman, & Feshbach, 1979). Each mother had at least one child between the ages of 2 and 5 years. The women were stratified by maternal employment and socioeconomic status, the latter determined by husband's level of occupation. There were 18 high-SES mothers, all of whom worked. Of the 36 low-SES mothers, 17 held jobs outside the home. Although all mothers were Israeli born, the high-SES mothers were from Western-oriented European family backgrounds while the low-SES mothers had Middle Eastern roots. This ethnic imbalance is an outcome of the generally strong relationship between SES and ethnicity among Israeli Jews (Habib, 1974).

Each mother was approached individually in a municipal work park by a trained Israeli female interviewer and asked to participate in a study on pressures facing mothers. As in the American study, content analyses were performed by submitting sets of 100 randomly selected responses to a panel of six judges. The judges were either native Israelis or had lived in Israel for long periods. All had extensive training in psychology and counseling.

Israeli and American Sources of Maternal Stress

A total of 12 categories emerged from the analysis of the Israeli responses by Israeli judges. Of these, eight were identical to those found in the American study: Children, Self, Husband, Work, Social Relations with Others, Finances, Housework, and Life Events. Three new areas of concern emerged from the Israeli sample and included the categories of Child Care Facilities, Community Services, and Living Environment. Community Services involved difficulties associated with inadequacies in such basic services as public transportation, health care, recreation, and shopping facilities. The category of Living Environment consisted of complaints associated with crowded or unkempt living conditions.

The category of Sociopolitical Milieu that appeared in the analysis of Israeli stress sources was similar but not identical to the category of Society found in the American sample. The Israeli concerns revolved around the imminent threat of war, as well as such issues as quality of the schools, crime, and inflation. The category of Time reflected in the American study did not emerge in the Israeli sample, although some items concerned with time were subsumed in the category of Self.

TABLE 2.3
Israeli Study
Percentage of Women Included in Each Category for Three Groups of Women

Category	High-SES Working (N = 18)	Low-SES Working (N = 17)	Low-SES Nonworking (N = 19)	Total (N = 54)
Children	94	76	89	87
Self	66	88	79	77
Husband	50	88	58	65
Finances	22	65	68	54
Housework	44	53	47	48
Child Care Facilities	33	47	53	44
Social Relations	33	41	53	63
Community Services	50	29	42	41
Sociopolitical Milieu	66	24	26	39
Living Environment	39	41	37	39
Occupation	39	53	32	41
Life Crises	33	24	6	24

The frequency of Israeli mothers citing each of the 12 categories is presented in Table 2.3. As in the American study, the areas associated with the greatest stress pertain to relationships within the family and include the caregiving relation with the child (cited by 87% of the mothers); the mother's relation to herself (77%); and the marital relationship (66%). The least frequent areas of chronic maternal stress in Israel involve infrequent life crises (39%) and the uncertain social climate outside the home (24%). Israeli mothers also cited the more moderate stress areas associated with home management, such as Finances (54%) and Housework (48%) in proportions roughly equal to their American counterparts.

Significant differences appeared in only three areas: Social Relations, Work, and Sociopolitical Milieu. Israeli mothers cited stress associated with relations with others at twothirds the frequency of American mothers (43% vs. 63%). In contrast, they were twice as likely to mention problems in the general social and political atmosphere (39% vs. 22%). Among the subsample of employed women, the Israeli mothers cited occupational difficulties at half the rate of their American counterparts (41% vs. 75%). Separate chi-square comparisons indicated that each of these differences was significant at the .05 level.

Maternal Employment and Socioeconomic Status

Comparison of the response distributions for the three subsamples of Israeli mothers replicates the stress effects found in the American study and points up differences associated with socioeconomic status as well (See Table 2.3). Qualitatively, the Israeli mothers' responses reveal striking parallels in the effect of employment in both countries. In the Israeli, as in the American sample, working mothers referred to difficulties at the job site and conflicts between job hours and home life, while their nonemployed counterparts cited problems with boredom and loneliness. Yet in contrast to their American counterparts, Israeli housewives also reported acutely felt personal frustrations over their inability to work outside the home. Close reading of these responses indicates that resistance from husbands as well as a lack of inexpensive child care were primary barriers to employment. Chi-square comparisons of stress responses in working and nonworking women at the low-SES level revealed that employed Israeli women had significantly more difficulties with their husbands than did housewives (88% vs. 57%).

More low-SES than high-SES working mothers cite difficulties with husbands (88% vs. 50%) and financial strains (65% vs. 22%), while more high-SES than low-SES mothers report broad concerns about the Sociopolitical Milieu.

The one aspect of the Israeli study not addressed by the American study was the influence of SES on chronic maternal stress. Contrary to suggestions of earlier writers (Dohrenwend & Dohrenwend, 1974), no qualitative differences appeared in the types of stress sources cited by working mothers at either end of the socioeconomic ladder. Moreover, no quantitative differences appeared in their relative emphasis on most aspects of stress connected to the care of their child, their homes, themselves, or their work. However, those differences that do appear include greater references to financial difficulty and marital strains among low-SES mothers, and less frequent references to tensions in the wider sociopolitical clime.

Although the financial press on low-SES mothers can readily be understood in strictly economic terms, their greater marital difficulties and lessened community concerns appear to be products of broader social considerations. In Israel, low socioeconomic status is associated with highly traditional and conservative patterns of family functioning.

The content analysis of the Israeli mothers' responses and its comparison with the American sample points out striking similarities in the difficulties and concerns facing women with young children in the two countries. When the responses of the American and the Israeli mothers are broadly compared, the similarities support the concept of an underlying structural pattern of stress sources associated with the roles of motherhood. The descriptive results rendered by the common qualitative methodologies of interviews and content analysis provide a first step toward more rigid quantitative assessments of the stress sources.

THE CHRONIC MATERNAL STRESS INVENTORY

The pilot American and Israeli studies provided a pool of recurrent or situational stress items organized into 10 comprehensive categories dealing with different life areas. Seven of these categories were basically homogeneous. These included: Housework demands; Time pressures of family management; Financial constraints; minor household Disruptions; relations with Kin; relations with Friends; and the quality of the general life Environment. The remaining three categories—Children (The Caregiving Relationship); Husbands (Marital Relationship); and Self (Strains in Fulfilling Personal Needs)—contained a much higher number of items and showed greater diversity. Hence, these latter three categories were further categorized. The category of children was divided into six subcategories and included: Faults; Motherwork (a term used by Bernard, [1974] to describe the chores associated with childcaring); Health Concerns; Developmental Concerns; Child-Rearing Decisions; and Child Care Arrangements. The category of Husband was divided into Faults; Lack of Help; Well-Being; Husband as Father. Self was divided into Overload; Personal Health and Well-Being; and Self-Actualization.

The inventory was devised by selecting four representative items for each category and subcategory out of the pool of American and Israeli responses. These items were edited to create parallel grammatical structures across items. The resulting questionnaire consisted of 80 items that asked the mother how much stress (tension, pressure, upset or hassled) she generally felt associated with each particular circumstance or situation. The following items are illustrative of the structure and content of the scale:

5. Children's fighting, noise, messes.
   1   2   3   4   5   6
6. Being rushed, too much to do in the time available.
   1   2   3   4   5   6
8. Money for essentials.
   1   2   3   4   5   6
17. Disagreements with husband over handling the children.
   1   2   3   4   5   6
36. Breakdown in the house—that is, appliances, plumbing.
   1   2   3   4   5   6
55. Concern over success as a parent.
   1   2   3   4   5   6
71. The state of public affairs that is, energy crisis, inflation.
   1   2   3   4   5   6

Mothers could indicate on a scale ranging from 1 (no stress) to 6 (extreme stress) the degree of stress elicited by each item. Average ratings across the four items in each category or subcategory are used as the outcome score for that category or subcategory. The average rating across categories in a life area serves as the life-area score. The unit of analysis selected depends on whether the purpose of the administration is for clinical or research use.

Reliability, internal consistency, and concurrent validity of the Source of Chronic Maternal Stress were evaluated in a number of subsequent studies. Hoffman (1983) administered the measure to 38 Anglo-American mothers of preschool children living in Los Angeles. Test–retest correlations for average response scores over a 1-week period ranged from .62 to .90 across the 10 life areas, with a mean correlation of .83. The test–retest correlation for the total sum was .94. These correlations point to a relatively high level of temporal consistency for the inventory. In terms of interitem correlations, Cronbach alphas for seven out of the 10 life areas were above .70. These results suggest a moderately strong level of internal consistency for most of the inventory's life-area scales.

In regard to validity estimates, two extensive dissertations were carried out evaluating the Chronic Maternal Stress Inventory. Before describing these two studies, it would be helpful to consider a shorter version of the Chronic Maternal Stress Inventory.

THE GLOBAL CHRONIC MATERNAL STRESS INDEX

A second instrument was constructed in conjunction with our efforts to develop procedures to assess chronic maternal stress. This latter measure focuses on mother's global perception of stress. This inventory consists of 10 questions regarding the 10 major categories of stress represented in the Chronic Maternal Stress Inventory. An additional item in the Index relates to overall or total amount of stress. For each of the 11 items, respondents are asked to estimate on a scale ranging from 1 (little or no stress) to 6 (extreme stress) the amount of stress she experiences. The obtained score is derived by summing the indicated stress amounts for each item divided by 11.

In regard to reliability estimates for the Index, Hoffman administered the measure to a sample of 20 Anglo-American mothers with preschool children twice over a 1-week period (Hoffman, 1983). Average test–retest correlations for the 11 items was .90.

A COMPARISON OF THE TWO STRESS MEASURES

The relationship between our two measures of chronic maternal stress—the detailed inventory and the shorter, global index was examined in conjunction with two doctoral dissertations (Hoffman, 1983; Jordon, 1982). In the first of these studies (Jordon, 1982), the measures were administered to 51 Caucasian, Anglo women who were the mothers of at least one child between the ages of two and five. All of the women resided in middle-class communities in the Los

Angeles area. With one exception, all had at least a high school diploma; 15 were college graduates and, at the time of the study, none of the mothers worked outside the home.

The correlations between the overall stress scores on the 80 item Chronic Maternal Stress Inventory and the Global Chronic Maternal Stress Index proved to be surprisingly high, with a Pearson r of .78. A comparison of the rank order yielded by each measure of the 10 stress categories further reflects the similarity of the two measures. The Spearman correlation for the rank orders is .80. Although these data indicate that the two measures are highly similar and equivalent in a number of respects, they are not identical. The range and mean absolute amount of stress are greater for Environment and, to a lesser extent, for Self, in the case of the more detailed inventory as compared to the Global Index, while those for the stress of Friends, Relatives, and Money are lower. The high ranking for Societal stress differs from the typical pattern that has been found for mothers. It reflects a special problem that was particularly salient in that community at that time—namely, tension in connection with compulsory school busing. The administration of these measures to a comparable sample in the same community by Hoffman (1983) 1 year later, by which time the busing issue had been resolved, yielded the more commonly found pattern of sources of maternal stress.

Hoffman's sample consisted of 80 Caucasian Anglo mothers. The criteria for inclusion in the study differed slightly from those used by Jordon. The mothers, as in the case of Jordon's sample, had to be married; their children were somewhat older, ranging from 3 years to 5½ years of age; and the outside employment of the mothers had to be less than 8 hours a week. Hoffman, like Jordon, also obtained high agreement between the two measures. In addition, he determined the degree to which each of the maternal stress areas, as assessed by the 80 item inventory, was correlated with the global index based on the single overall stress estimate item. Variations in the areas with the highest mean ratings for stress— Self, Children (especially childrearing), Housework, correlated most highly with the Global Stress score, these correlations ranging from .79 to .72. Most of the other correlations of the Global Stress score with each of the stress components were between .7 and .6, again reflecting the consistency of the two methods of assessing chronic maternal stress.

RELATIONSHIP OF THE CHRONIC MATERNAL STRESS INVENTORY AND GLOBAL CHRONIC MATERNAL STRESS INDEX TO OTHER STRESS INDICATORS

The data that have been reported thus far attest to the reliability of the two chronic stress indicators and, to a lesser degree, to their validity or meaning. These are several different kinds of data from the Jordon and Hoffman disserta-

TABLE 2.4
Mean Scores and Ranks of Sources of Chronic Maternal Stress

Sources of Stress		Maternal Stress Inventory (Long Form) Categories		Global Maternal Stress (Short Form) Items	
		Mean Score	Rank	Mean Score	Rank
FINANCES		2.48	5	3.01	3
HOUSEWORK		2.26	7	2.60	6
TIME		2.73	2	3.13	2
FRIENDS/RELATIVES		2.15	10	2.47	7
DISRUPTIONS		2.17	8	2.43	8
ENVIRONMENT		2.43	6	1.84	10
SOCIETY		3.13	1	3.43	1
HUSBAND (MEN)		2.14	9	2.31	9
faults	2.25				
help	2.02				
well-being	2.26				
as fathers	2.04				
CHILDREN		2.58	3.5	2.78	4
mother work	2.27				
faults	3.38				
health	2.19				
child rearing	2.73				
child care	1.60				
SELF		2.58	3.5	2.64	5
overload	2.75				
health	2.55				
self-actualization	2.44				

NOTE: Jordan, 1982.

tions that bear on the validity and utility of the stress measures. Several sets of observations involve maternal behaviors that are predicted consequences of chronic stress. These data bear on the construct validity of the measures. Other observations addressed to variables that are hypothesized to mediate the intensity or negative consequences of stress, such as availability of social supports, also bear on construct validity. Before reviewing these findings, the relationship of the chronic stress measures to other stress indicators will be examined. These latter relate to both criterion and construct validity issues.

In addition to administering the two chronic stress forms, Jordan (1982) through daily telephone interviews, assessed the level and sources of stress experienced by the participating mothers over an 8 day period. These interviews were initiated on the day following the administration of the stress inventories. During the telephone interview, the mother was queried concerning the amount of stress she had experienced that day, and, in addition, the discipline events that had occurred. This daily telephone report of stress followed the format of the Global Stress Index in that the mother was requested to indicate on a scale of 1 to 6, the amount of stress she had felt during the past 24 hours in regard to each of the 10 categories of stress sources, and how much stress she had felt overall.

The mean responses on the Daily Stress Report are indicated in Table 2.5. Inspection of the table indicates that while there was some day to day fluctuation, on the whole there was relatively little change over the 8 days of observation. An examination by day of the week, rather than by day of observation, yielded a similar pattern. There was no evidence that mothers experience different levels of stress on weekdays than on weekends. The Daily Stress Reports were averaged across all 8 days to yield a mean stress level for each stress source and overall global stress index. The rank order of the stress categories closely corre-

TABLE 2.5
Mean Responses on the Daily Stress Report for Each Day of Observation

STRESS CATEGORIES	DAY OF OBSERVATION							
	1	2	3	4	5	6	7	8
FINANCES	2.13	2.07	2.23	1.96	1.74	1.84	1.94	2.07
HOUSEWORK	1.98	1.76	1.83	2.05	1.82	2.04	1.88	2.12
TIME	2.35	2.29	2.25	2.25	2.45	2.45	2.19	2.41
FR/REL	1.84	1.53	1.66	1.66	2.01	1.80	2.04	1.94
HUSBAND (MEN)	2.16	1.63	1.96	1.45	1.73	1.65	1.70	1.96
DISRUPTIONS	1.92	1.65	1.83	2.00	1.98	1.86	1.68	1.90
CHILD	2.31	2.39	2.25	2.45	2.63	2.63	2.29	2.27
ENVIRON	1.65	1.49	1.64	1.55	1.57	1.57	1.57	1.60
SOCIETY	2.43	2.23	2.22	2.30	2.05	2.31	2.43	2.29
SELF	2.00	2.00	1.96	2.11	2.09	2.15	2.21	2.27
OVERALL	2.45	2.47	2.45	2.41	2.56	2.51	2.45	2.80
MEAN	2.11	1.95	2.03	1.99	2.06	2.05	2.03	2.15

NOTE: Jordon, 1982.

sponded with that of the Chronic Maternal Stress Inventory and of the Chronic Maternal Stress Global Index, the respective rank order correlations being .80 and .88. The Pearson correlations of the total scores are much lower, the correlations of .26 with the inventory approaching significance and that of .42 with the Global Index being significant at the .01 level.

Both Jordan (1982) and Hoffman (1983) included the Life Experiences Survey (LES) developed by Sarason and his coworkers (Sarason, Johnson, & Siegel, 1978) among the measures that were completed by the mothers. The LES is an adaptation of the Holmes and Rahe (1967) Schedule of Recent Experiences and of other life-events schedules that are widely used as indicators of acute stress. The LES is a self-report measure containing 47 life events such as family death, job loss, and financial reversal. Respondents indicate which items occurred in the previous year and rate the associated degree of positive or negative impact on their lives.

The responses of both samples of mothers on the LES were comparable. The 51 mothers in the Jordan sample reported an average of 5.24 significant life events per mother while the 80 mothers in the Hoffman study reported an average of 6.21 such events. Serious illness of a family member, a major change in number of arguments with spouse, a change in husband's work, major change in social activities, borrowing more than $10,000, and pregnancy were among the most frequently cited events in both samples. Hoffman compared the annual life event frequencies of his maternal sample with those that have been reported for a normative sample and found significant differences in report frequency for only 4 of 18 events that were compared. Changes in family closeness, the borrowing of more than $10,000 (mortgage or loan), and "trouble with in-laws" were cited more often by these young mothers while changes in work conditions were cited twice as often by the normative sample.

The LES is a measure of acute stress and is not likely to be strongly correlated with the measures of chronic maternal stress. However, one might expect some overlap between the events that contribute to acute stress and those that become sources of chronic stress. Thus, Jordan finds a small but significant correlation (.29) between the LES and the Chronic Maternal Stress Inventory. While Jordan did not obtain a significant relationship between LES and either the Daily or Global Stress measure, Hoffman found a quite significant correlation between the total number of reported life events and the global stress score ($r = .34$, p .01).

Hoffman, carrying out a more detailed analysis, noted that the relationship between the degree of the global chronic stress rating and the number of reported life events is a function of the number of negative events reported; that is, variations in the number of high-frequency events are correlated with global stress while variations in low-frequency events were generally unrelated to stress. The number of negative events was moderately associated with global stress scores ($r = .36$, p .01) while positive events frequency was essentially

TABLE 2.6
Correlations Between Maternal Chronic Stress Inventory
Category and Subcategory with Reported Negative,
Positive and Total Life Event Frequencies

| | LIFE EVENT | | |
CHRONIC STRESS SOURCE	NEGATIVE	POSITIVE	TOTAL
HUSBAND (MEN)	.36**		.37**
SELF	.33**	.22	.36**
TIME	.32**	.29*	.36**
CHILD	.31**	.18	.34**
RELATIVES	.26*		.28*

NOTE: Hoffman, 1983.
    *$p < .05$
    **$p < .01$

unrelated to chronic stress ($r = .10$, p .10). Negative events that were particularly related to maternal stress were those involving the husband ($r = .29$), financial stress ($r = .25$), social activity ($r = .22$) and relatives ($r = .22$).

Hoffman also examined the relationship of negative and positive life event frequencies to the more detailed Maternal Chronic Stress Inventory. He found several specific components and subcomponents of chronic stress to be significantly associated with acute life event experiences, especially negative experiences. These are summarized in Table 2.6. From Table 2.6, it can be seen that only one life-area category—time pressure—is significantly correlated with the number of positive events that occurred the previous year. Because time pressure permeates so many life-area stress sources, it may well be a significant factor mediating the relationship between positive life events and stress. Whereas theoretical discussion of the stressful consequences of positive significant life events has implicated emotional arousal and disruption as the primary cause of stress, increased time demands resulting from new opportunities and relationships may well be a critical factor contributing to stress.

At the same time, Hoffman's data suggests that negative life events are much more potent contributors to stress than positive life events. With regard to sources of chronic stress for mothers that are linked to negative events that occurred the previous year, problems in martial relations, personal health and other self-related issues, difficulties in the child-rearing area, problems with relatives, and time pressures are the areas found to be significantly correlated with negative event frequencies.

Thus, both Hoffman and Jordon find a significant relationship between Maternal Chronic Stress Inventory and the LES measure of acute stress. In the case of the Global Maternal Stress Index, the relationship with LES is less consistent. Global maternal stress is significantly correlated with frequency of negative events on the LES in the Hoffman study, while Jordon, using the total LES score, did not carry out this particular analysis. However, Jordon did find a significant relationship between the Global Maternal Stress Index and daily reports by mothers of stressful experiences. The evidence of concurrent validity provided by both the Hoffman and Jordon studies increases one's confidence in the utility of the chronic maternal stress measures.

In addition to bearing on the methodological question of the validity of the measures, the data also suggest that the chronic stress measures can be useful tools in exploring theoretical and empirical questions regarding the processes by which significant life events become sources of stress. There is probably a reciprocal relationship between chronic stress and the stressful consequences of significant life events such that areas of chronic stress increase one's vulnerability to the stress-inducing effects of a major life change, and major life events in turn will become reflected in and exacerbate sources of chronic stress. It would be revealing to carry out longitudinal studies that would permit the analysis of this likely interaction between chronic and acute stress.

CHRONIC MATERNAL STRESS AND SOCIAL SUPPORT

One of the factors that has been hypothesized to influence the degree to which potential stressful events and experiences become sources of stress is the amount and kind of social support that is available to the individual. Social support can help prevent or mitigate the amount of stress ensuing from a potentially stressful event; or it may enter into the stress dynamic at a later point, helping the individual to cope with a severe or chronic stress and thereby reducing the subsequent intensity of the stress. In either case, social supports should foster lower stress. An inverse relationship between social supports and stress should hold for chronic stress and for acute stress.

The role of social supports in stress was examined by both Jordon and Hoffman. In each study, a social support interview developed by Miller (1979) was administered to the mothers. The interview elicits information as to the availability of confidantes with whom problems could be shared. The instrument was modified so as to ensure that child-related problems were among those that could be discussed. In addition, Jordan asked her subjects to indicate the availability and actual utilization of confidantes within the previous 2 weeks.

Jordon did not find the availability of a confidante to be related to the stress measures. Some negative relationships were found between actual help received during the previous 2-week period and degree of stress indicated for various stress categories. However, the Jordon findings, at best, provide only marginal support for the hypothesized inverse relationship between social supports and amount of stress.

TABLE 2.7
Correlations of Social Confidante Indices With
Chronic Maternal Stress and Acute Life Events

| | Confidantes | | | |
Source Type	Friends	Family	Husband	Total
CHRONIC MATERNAL STRESS INVESTORY TOTAL	-.27*			-.30**
Childrearing	-.22*			-.27*
Husband			-.30*	
Self	-.26*			-.30*
Environ	-.22*			-.29**
Housework	-.32**			-.28*
Time Press	-.32*			-.36**
Financial				
Events				
Relatives				
Friends				
LIFE EVENTS TOTAL				-.23*
Negative Total		-.27*	-.27*	
Positive Total			-.27*	

NOTE: Hoffman, 1983.
   *$p<.05$
  **$p<.01$

Jordon's data are primarily based on the presence or absence of social supports. Hoffman, using measures of the number and type of social supports, finds much more evidence indicating that the social supports available to the mother play an important role in helping her cope with stressful experiences. Hoffman distinguishes between "Confidantes"—individuals with whom major problems can be shared and discussed, and "Aids"—reliable sources of physical aid and assistance in times of need. Each of these groups are further categorized according to whether the support is a friend, extended family member, or husband. While the index of friend support was based upon the number of friends who served in this role, the husband support index and that for the family members were based upon presence versus absence.

Correlation analyses of the relationship between social supports and the Chronic Maternal Stress Inventory and LES measures were carried out and are reported in Tables 2.7 and 2.8. It can be seen from these tables that chronic maternal stress is significantly related to amount of social supports. The more supportive friends the mother has who can function as confidantes, the less stress she experiences in regard to childrearing, her husband, her immediate environment, housework, and time pressures. They do not affect financial stress, or the stress from relatives, disruptive events, and surprisingly, friends, although, in the case of the latter, the negative correlation approaches significance ($r = .19$, p .10). The number of family confidantes is unrelated to chronic maternal stress,

TABLE 2.8
Correlations of Potential Aid Indices With
Chronic Maternal Stress and Acute Life Events

| | Potential Aids | |
	Friends	Family
CHRONIC MATERNAL STRESS INVENTORY TOTAL	-.34*	
Childrearing	-.28*	
Husband	-.37**	
Self	-.31**	
Environ		
Housework	-.36**	
Time Press	-.25*	
Financial		
Events	-.34*	
Relatives		
Friends		
LIFE EVENTS TOTAL		
Negative Total		
Positive Total		

NOTE: Hoffman, 1983.
*$p<.05$
**$p<.01$

and the availability of the husband as a confidante is associated, as one would expect, with a lesser amount of stress stemming from the marital relationship with the husband.

The correlations of the Chronic Maternal Stress Inventory with the number of Potential Aids yields essentially similar relationships to those obtained for confidantes. (Husbands were not included in the queries concerning Aids). For the Life Events measure, the correlations with support available from Aids were insignificant and those with Confidantes inconsistent. The number of friends as confidantes is unrelated to acute, life-event stress. When husbands are available as confidantes, negative life-event scores are lower. When family members are available, negative event scores are higher. Given the general absence of relationships between amount of stress and availability of family members as sources of support, the obtained correlations may be spurious. It might possibly reflect the occurrence of negative family events (e.g., illness or death of parents or other relatives) that foster greater closeness between the mother and her kin.

Overall, these findings suggest that the availability of social supports from friends may play an important role in ameliorating the amount of chronic stress that mothers experience and are consistent with the work of Bronfenbrenner (1979) on family support and family stress. These data further bear on the construct validity of the Chronic Maternal Stress Inventory, and point to its potential utility.

MATERNAL STRESS AND MATERNAL ATTITUDE AND BEHAVIORS

The initial impetus to develop the Chronic Maternal Stress Inventory was the proposition that maternal use of aversive or negative reinforcement as compared to positive reinforcement was linked to heightened maternal stress. Having developed reliable indices to assess such stress, we can now consider the relationship between maternal stress and maternal attitudes and behavior. The relationship between stress and the use of punitive or aversive methods for controlling and instructing children was explored in the Jordon (1982) and Hoffman (1983) dissertations. In Jordon's dissertation, the observations focus on mother's preferred methods of discipline as reflected in responses to hypothetical and actual discipline situations. In Hoffman's dissertation, the observations focus on the mother and child behavior in teaching situations.

Jordon, utilizing a method developed by Loveland (1977), asked each mother to respond to brief descriptions of 15 situations of child misbehavior, ranging from meal refusal and toilet accidents to aggression toward the parent. The mother is asked to describe how she would handle this situation if it occurred; how she would respond to it if her first option failed; and how she would respond to it if her second option failed. Prior to the analysis of the maternal responses, a panel of judges sorted the responses into categories. Eleven discipline techniques emerged from their categorization. Five could be clustered as Power Assertive: Physically Moving the Child; Physical Punishment; NonPhysical Punishment; Command; and Threat. Four were designated as Cooperative: Reasoning; Restructuring (or changing a situation that caused difficulty); Reward for Compliance, and Labeling the Negative Effects (of the behavior). The remaining two disciplinary practices, No Action or Ignoring (the behavior), and giving up and letting the child have his or her way, (yielding) were considered as Avoidance. Maternal responses were scored for the number of times each discipline technique was mentioned and for the presence of escalation in each of the 15 discipline episodes. In addition to applying this coding procedure to the responses to the hypothetical discipline situation, it was also used to score the mother's responses to the eight daily telephone interviews.

Table 2.9 presents the relative frequencies of the various disciplinary responses to the hypothetical situations and to the reported daily incidents. It can be seen there is a substantial overall correspondence between responses in the two contexts. The majority of discipline procedures used are Power Assertive: 61% for the hypothetical situations and rising to 69% for the daily incidents. Cooperative strategies accounted for 25% and 20% of the responses to the

TABLE 2.9
Maternal Discipline Usage in Hypothetical Discipline
Situations and Reported Daily Discipline Events

	Discipline Situation	Daily Discipline
POWER ASSERTIVE	61%	69%
Move	3%	10%
Physical Pun.	11%	10%
Punishment	18%	11%
Command	22%	28%
Threat	7%	10%
COOPERATIVE	25%	20%
Reasoning	13%	9%
Restructure	8%	7%
Reward	.5%	2%
Effect on Mother	5%	2%
AVOIDANCE	13%	11%
No Action	12%	9%
Give Up	.9%	2%
ESCALATE	16%	15%

NOTE: Jordon, 1982.

situational test and to the actual incidents, respectively, with Avoidance approaches accounting for 13% and 11% of the maternal disciplinary behaviors. However, despite the consistency of the rank order of responses in the hypothetical and actual situations, the correlations between the frequency with which a mother reported a particular discipline cluster or procedure in response to the hypothetical situation and in response to actual situation were negligible. The one exception was Physical Punishment—the correlation between hypothesized and actual use of physical punishment being .56 (p .01).

Data bearing on the relationship between disciplines practices and the measures of chronic maternal stress are reported in Table 2.10. It can be seen from inspection of Table 2.10 that the correlation of discipline techniques with stress occur primarily in relation to the use of Power Assertion. These correlations, while not large, are in the predicted direction. The correlation of the total Power Assertion score based on actual incidents with the Stress Inventory and Global Stress measures are significant at the .10 level (two-tailed test), while the correlation of the hypothetical situation score with Global Stress is significant at the .05 level. The use of physical punishment is significantly correlated with Global Stress and approaches statistical significance for the Daily Stress Index.

It is noteworthy that with the exception of the Labeling the Effect response, none of the correlations with the Cooperative and Avoidance disciplinary tech-

TABLE 2.10
Summary of Significant Correlations Between Discipline Techniques and
Over-all Stress on the Three Measures of Chronic Maternal Stress

	Stress Inventory	Global Stress	Daily Stress
POWER ASSERTIVE	.31*(DR)	.30*DR; .34*(ST)	.29*(DR); .29*(ST)
Physical Move	.40***(DR)	.45***(DR)	
Physical Pun.		.35**(DR)	.29*(DR); .29*(ST)
Nonphysical Punishment			
Command	.28*(DR)		
Threat			
COOPERATIVE			
Reasoning			
Restructuring			
Reward Labeling	.28*(DR)		.30*(ST)
AVOIDANCE			
Yielding			
No Action			

NOTE: Jordon, 1982.

   * .10 level   DR: Daily Reports of Discipline Incidents
  ** .05 level   ST: Hypothetical Situation Test
 *** .01 level

niques approach significance. The Labeling Effect on Mother correlation, while only significant at the .10 level, is suggestive of the ambiguous properties of this tactic as a method for inducing a child to desist from some undesired activity. This approach may point out to the child the negative consequences of the behavior for the mother. And while it may sensitize the child to the effects his or her action has on others, it can also be a powerful method for guilt induction as well as an appeal for sympathy for the stressed mother.

The relationship between the Effect on Mother tactic and maternal stress is more evident when the correlates of specific sources of stress are analyzed. The stress of Housework, Time, and Self are significantly related to the Labeling the Effect on Mother strategy while the correlations of that tactic with most of the other stress categories approach statistical significance. Housework, Time, and Self stress scores are also highly correlated at p .01 levels with the frequency of physically moving of the child for both the Chronic Maternal Stress Inventory and the Global Maternal Stress Index. Stress from Friends and from Children are additional stress sources, based on the Stress Inventory, that are significantly related to Physical Movement.

For Physical Punishment, the only significant correlation is with Self as a source of stress, as assessed by daily interviews (r = .33, p .01). However, if the mothers are divided into two groups—the 27 who actually used physical punishment during the 8 days of telephone contact and the 24 who did not—then significant differences in sources of stress from child emerge, with the physical punishment group obtaining significantly higher mean scores than the other group of mothers on each of the stress measures. The only other disciplinary procedure to display consistent correlations with specific stress categories was punishment. Here, financial stress emerged as a significant correlate (r = .36, when derived from Global Index and r = .39 when derived from Stress Inventory) in addition to Housework and Time.

In summary, the Jordon findings are consistent with the hypothesis that mothers under stress tend to use aversive disciplinary procedures. Although the correlations tend to be small, they are in the predicted direction, and many are statistically reliable.

Hoffman's direct observations of the mothers in teaching situations provide another test of the relationship between stress and parental discipline. Following administration of the stress questionnaire, he selected a subsample of 40 mothers from the initial stress inventory group for participation in the observational phase of the study. Mothers were chosen by dividing them into four groups based on quartile scores for the Global Maternal Chronic Stress Index, and then randomly selecting 10 mothers from each quartile. A home visit, made approximately 3 weeks after the initial session, allowed observations in three contexts. First, the mother was given questionnaires to complete while the child played adjacently. The next two tasks (Phinney & Feshbach, 1980), entailed interactions between the mother and child. One of these utilized a set of wooden miniature houses, other structures, people, and animals. The mother was asked to have the child set up a village, a task in which she could help the child as much or as little as she desired. For the second task, the mother was asked to teach her child the meaning of "live" or "living" by having the child sort the village pieces into separate piles of living and nonliving items.

Systematic recordings were made of the verbal and nonverbal behaviors of the mother and child. Reliable scoring categories were established and, in regard to maternal behaviors, were grouped into four clusters reflecting the degree of maternal involvement, extent of information conveyed, degree of maternal control, and use of reinforcement. The last cluster bears most directly upon the hypothesized effects of stress. Three indices of maternal reinforcement were employed: Positives—the average number of positive statements and physical acts of warmth and affection made during a 6-second scoring interval; Negatives—the average number of negative or rejecting statements made during a 6-second scoring interval; and Positive emphasis—the percentage of positive acts out of the total number of positives and negatives. This last index controls for differences in frequency of reinforcements and focuses on the relative use of positive versus negative reinforcements.

The correlations between total scores on the Chronic Maternal Stress Inventory with maternal reinforcement usage are presented in Table 2.11. In accordance with the stress–maternal behavior hypothesis, a significant positive correlation (r = .32, p .05) was obtained between amount of reported stress and maternal use of negative responses with her preschool child in the instructional task and play situations. Also, while the use of positive reinforcement is not significantly

TABLE 2.11
Correlations of Maternal Use of Reinforcement With
Total Scores on the Chronic Maternal Stress Inventory

Reinforcement	Partial r (Controlling for Child Misbehavior)
Negative r = .32; $p<.05$	r = .27; $p<.10$
Positive r = -.14; $p<.10$	r = -.15; $p<.10$
% Positive r = -.38; $p<.05$	r = -.31; $p<.05$

NOTE: Hoffman, 1983.

related to stress, the proportion of positive reinforcers is negatively correlated with chronic maternal stress, the r of −.38 being significant at the .05 level.

It is possible that both maternal stress and the greater maternal use of negative reinforcement could be a consequence of the mother having to cope with a difficult, misbehaving child. During the observation situations, the child's behavior was coded along with the mother's, and a measure of child misbehavior was derived. Table 2.11 also presents the correlations of maternal stress with reinforcement usage, with the effects of child misbehaviors partialled out. While the correlations are somewhat smaller, the relationship of stress to percentage of positive reinforcers used remains significant, while that with negative reinforcement is significant at the .10 level. An analysis of the relationship of reinforcement usage to specific sources of stress did not indicate that there were particular stress sources that were primarily responsible for the obtained relationship between stress and greater negative and relatively less positive reinforcement usage. The stress appeared to be stemming from a variety of different sources that, in combination, were related to the mother's behavior.

Analyses of maternal stress, as reflected by the LES measure, yielded essentially similar relationships. The correlations of the acute stress scores to the negative reinforcement scores were significant at the .05 level without and with child misbehavior controlled (r = .42; r = .36). The relationships with absolute use of positive reinforcers were negligible, and while those with percentage of reinforcers were larger, they were not significant (r = −.22; r = −.17). A separate analysis of acute stress scores for positive and for negative events resulted in similar patterns of relationships, with the correlation of positive event stress scores with negative reinforcement being somewhat higher (r = .42, p < .05) than that obtained for negative events (r = .29, p < .10). The difference between the two correlations was not significant.

It is clear from both the Hoffman and Jordon studies that chronic maternal stress, while not a powerful determinant of maternal behaviors, is a significant and theoretically consistent correlate of maternal behavior. The greater the degree of maternal stress, the more likely is the mother to employ punitive discipline techniques and to use negative reinforcing procedures when instructing her child. These findings, in addition to providing empirical support for the hypothesized relationship between stress and maternal behavior, also bear upon the construct validity of the chronic maternal stress measures. Support for the predicted correlates of the Chronic Maternal Stress Inventory was found by both Jordan and Hoffman. Although the behavioral correlates of the Global Maternal Stress Index were not examined in the Hoffman study, the global stress measure did relate in a consistent manner to the measures of maternal discipline obtained in Jordan's investigation.

PARENTAL CHRONIC STRESS SCALE

The Parental Chronic Stress Scale is an adaptation of the Global Chronic Maternal Stress Index. The latter instrument was used as the basis for the development of a measure that would be equally appropriate for use with fathers as well as mothers. Five researchers of paternal behavior were asked to evaluate each item of the index in terms of its applicability to fathers. On the basis of this procedure, a number of items from the original index were modified. The revised scale was then discussed by father and mother participants in a number of parent groups. This procedure contributed to the editorial clarification of several items.

The revised Parental Scale has a similar structure to the Maternal Index. Parents are asked to rate 12 items on a six-point scale in regard to the amount of stress experienced. The major categories of stress covered by the items include: Money; Household Chores; Time Demands; Relationship with Spouse or Partner; Relationship with Others; Occurrence of Unusual or Unplanned Events; Children; Family Health; Personal Health; Self Problems and Worries, Pressures and Duties from Job.

At the current time, the Parental Chronic Stress Scale is being used and validated in a number of studies here at UCLA and at CHILDHELP, International. Dr. Carollee Howes and myself are investigating a broad array of child and parental interaction behaviors and attributes in abusive and nonabusive families. We are exploring the relationships among a number of dimensions of peer and mother–child interactions, parental and spousal empathy, parental awareness, parental attributions, family support, social desirability, and chronic parental stress. While most of the participants are mothers, we do have a number of fathers in the sample.

A more extensive father population is included in a study being carried out by Jennifer Gilly and myself. In this latter study, we are looking at the relationship between chronic stress, acute stress, empathy, marital intimacy, and family support in 100 pairs of mothers and fathers. Both of these projects are in the active data collection phase, and findings from these studies will bear on the validity of the Parental Chronic Stress Measure.

FUTURE DIRECTIONS

The original impetus to develop the measures described above was an interest in the relationship between parental socialization practices and child behaviors on the one hand, and parental stress and parental socialization practices on the other hand. The child abuse project being carried out by Dr. Howes and myself is an extension of that interest. There are other topics of interest that we plan to pursue, such as the relationship of adequate and available child care to parental stress; the relationship between chronic stress and health; and the relationship between parental stress and child stress. It is in the context of these studies that the particular advantages and properties of chronic stress measures as compared to acute stress measures will be reflected. However, I believe the most important outcome of these chronic stress studies lies in their potential application to stress reduction programs. In particular, we plan to address the issue of stress reduction in our mothers for their sake and for their children's sake.

REFERENCES

Bee, H. L., Egeren, L. F., Streissguth, A. P., Nyman, B. A., & Leckle, M. S. (1969). Social class differences in material teaching strategies and speech patterns. *Developmental Psychology, 1,* 726–734.

Bercovici, A., & Feshbach, N. D. (1973, February). *Teaching styles of mothers of successful and problem readers.* Paper presented at the meeting of the American Educational Research Association, New Orleans.

Bernard, J. (1974). *The future of motherhood.* New York: Penguin.

Bronfenbrenner, U. (1979). *The ecology of human development.* Cambridge, MA: Harvard University Press.

Brophy, J. (1970). Mothers as teachers of their own preschool children: The influence of socioeconomic status and task structure on teaching specificity. *Child Development, 41,* 79–94.

Campbell, A., Converse, P. & Rogers, C. (1976). *The quality of American life: Perceptions, evaluations, and satisfactions.* New York: Russell Sage.

Dohrenwend, B. S. & Dohrenwend, B. P. (Eds.) (1974). *Stressful life events: Their nature and effects.* New York: Wiley.

Feld, S. (1963). Feelings of adjustment. In F. I. Nye & L. W. Hoffman (Eds.), *Employed mothers in America.* Chicago: Rand McNally.

Feshbach, N. D. (1973a). Teaching styles in four-year-olds and their mothers. In J. R. Rosenblith, R. & W. Allinsmith (Eds.), *The causes of behavior: Readings in child development and educational psychology* (3rd ed.). Boston: Allyn & Bacon.

Feshbach, N. D. (1973b). Cross cultural studies of teaching styles in four-year-olds and their mothers. In A. Pick (Ed.), *Minnesota Symposium in Child Psychology, 7.*

Feshbach, N. D., & Devor, G. (1969). Teaching styles in four-year-olds. *Child Development, 40,* 183–190.

Feshbach, N. D., & Jordon, T. S. (1980). *The relationship between material stress and discipline patterns.* Paper presented at a meeting of the Western Psychological Association, Waikiki.

Garbarino, J. (1975). Some ecological correlates of child abuse: The impact of socioeconomic stress on mothers. *Child Development, 47,* 178–185.

Gavron, J. (1966). *The captive wife.* London: Rutledge & Keagan.

Habib, J. (1974). *Children in Israel.* Jerusalem, Israel: Henrietta Szold Institute.

Hess, R. D., Shipman, V. C., Brophy, J., & Bear, R. (1968). *The cognitive environments of urban preschool children.* Chicago: University of Chicago.

Hoffman, M. A. (1983). *Maternal stress and mother child interactions.* Unpublished doctoral dissertation, UCLA, Los Angeles.

Hoffman, M. A., Hoffman, A. M., & Feshbach, N. D. (1979). *Chronic stress in Israeli mothers: The effects of socioeconomic status and maternal employment.* Paper presented at the 59th meeting of the Western Psychological Association, San Diego, CA.

Holmes, T. H., & Rahe, R. H. (1967). The social readjustment rating scale. *Journal of Psychosomatic Research, 11,* 213–232.

Jordon, P. S. (1982). The relationship between maternal stress and maternal discipline, attitudes and practices. *Dissertation,* University of California, Los Angeles Library, Los Angeles, California.

Jordon, P. S. & Feshbach, N. D. (1979). *Chronic stress in mothers of young children.* Paper presented at the meeting of the Western Psychological Association, San Diego, CA.

Laws, J. L. (1971). A feminist review of the marital adjustment literature: The Rape of the Locke. *Journal of Marriage and the Family, 33,* 483–516.

Lazarus, R. S. (1981). The stress and coping paradigm. In C. Eisdorfer, D. Cohen, & A. Klemman (Eds.). *Clinical models for psychopathology* (pp. 188–209). New York: Spectrum.

Loveland, R. J. (1977). Distinctive personality and discipline characteristics of child neglecting mothers. *Dissertation Abstracts International, 38*(1-B), 368.

McLean, P. (1976). Depression as a specific response to stress. In I. G. Sarason & C. D. Spielberger, (Eds.), *Stress and anxiety III.* New York: Hemisphere.

Miller, J. (1979). *Corporal discipline and stress.* Unpublished doctoral dissertation, Cornell University, Ithaca, NY.

Oakley, A. (1974). *Woman's work: The housewife past and present.* New York: Pantheon.

Pearlin, L. I., & Lieberman, M. A. (1977). Social sources of emotional distress. In J. Simmons, (Ed.), *Research in community and mental health.* Greenwich, CN: AI Press.

Phinney, J. S. & Feshbach, N. D. (1980). Non-Directive and intrusive teaching styles of middle- and work-class English mothers. *British Journal of Educational Psychology, 50,* 2–9.

Radl, S. L. (1973). *Mother's day is over.* New York: Charterhouse.

Richman, W. (1976). Depression in mothers of preschool children. *Journal of Child Psychology and Psychiatry, 17,* 75–78.

Rosenberg, M. S. & Repucci, N. D. (1983). Child abuse: A review with special focus on an ecological approach to rural communities. In A. Childs & G. Melton, (Eds.), *Rural psychology.* New York: Plenum Press.

Sarason, I. G. & Johnson, J. H., & Siegel, J. M. (1978). Assessing the impact of life changes: development of the Life Experiences Survey. *Journal of Consulting and Clinical Psychology, 46*(5), 932–946.

3 Recent Advances In Anger Assessment

Mary Kay Biaggio
University of Idaho

Roland D. Maiuro
University of Washington School of Medicine

In recent years research efforts have focused increasingly on anger arousal and expression. Such research has important implications for the study of anger as an instigator of aggression (Konecni, 1975; Zillman, 1978); the anger-prone personality (Novaco, 1977); the relationship between anger inhibition and some psychosomatic disorders (Holt, 1970); anger related disorders, such as depression (Novaco, 1977); and interpersonal relationships fraught with anger related communication problems (Holt, 1970). Of course, reliable study of anger arousal and expression is predicated on the availability of adequate means of anger assessment.

One of the primary problems in the measurement of anger is that research has progressed in this area without a systematic and comprehensive definition of the term. Most research in the area has focused on behavioral manifestations of anger in the form of aggression and has thus viewed anger as a minor part of the aggressive response (Biaggio, 1980; Rothenberg, 1971). Moreover, in cases where attempts have been made to assess or measure some aspect of anger, the terms anger, aggression, and hostility have often been used interchangeably, suggesting a lack of differentiation between these constructs.

Our purpose is to provide a comprehensive review of current approaches to the assessment of anger and to discuss issues of relevance to researchers in this area. The individual assessment devices are discussed in terms of their purpose, derivation, and format, as well as their practical utility and published methodological and empirical support. For purposes of organization, the measures are categorized according to the major system that they tend to assess—cognitive, behavioral, or physiological. Two major problems confronting investigators in this field are discussed in the conclusion: difficulties inherent in assessing a multifacted phenomenon and the need for a differentiation between the constructs anger, hostility, and aggression.

COGNITIVE MEASURES OF ANGER AROUSAL— OBJECTIVE TECHNIQUES

Most objective questionnaires and projective measures may be categorized as cognitive on the basis of the method used and the experiential system tapped. Items on such questionnaires may provide indirect or self-reported assessment of overt behavioral and physiological systems but still represent cognitive measures. Thus, they may tap cognitive perceptions of hostile attitudes, inclinations to act or behave in angry/hostile ways, past history of behaving in angry/hostile ways, and psychophysiological feeling states. Whether such measures of anger are related to other constructs, such as destructive aggression, depends on a host of factors including the nature and construction of the items, the frequency and intensity of their endorsement, the specificity of the situations covered, the timing of the test administration, the specific choice and base rate of the targeted behavioral referents, and the type of individuals assessed (cf. Bem & Allen, 1974; Mischel, 1968).

The Buss-Durkee Hostility Inventory

The Buss-Durkee Hostility Inventory (BDHI) (Buss & Durkee, 1957) is probably the best known and most frequently used inventory of its kind. The BDHI attempts a descriptive and quantitative analysis of an individual's preferred mode of hostility expression. In developing the inventory the authors first defined subclasses of hostility that are typically delineated in clinical situations: Assault, Indirect Hostility, Irritability, Negativism, Resentment, Suspicion, Verbal Hostility, and Guilt. A pool of 105 true–false items was then constructed, with the developers considering specificity of item content, minimization of defensiveness in responding, and response set. This version was administered to 159 college students and items were discarded on the basis of high frequency set and low internal consistency. Only 60 of the original items remained; these were supplemented with 34 newly written items and the second version was administered to a sample of 120 college students. After the reapplication of the frequency set and internal consistency criteria, the final form of the scale consisted of 75 true–false items. Factor analysis of the inventory produced two factors: an attitudinal component of hostility (Resentment and Suspicion subscales) and a "motor" component (Assault, Indirect Hostility, Irritability, and Verbal Hostility subscales). The authors provide normative and descriptive data for a sample of 85 male and 88 female college students but no reliability data are calculated. Biaggio, Supplee, and Curtis (1981) do report 2-week test–retest reliability coefficients for the subscales ranging from .64 to .82 (all significant at the $p<.01$ level).

Buss and Durkee (1957) also scaled individual items for social desirability and then correlated social desirability with the probability of endorsement (in accordance with a technique recommended by Edwards, 1953). Correlation coefficients of .27 for males and .30 for females were significant at the .05 level, indicating a small but significant effect of social desirability on responding. Sarason (1961), using a similar method, noted a significant negative correlation ($r=-.47,p<.01$) between the BDHI and social desirability. Other researchers have examined the correlation between the BDHI and the Marlowe-Crowne Social Desirability Scale (Crowne & Marlowe, 1960). Leibowitz (1968) arrived at a sizable negative correlation ($r=-.68,p<.01$) and Heyman (1977) also found significant negative correlations for both males ($r=-.44,p<.001$) and females ($r=-.50,p<.001$). Biaggio (1980) and Russell (1981) found significant negative correlations of the same magnitude as those reported by Heyman. Although the scale appears to be confounded by social desirability, several researchers have found a real difference between subjects high and low on social approval in tendency to express or experience hostile feelings (Conn & Crowne, 1964; Novaco, 1975; Young, 1976).

A few studies have addressed construct validity of the BDHI. Heyman (1977) found negative and significant correlations between the BDHI and dogmatism for both males and females. In a study examining the aggressive behavior of high and low authoritarians the BDHI was employed in order to obtain an estimate of aggression independent of the experimental manipulation (Lipetz & Ossorio, 1967). A low but significant positive correlation was obtained between the BDHI and a measure of authoritarianism ($r=.25,P<.05$), which the authors note to be consistent with the theoretical concept of authoritarian aggression.

Fairly extensive data regarding concurrent validity are available for the BDHI. Sarason (1961) found significant relationships between the BDHI and two other measures of hostility, although these measures are subscales of tests no longer in popular use. Sarason also noted that correlations between BDHI subscales were generally nonsignificant; he attributes this to the unreliability of the relatively small number of items per BDHI scale. Biaggio et al. (1981) have also noted that the subscales do not seem to possess a high degree of discriminant validity. In another study, Biaggio (1980) found that the BDHI scales correlated with a number of scales from the Anger Self-Report (Zelin, Adler, & Myerson, 1972).

Studies of predictive validity have been mixed in their results. Lipetz & Ossorio (1967) found no differences in intensity and duration of shock administered by high and low BDHI scorers. In another study, subjects were given an aggression rating on the basis of role-playing and were placed in a condition in which they simulated delivery of shock (Leibowitz, 1968). The total BDHI score correlated with the role-playing aggression score ($r=.36p<.05$), but none of the

BDHI subscales correlated with the amount of shock delivered. A similar study placed high and low scorers on the BDHI in a situation in which they were angered and could retaliate by shocking others (Knott, 1970). The high and low scorers differed significantly from each other on measures of number and intensity of shocks used and in terms of the first trial on which they retaliated. Buss, Fischer, and Simmons (1962) found that psychiatrists' ratings of aggression in patients correlated significantly with all subscales except Assault, Indirect Hostility, and Suspicion. On the other hand, Edmunds (1976) reported that correlations between ratings by psychiatric staff and patients' scores on the inventory did not attain statistical significance. Miller, Spilka, and Pratt (1960) reported that there were no significant differences on the BDHI total score between violent and nonviolent paranoid schizophrenics. Edmunds (1976) similarly found that the BDHI failed to correlate with staff ratings of aggression for male inpatients.

While the BDHI has been a much used research tool, data on its validity are somewhat equivocal. While studies of concurrent validity generally yield positive results, some of the research on predictive validity does not. Further, though a number of researchers have found the total BDHI score to be fairly reliable, the reliability and validity of the subscales have been questioned.

The Overcontrolled-Hostility Scale

Megargee and his associates (Megargee, 1973; Megargee, Cook, & Mendelsohn, 1967; Megargee & Mendelsohn, 1962) have suggested that some persons who commit acts of physical aggression are chronically overcontrolled; that is, they have very rigid inhibitions against the expression of any form of aggression. Typically these individuals do not respond at all to instigation, but occasionally, when the instigation is intense enough, they may act out in an extremely aggressive manner. The Overcontrolled-Hostility (O-H) Scale was developed to identify such chronically overcontrolled persons (Megargee et al., 1967). Items for a provisional form of the scale were selected from the Minnesota Multiphasic Personality Inventory (MMPI) item pool by comparing response frequencies of four groups of male subjects. That is, items had to differentiate between assaultive and nonassaultive men but not between nonviolent prisoners and men who had not been convicted of any crime. When a cutoff score of 22 was used for the provisional 55 item O-H Scale, all of the extremely assaultive, 25 of the 28 moderately assaultive, and 40 of the 44 nonviolent criminals used to select items were correctly identified. The scale was then cross-validated on new groups of extremely assaultive, moderately assaultive, and nonviolent male prisoners. The three cross-validational groups differed significantly on the O-H Scale, with extremely assaultive prisoners scoring higher than moderately assaultive and nonviolent prisoners, but with the two latter groups not differing significantly from each other. The item responses of the cross-validational groups on the original O-H Scale were analyzed, the items that did not discriminate between the assaultive and nonviolent groups were eliminated. The final O-H Scale thus contained 31 true–false items.

Megargee et al. (1967) report on internal consistency coefficient (Kuder-Richardson 21) of .56 for the O-H Scale for a combined group of criminals and college students. While this coefficient is lower than most of those reported for the other special scales published by Psychological Assessment Resources, Inc. Megargee et al. point out that it is comparable to the median split-half reliability of the non-standard clinical scales of the MMPI. Megargee et al. also report significant negative correlations between O-H scores and the MMPI Impulsivity, Manifest Hostility, Hostility, Hostility Control, and Repression-Sensitization scales and significant positive correlations with the MMPI Inhibition of Aggression and Ego Overcontrol scales.

Some research has correlated the O-H Scale with other personality measures. In a study cross-validating the O-H and a number of other MMIP scales assessing aggression (Deiker, 1974), it was noted that the results appear to confirm Megargee et al.'s (1967) predictions about the overcontrolled personality. However, the researchers question the validity of this conclusion on the basis of a naysaying response style among aggressive subjects and call for a reexamination of the possibility of a response set on the O-H Scale. Other studies have employed criterion measures that do not share common methods with the O-H Scale, however. White (1975) administered the Rosenzweig Picture-Frustration Study to high and low O-H youthful offenders. Results indicated that high O-H subjects were significantly more impunitive than low O-H subjects and, conversely, that low O-H subjects were more extrapunitive than high O-H subjects. That is, high O-H subjects demonstrated a significantly higher level of control when contrasted with low O-H subjects whose verbalizations to the Rosenzweig stimuli were characteristically extrapunitive. Such findings are consistent with the O-H personality typology, indicating that the O-H Scale is associated with distinctive styles of dealing with hostility. In another study (White, McAdoo, & Megargee, 1973), Megargee selected seven of the factors assessed by the 16 Personality Factor Questionnarire as being ones on which high and low O-H offenders should clearly differ if the O-H Scale validly assesses the construct. All predictions were confirmed, with the youthful offender who scored high on the O-H Scale characterized as more mature, stable, responsible, well-organized, conscientious, and cautious than the low O-H scorer. Further, he is more considerate and adaptable and makes a good team member, rarely asserting himself but instead going along with the majority. He is a careful, cautious, more conforming individual who is rather naive and anxious to do the right thing.

A number of studies have examined validity of the O-H Scale against behavioral indices. For instance, Lane and Kling (1979) administered the O-H Scale to 110 male forensic psychiatric patients at a state hospital. Anamnestic data (hospital records which included state and FBI rap sheets) were used to divide subjects with a criminal record of assault into overcontrolled or undercontrolled personality types. The O-H Scale significantly discriminated between these two criterion groups, thus supporting its construct validity. High O-H patients were characterized by rigidity, excessive control, repression of conflicts, the ability to delay immediate gratification, and a reluctance to express psychiatric symptoms. High O-H patients also reported less alienation, anxiety, and anger than did low O-H patients. In a study correlating O-H scores with behavioral ratings and subject self-reports (Walters, Greene, & Solomon, 1982), a number of personality characteristics of O-H scorers emerged. Patients scoring high on the O-H Scale were found to be chronically angry and to exert rigid control over their hostile and aggressive impulses. They also displayed excessive concern over the issue of self-control. Although high O-H patients were no more defensive than controls, they did exhibit greater denial. The fact that these patients were both defensive and reported little discomfort in social situations was thought to reflect a denial of social anxiety.

Thus, available research attests to the construct validity of the O-H scale. A number of studies note correlations between high O-H scores and chronic anger, rigid control over aggressive impulses, and impunitiveness. Though reliability should be further assessed, particularly for clinical use of the scale, the O-H Scale does have good research utility. One other minor problem warrants consideration. The scale was developed with male subjects and much of the subsequent research has utilized male groups. It thus seems understood that the O-H Scale is more applicable to males than females, though researchers have failed to examine the possibility of behavioral differences between male and female subjects scoring high on O-H. Also, since significant racial differences have been found on the O-H Scale (Haven, 1969), it seems that further profileration of norms and exploration of any differences in behavioral correlates of high O-H scores for these populations is advisable.

The Hostility and Direction of Hostility Questionnaire

According to its authors (Caine, Foulds, & Hope, 1967), the Hostility and Direction of Hostility Questionnaire (HDHQ) was designed to sample a wide, though not exhaustive, range of possible manifestations of aggression, hostility, or punitiveness. It apparently originated from Foulds' (1965) theory of personality, which views punitiveness as a primary symptom of psychological disturbance. Foulds defined hostility as a unitary drive or entity which could be directed inward toward the self or outward against other people or inanimate objects; he adopted Rosenzweig's (1934) terms for these frustration reaction tendencies—intropunitiveness and extrapunitiveness.

The HDHQ is comprised of 51 true–false items derived from the MMPI and is organized into five subscales. Two subscales (Delusional Guilt and Self-Criticism) were designed to measure intropunitiveness (Foulds & Caine, 1959), while the other three (Delusional Hostility, Criticism of Others, and Acting Out Hostility) were designed to assess extrapunitiveness (Foulds, Caine, & Creasy, 1960). The test construction sample consisted of a normal sample of hospital employees and surgical ward patients and a psychiatric sample of patients admitted to two hospitals in Great Britain. The authors reported positive correlations between all five subscales, with generally higher correlations observed within the intropunitive and extrapunitive dimensions than between the directional dimensions. Philip (1968) conducted a principal components analysis of the HDHQ with normal and neurotic samples and the results supported the idea of a general hostility component that could be further broken down into a bipolar or directional component. Measures of internal consistency are not reported by the authors. Test–retest correlations for 1-year period varied widely and were reported to range from .23 to .70 for the five specific subtests and are listed at .75 and .51 for the general hostility and direction of hostility components respectively.

Evidence supporting the validity of the HDHQ is largely based on clinical sampling. Caine et al. (1967) hypothesized that psychotically disturbed patient samples should exhibit more hostility than neurotically disturbed samples and that both groups should score higher than normals; their data supported this assertion. In the same study the directionality component of the HDHQ was examined for construct validity by comparing highly paranoid and paranoid subjects to normal and neurotic samples on the extrapunitive dimensions. Predicted differences in extrapunitiveness were found between the paranoid and normal samples, with the normals scoring higher on the extrapunitive scale than self-defeating neurotic samples. A number of other studies on clinical samples have reported similar results, thus providing some additional support for the construct validity of the HDHQ by independent researchers (Philip, 1969). It should be noted, however, that most of the clinic research supporting the HDHQ has been performed by investigators in Great Britain where diagnostic labeling practices may differ from those applied in the United States, raising questions regarding the generalizability of the findings.

Some limited support exists for the HDHQ in terms of empirical validity. In a study of 19 depressed inpatients, Blackburn, Lykelsos, and Tsiantis (1979) reported significant correlations between the HDHQ and nurse's observational ratings of anger and also found that intropunitiveness scores decreased with therapeutic improvement of the patients. In a recent study of 44 male outpatients with documented histories of maladaptive anger and destructive aggression, Maiuro, Hall, Patterson, and Vitaliano (1983) found the HDHQ useful as a general measure of anger/hostility but noted that the subscales did not differentiate depressed and nondepressed subjects in commonly theorized directions. This finding, however, may have resulted more from the inadequacy of current anger/depression theory than from the inadequacy of the HDHQ. No large-scale studies investigating the empirical validity of the HDHQ have been reported to date.

One of the advantages of the HDHQ stems from the fact that it is easily derived from the MMPI. Thus, in clinical or research settings where the MMPI is in use, the HDHQ can be easily culled from the full scale and can provide some interesting theoretical perspectives related to anger and hostility. If used apart from the MMPI, however, the HDHQ does not include any indices of response set and/or defensiveness such as those available with the MMPI validity scales and may be especially prone to social desirability effects due to the pathognomic quality of some of its items. That is, the questionnaire not only includes items relevant to anger/hostility response tendencies but items related to clinical levels of paranoia and perceptual distortions. Moreover, there appears to be a broad range of variability for the reliability coefficients of the subscales of the HDHQ, with some reported to be quite low. The inclusion of a delusional guilt subscale as a factor of the "inner directed anger" index may also be questionable to those who view guilt as a separate and distinguishable emotional state. Clinicians and researchers who are interested in the theoretical constructs assessed by the HDHQ might also consider the Gottschalk-Gleser hostility scales or the Speilberger Anger Expression Scale as alternative instruments that address similar facets of anger and hostility.

The Reaction Inventory

Evans (1970) has suggested that the relationship between anger and aggression is analogous to the relationship between fear and anxiety, thus hypothesizing that: 1)Anger is stimulus specific and differs from fear only in the behavior that results; and 2)Aggressive behavior can be modified by reciprocal inhibition therapy. The Reaction Inventory (RI) (Evans & Stangeland, 1971) was developed to isolate, in individuals, the specific stimulus situations that result in anger in order to test the above hypotheses.

The two authors first wrote 100 items each for the RI on an intuitive basis and selected the 76 similar items. The inventory is a Likert-type questionnaire in which the individual responds to each item on a five-point scale ranging from "not at all" to "very much," depending upon the degree of anger the situation is judged to provoke. A single score is obtained by summing the individual item scores, with high scores indicating higher degrees of anger.

For the purpose of obtaining normative data the RI was administered to a sample of 275 subjects, most of whom were college students, with a median age of 21 years and median education of 13 years. A mean item-test correlation coefficient of .46 indicated fair internal consistency. The authors, using a formula suggested by Gaylord (1969), estimated the internal consistency coefficient to be .95 ($p<.01$). An orthogonal rotation by varimax method yielded 10 factors with eigenvalues greater than 1.5: minor chance annoyances, destructive people, unnecessary delays, inconsiderate people, self-opinionated people, frustration in business, criticism, major chance annoyances, people being personal, and authority. The authors correlated the RI and the BDHI for two samples; correlations of .52 and .57 were both significant at the .01 level.

In a study intercorrelating anger measures, Biaggio (1980) found significant correlations between the RI and the BDHI ($r=.45$, $p<.01$) and between the RI and the Novaco Anger Inventory (Novaco, 1975) ($r=.82$, $p<.01$). Biaggio concluded that the RI seems to be assessing the propensity for anger arousal and the extent to which one is willing to admit angry feelings. In this same study a low but significant correlation was obtained between the RI and the Marlowe-Crowne Social Desirability Scale.

In a study examining reliability and validity of a number of anger measures (Biaggio et al., 1981), a test–retest reliability coefficient of .70 ($p<.01$) was obtained for a 2-week period for the RI. The RI was also found to correlate positively with subject self-reports of verbal and physical antagonism and negatively with constructive action, lending some evidence to the RI's ability to predict anger expression.

The RI was originally devbloped to facilitate testing of Evan's hypotheses relevant to the relationship between anger and aggression and the value of reciprocal inhibition therapy. It has not been widely used for either research or clinical purposes. Though there is little validity data available on it, the RI does seem to adequately assess one aspect of anger, that is, propensity for anger arousal.

The Novaco Anger Inventory

The Anger Inventory (AI) was developed by Novaco (1974) as an index of anger reactions to a wide range of provocations and served as one of the measures of such expression in his study of anger control (Novaco, 1975). The original version was composed of 90 statements of provocation incidents for which the person rated, on a five-point scale, the degree of anger he or she would experience had the incident actually happened. The items were intuitively derived and partially based upon interviews with students about the things that make them angry.

In a preliminary study, the inventory was administered to 138 male and 138 female undergraduates. Item analysis showed the inventory to be internally consistent (Cronbach alpha = .94 for males and .96 for females). Novaco (1975) found significant sex differences on the AI, with males giving consistently higher anger ratings for items having physical content and females giving higher ratings for items describing unfair or unjust actions or practices.

The inventory has subsequently been revised so that it now consists of 80 items (Novaco, 1977). For a sample of 353 students, the author reported a reliability coefficient (Cronback alpha) of .96. No significant correlations between scores on the AI and the Marlowe-Crowne Social Desirability Scale were obtained for samples of students and psychiatric patients. Novaco administered the revised inventory to 16 psychiatric patients, several of whom were identified as having anger problems. The difference between means on the AI for the normal and psychiatric sample was significant ($p<.02$).

Biaggio (1980) has noted correlations between the AI and the BDHI ($r=.39$, $p<.01$), the RI ($r=.82, p<.01$), and the Marlowe-Crowne Social Desirability Scale ($r=-.26p<.01$). In this study it was concluded that the AI and RI, which are almost identical in format, are measuring the extent to which one is willing to admit angry feelings. The low but significant correlation with social desirability was not considered problematic since researchers (Conn & Crowne, 1964; Novaco, 1975) have found subjects low and high on need for approval to vary in hostility expression.

Biaggio et al. (1981) report a test–retest reliability coefficient of only .17 for the AI over a 2-week period. In this same study no significant correlations were obtained between the AI and subject self-reports of actual anger experiences. The scale's reliability and ability to predit individual differences in tendency to experience and express anger are thus questionable.

The Anger Self-Report

The authors of the Anger Self-Report (ASR) contend that the items and scores of existing aggression inventories confound the awareness of angry feelings with the behavioral expression of hostility and anger (Zelin et al., 1972). Since the awareness or consciousness of aggressive feelings and impulses has been stressed in the literature on psychotherapy, an adequate objective anger questionnaire that gives attention to these considerations would be helpful in psychotherapeutic work. The developers of the ASR thus intended that it differentiate between the awareness and expression of aggression.

The subscales of the ASR were designed to assess a number of dimensions of anger awareness and expression: (1)Awareness of Anger; (2)General Expression; (3)Physical Expression; (4)Verbal Expression; (5)Guilt; (6)Condemnation of Anger; and (7)Mistrust. A Total Expression score is also obtained by summing scores for General, Physical, and Verbal Expression. The provisional form of the scale contained 89 items (the authors drew most of the items from a number of existing scales and wrote the remainder of the items). After administering this form to 138 subjects and examining the correlations between individual items and both the scale as a whole and the subscale from which the item was drawn, 25 items were discarded. The final form of the ASR thus consists of 64 items which are responded to on a six-point Likert scale ranging from "strongly agree" to "strongly disagree."

Split-half reliability coefficients for the subscales range from .64 to .82 and the authors contend that scale intercorrelations indicate sufficient independent variance so that an ASR profile based on the subscales can be validly employed for predictions about individuals. Zelin et al. (1972) also report validity data for psychiatric and student samples. Differences between students and patients on the ASR were highly significant on all subscales except Mistrust. The 82 psychiatric patients were rated by psychiatrists on relevant scales of the Problem Appraisal Scales (Endicott & Spitzer, 1972). Analysis of the correlations between scales yielded substantial convergent and discriminant validities for the ASR scales. ASR scores and peer ratings were also correlated for the student sample. The highest correlation for the Awareness of Anger score was with ratings of "To what extent does this person feel anger?" ($r=.20$, $p<.01$). The highest correlation for Verbal Expression was with ratings of the extent to which the subject "provoked arguments" ($r=.29$, $p<.01$).

In independent research (Biaggio, 1980) the ASR has been found to correlate with a number of BDHI scales: ASR General Expression, Physical Expression, and Verbal Expression with BDHI Total Hostility; ASR Total Expression with BDHI Assault and Verbal Hostility; ASR Physical Expression with BDHI Assault; ASR Verbal Expression with BDHI Verbal Hostility; ASR Awareness of Anger with BDHI Assault, Indirect Hostility, Irritability, Negativism, Resentment, Verbal Expression, and Total Expression; and ASR Guilt with BDHI Guilt (all correlations significant at the .01 level). Also, all ASR subscales except Guilt and Condemnation of Anger were found to correlate negatively with the Marlowe-Crowne Social Desirability Scale ($p<.01$). The Condemnation of Anger scale correlated positively with social desirability. Significant sex differences were also observed for all ASR subscales except General Expression.

In a study examining the reliability and validity of selected anger scales (Biaggio et al., 1981), test–retest reliability coefficients for the ASR scales over a two-week period were moderate but significant. Reliability for the Verbal Expression and Guilt subscales was thought to be questionable however. In this same study the anger scales were correlated with subject's self-reports of anger arousal during a laboratory provocation and with reports of actual instances of anger arousal in their day-to-day lives. Evidence for predictive validity was especially good for Awareness of Anger, General Expression, Physical Expression, Condemnation of Anger, and Total Expression. No significant correlations were noted for Verbal Expression, for which test–retest reliability was also low. Only two significant correlations were obtained for ASR Guilt, but more importantly, it failed to correlate with ratings of actual guilt experiences and test–retest reliability was low. There was only one significant correlation for ASR Mistrust and this subscale did not correlate with ratings of actual suspicion or mistrust. Thus, though some of the ASR subscales appear to measure the purported constructs, others are of questionable reliability and validity.

The State-Trait Anger Scale

Spielberger and his associates (Spielberger, Jacobs, Russell, & Crane, 1983) contend that anger can be conceptualized as an emotional state that varies in intensity as well as a relatively stable personality trait. They note that this state–trait distinction has typically not been taken into account in the research on the measurement of anger and hostility. Speilberger et al. invoke this distinction in the development of their State–Trait Anger Scale (STAS), which is analogous in conception and similar in format to the State-Trait Anxiety Inventory (Spielberger, Gorsuch, & Lushene, 1970).

The first step in their methodical approach to the development of the STAS (Spielberger et al., 1983) was a formulation of working definitions of state and trait anger. State anger (S-Anger) was defined as a emotional state or condition that consists of subjective feelings of tension, annoyance, irritation, fury and rage, with concommitant activation or arousal of the autonomic nervous system. Trait anger (T-Anger) was defined in terms of individual differences in the frequency with which S-Anger was experienced over time.

The authors assembled a pool of 22 items consistent with their working definition of T-Anger by adapting some items from the BDHI and other measures of anger and hostility and by writing some new items. These items were administered to a sample of students who were instructed to rate themselves according to "how you generally feel" on a four-point scale ranging from "almost never" to "almost always." The 15 items with the highest item-remainder correlations and with relatively low correlations with measures of anxiety and curiosity were selected for the T-Anger scale. Alpha coefficients for this 15 item scale were .87 for both males and females.

A list of 20 items consistent with the working definition of S-Anger was derived by identifying synomyms and idioms for anger. Subjects were asked to report the intensity of their feelings "right now" by rating themselves on a four-point scale ranging from "not at all" to "very much so." After administering these items to 270 subjects, the 15 S-Anger items with the highest item-remainder correlations and lowest correlations with anxiety and curiosity were retained. An alpha coefficient of .93 was obtained for males and females on the S-Anger scale.

Since correlations of individual S-Anger and T-Anger items with state and trait anxiety scores were substantially higher than expected and since both anger scales evidenced high internal consistency, the authors attempted to shorten both anger scales so as to minimize correlations with anxiety. Only those items with the highest item-remainder correlations and the lowest correlations with anxiety were retained, resulting in 10-item S-Anger and T-Anger scales. Correlations between the 10-and 15-item S- and T-Anger scales were uniformly high, suggesting that the scores on the 10-item forms provided essentially the same information as scores for the longer forms.

The S- and T-Anger scales were subjected to a principal factors analysis in order to investigate their factor structure. A single factor for both males and females was obtained for S-Anger, suggesting that this scale measures anger as a unitary emotional state that varies in intensity. Two factors were derived for T-

Anger; on the basis of the content of the four items loading on each factor, these factors were labeled Angry Temperament and Angry Reaction.

The authors (Spielberger et al., 1983) provide normative data for the STAS for large samples of high school students, military recruits, college students, and working adults (the total number of subjects for which this data is provided exceeds 8000). Data are presented separately for the sexes, with some sex differences obtained for both S-Anger and T-Anger. Alpha coefficients range from .88 to .95 for the S-Anger scale and .81 to .92 for the T-Anger scale, suggesting a high degree of internal consistency for the two scales.

Some validity date is presented in the author's original report (Spielberger et al., 1983). The STAS was correlated with the BDHI and two MMPI hostility scales: the Hostility (Ho) Scale developed by Cook and Medley (1954) and the Overt Hostility (Hv) Scale constructed by Schultz (1954). Correlations between the T-Anger scale and the Hv Scale were low but significant, suggesting that the T-Anger scale does measure a hostility trait. The STAS was also correlated with measures of anxiety, curiosity, and the Eysenck Personality Questionnaire (Eysenck & Eysenck, 1965). Though the authors speculate about the implications of the obtained correlations, some of their statements presume rather than prove construct validity of the STAS. A small negative correlation between T-Anger and the Eysenck Lie scale suggests that anger scores may be slightly reduced by test-taking attitudes that lead some people to inhibit reports of negative characteristics such as anger, a finding that is in line with previous researchers contentions about the relationship between social desirability and hostility (cf., Conn & Crowne, 1964; Novaco, 1975).

The STAS is a newly published scale and there is little independent research on its reliability and validity. Crane (1981) has, however, reported higher T-Anger scores among hypertensive patients than a control group of medical and surgical patients; hypertensives also had higher S-Anger scores after performing on a mildly frustrating task. The notion of a distinction between state and trait anger appears to have good research and clinical utility. Further exploration of the validity of the STAS is thus warranted.

COGNITIVE MEASURES OF ANGER AROUSAL— PROJECTIVE TECHNIQUES

The Rorschach Method of Personality Assessment

Recent years have witnessed renewed interest in the use of the Rorschach as a psychometric tool. First published in 1921 as "The Form Interpretation Test," the Rorschach method of assessment (Rorschach, 1942) was initially used as a general personality test and has since been the focus of much research and theoretical controversy. The Rorschach has its origins in psychodynamic and projective theory, which holds that subjects will perceive ambiguous stimuli in a manner consistent with their cognitive style, emotional needs, and conflicts.

The test consists of a standard series of 10 ink blots, some in black and white and some colored. The ink blot cards are shown one at a time to a subject who is instructed to tell the examiner what the blot looks like or of what it reminds him or her. Responses are recorded verbatim and, if a formal and orthodox scoring system is used, the subject is taken through the blots a second time for an inquiry regarding the specific determinants (e.g., use of form, color, and white space) of the response given. Two types of scoring have been employed in Rorschach studies of anger and hostility: The traditional method of scoring formal determinants and elements, and a more recently developed and practiced approach of scoring stimulus or thematic content of the response given.

Although a number of different systems have been proposed for the scoring of anger/hostility content (Arnaud, 1959; Elizur, 1949; Finney, 1955; Hafner & Kaplan, 1960; Murstein, 1958), Elizur's (1949) scoring criteria have been used more often than any other approach and have generated the most data. In fact, other approaches essentially represent modifications and elaborations of the Elizur system. Elizur's technique purports to assess hostility, which he defines quite broadly to be: (1)an emotional state with drive, arousal, and motivational properties; (2)an inclination towards aggressive instrumental behavior; and (3)a generalizable personality trait characterized by an enduring, negative attitude with which the person views and responds to the environment. Six general categories of scorable responses are articulated in the Elizur system, including descriptions of angry, hostile, or aggressive behavior, negative attitudes or emotions, objects and devices typically used for aggressive purposes, responses that are symbolically associated with anger or aggression, responses characterized by ambivalence or double connotation (usually anxiety versus anger/hostility), and neutral responses that do not typically provide indications of anger, hostility, or aggression. Weights may be additionally assigned, depending on whether the response is obviously expressed or symbolically and less obviously expressed.

When the Rorschach is simply scored for content using the Elizur (1949) system the interrater reliability and agreement appears to be quite high. Elizur originally reported correlation coefficients ranging from .82 to .93 and subsequent studies have commonly reported reliability figures in the neighborhood of .96 for both clinically experienced and inexperienced raters (Cummings, 1954; Forsyth, 1959; Sanders & Cleveland, 1953). Studies of test–retest reliability, however, are limited (Epstein, Nelson, & Tonofsky, 1957; Lucas, 1961), with no solid data reported for large or heterogeneous populations.

Most of the studies examining the construct validity of the Elizur content analysis method have been supportive. Clinical and institutional samples with histories of psychological conflicts or acting out in a destructive and aggressive fashion have been found to score higher on hostility content indices than those without such histories. Although the predicted relationships of anger and hostility to the criterion population have been characterized by questionable psycho-dynamic assumptions in some cases (e.g., interpretations of "repressed anger" in cases where the sample scored lower than controls), differential and significant findings have been independently reported for nail-biting samples (Cummings, 1954); psychosomatic disorders such as neurodermatitis (Cleveland & Fisher, 1956); patients afflicted with coronary heart disease (Cleveland & Johnson, 1962); teeth-grinding or bruxism samples (Vernallis, 1955); students placed on probation by college authorities (Lit, 1956); male inpatients (Sommer & Sommer, 1958); and assaultive versus nonassaultive adolescents (Gorlow, Zimet, & Fine, 1952). These findings have received some additional support in studies of concurrent and divergent validity (Elizur, 1949; Walker, 1951), in which hostility content scores have been found to be related in predictable ways to self-ratings and questionnaires of hostility as well as theoretically independent traits (cf. Campbell & Fiske's multitrait-multimethod approach to test validation, 1959). Studies of the relationship between hostility content scores and behavior ratings of hostility and aggressiveness have yielded mixed results, with some researchers reporting significant and positive relationships for therapist-based ratings (Rader, 1957; Haskell, 1961; Walker, 1951), while others have reported nonsignificant correlations (Buss, Fischer, & Simmons, 1962).

Little research exists to support the use of the Rorschach hostility content in terms of predictive validity. In a recent study using a modified version of Elizur's scoring system called the Palo Alto Destructiveness Content Scale (Rose & Bitter, 1980), an attempt was made to differentiate reoffenders and nonreoffenders among a male patient sample institutionalized for crimes of violent assault. While this study suggests that the Rorschach hostility content analysis technique may have potential for differentiating reoffenders from non-reoffenderson a short-term release basis, the study samples reported were not sizeable ($n=$ 11 to 20) and more research of this type is needed to critically evaluate the use of the test for such purposes.

The traditional and formal scoring methods for the Rorschach have generally yielded weak and inconsistent results (Buss, 1961; Storment & Finney, 1953; Lit, 1956), whereas content scoring systems have shown some ability to differentiate angry, hostile, and assaultive subject samples from those without such behavioral histories (Kane, 1955; Rose & Bitter, 1980; Sommer & Sommer, 1958; Wolf, 1957). The use of content methods tends to significantly shorten administration time and to greatly simplify the rather unwieldy traditional scoring procedures. Potential advantages of the Rorschach stem from the fact that it is a clinically individualized measure which is supposedly less subject to social desirability distortions since the culturally "correct" answer is neither apparent nor embedded in a forced-choice format. Since the test stimuli are visually processed ink blots, they do not require that the subject read or write. Among the test's disadvantages is a continued and serious lack of psychometrically usable normative data for specific populations and demographic groups. Some recent writers have suggested the use of a relative percentage computation based on the amount of hostile content in comparison to the number of responses given by the subject (Goldfried, Stricker, & Weiner, 1971). However, this procedure has not been adopted in any standardized or systematic way and would still need to address the problem of variable numbers of responses associated with the test's relatively unstructured administration. The use of the Rorschach also appears to be limited to measuring a general level of anger and hostility and its use has not been demonstrated in terms of differentiating subtypes of anger or differential modes of expression.

The Rosenzweig Picture-Frustration Study

The Rosenzweig (1950) Picture-Frustration (P-F) Study is a semiprojective technique, originally developed to study frustration in the context of psychoanalytic theory. Rosenzweig defines frustration ''as occurring whenever the organism encounters an obstacle or obstruction en route to the satisfaction of a need;'' (1978a p. 9)with frustration, an increase in tension occurs and ''aggression in some form is entailed.'' Rosenzweig views aggression as ''stepping or moving forward to achieve goals and overcome obstacles;B' (1978a, p. 2) Aggression involves constructive as well as destructive actions. According to the author, the P-F Study does not assess personality types or traits, but rather the subject's repertoire for coping with frustration.

The P-F Study is comprised of a self-administering booklet that includes written directions and a series of 24 cartoon-like pictures, which depict a variety of frustrating interpersonal situations. In each picture, one person is shown saying something that either describes the frustration of the other person or serves to frustrate him. The other person has a blank balloon above his head and the subject is instructed to imagine what that person would answer and then write the first reply that occurs to him. Currently, three forms are available: one for children, adolescents, and adults. Basic manuals and updated supplements (Clarke, Rosenzweig, & Fleming, 1947; Rosenzweig, 1950, 1976, 1977, 1978a, 1978b, 1978c; Rosenzweig, Fleming, & Rosenzweig, 1948) provide information on standardization, scoring samples and principles, and norms for all three forms. Although the P-F Study can be administered to individuals or groups, individual administration is preferred because an inquiry is then possible.

The pictured situations in the P-F Study include 16 ''ego blocking'' situations that directly frustrate the subject and 8 ''superego blocking'' situations that serve to accuse, charge, or incriminate the subject (Rosenzweig, 1945). The test's lack of systematic or empirical item selection procedures has been frequently criticized, but Rosenzweig (1978a) defends the inherently large item variance that results from the semi-projective nature of the test. Each response is scored in two main categories: Direction of Aggression and Type of Aggression (Rosenzweig, 1978a). Included under Direction of Aggression are extra-aggression (E-A) or aggression toward the environment; intra-aggression (I-A) or aggression toward the self; and im-aggression (M-A) or the avoidance of aggression. Included under Type of Aggression are obstacle-dominance (O-D), in which the subject's reactions are attributed to the object; ego- or etho-defense (E-D), in which the subject's reactions are characterized by attack, blame, or censoring; and need-persistence (N-P), in which a solution or amends is sought. The subject's reactions are tallied to obtain relative percentages for the six scoring categories. Investigators focusing on anger, hostility, and aggression have typically narrowed the scoring to two factors, extrapunitive (E) and intropunitive (I), which reflect outer- and inner-directed ego-defense reactions. A Group Conformity Rating (GCR) allows comparison with the modal responses of the standardization population. The adult standardization sample included 236 males and 224 females. Children's norms are provided for 131 boys and 125 girls.

Clarke, Rosenzweig, and Fleming (1947) report three separate projects investigating inter-scorer reliability of the Adult form. In the first study, response records for 82 student nurses were scored by four persons. Each rater achieved an average agreement of at least 70% of the responses with the other three raters. In the next project, a total of 136 records from 68 medical students were scored by two examiners who agreed in 81% of their scores. In the third study, the two examiners scored 125 records in groups of 25 and showed agreement for at least 75% of the responses. Franklin and Brozek (1949) report inter-rater reliability coefficient- of .86, .87, and .82 for extrapunitive, intrapunitive, and impunitive categories, though these ratings may not have been independent, given reports of some discussions between raters during the scoring. However, reliability studies investigating internal consistency (Taylor, 1952; Taylor & Taylor, 1951; Sutcliffe, 1955) by analysis of variance, item analysis, or intercorrelation methods generally yield low reliability for the scoring categories.

With respect to test–retest reliability, which Rosenzweig considers more relevant to the test's reliability, Rosenzweig, Ludwig, and Adelman (1975) report results from an investigation completed some 20 years ago involving groups of 35 adult females tested twice in a 2-month interval and 45 males tested twice in 7½-month interval. In the female group all test–retest correlations except GCR were significant. For males all correlations were significant. Test–retest reliability coefficients for the Adolescent form over a 1-month period were significant. Coefficients for the Children's form over a 10 month period were significant for E-A, M-A, E-D, and N-P. Bernard (1949) reported retest reliability coefficients for 175 college students after 4 months ranging from .50 to .75 for the categories and .45 for GCR.

Since the Rosenzweig P-F Study was developed to validate psychoanalytic concepts, much of the research has focused on construct validity. Rosenzweig and Adelman (1977) cite data from the standardization sample indicating different reactions to P-F stimuli as the age of the subject increases. In particular, they note a steady and significant decrease in E-A and increases in I-A, M-A, and

GCR between the ages of 4 and 13. These results are felt to be in line with developmental psychology findings that a child learns to inhibit hostile reactions and to conform socially during this age period. Rosenzweig and Braun (1970) found E-A scores for 85 male adolescents to be relatively higher than those reported for children. Furthermore, the males showed significantly higher E-A scores than the females. Such findings are thought to be in line with observed dependence–independence conflicts, rebelliousness, and sex differences during this age period. Rosenzweig (1950) indicates that all scoring categories stabilize in young adulthood.

A variety of criterion measures have been used in attempts to compare P-F scores with overt behavior. Albee and Goldman (1950) compared the P-F scores of 65 patients classified as either extrapunitive or intropunitive and found no significant differences.Holzberg and Posner (1951) compared the extrapunitive P-F responses of 47 student nurses to three measures of overt behavior and one measure of fantasy; correlations were nonsignficant. Lindzey and Goldwyn (1954) attempted to assess the ability of the P-F Study to differentiate between delinquents and nondelinquents. Forty male delinquents were compared to 50 controls matched for age, socioeconomic status, and intelligence. The delinquents had significantly lower extrapunitive scores than the controls. Rosenzweig and Rosenzweig (1952) similarly compared 162 problem children with the normal child standardization sample and found the problem children had significantly higher E-A scores than normals at lower age levels. Mercer and Kyriazis (1962) reported no significant differences on the P-F in a study comparing 32 male prisoners with known histories of physical aggression to 35 male controls matched for age, intelligence, and educational level. Kaswan, Wasman, and Freedman (1960) related the quantity and intensity of aggressive responses obtained on the P-F Study to findings from the Rorschach, an attitude scale, psychiatrists' ratings of aggressive behavior, and prison records for 121 male prison inmates. Twenty-three out of 73 relationships were significant. The extrapunitive measures showed the most significant correlations with the various reports of overt behavior. Rosenzweig (1963) has suggested that the failure to find positive correlations between the outer-directed P-F variables in some populations might be due to the ability or tendency of those subjects to present themselves in a positive light or to deny hostile tendencies.

A number of studies have explored the validity of the P-F Study by examining the relationship between P-F scores and differential reactions to induced frustration. Nisenson (1972) classified 36 Jewish adolescents according to three levels of extrapunitiveness on the P-F Study. After reading an antiSemitic communication, subjects were assessed for overt verbal aggression on an attitude scale adapted from Feshbach (1955) and the results indicated a significant and linear relationship between extrapunitive scores and attitude scale scores. Lindzey (1950) studied 10 subjects who were experimentally frustrated and then given feedback regarding personal failure in a group setting. Significant increases in extrapunitive scores were noted for the experimental subjects. Other studies suggest that the P-F Study is insensitive to environmentally imposed frustrations (Franklin & Brozek, 1949; Loveland & Singer, 1959).

Use of the Rosenzweig P-F Study has declined in recent years. This pattern appears to be attributable in part to the general decline in use of projective techniques among psychologists (Garfield & Kurtz, 1974, 1976) as well as the diminished popularity of the frustration-aggression hypothesis (Berkowitz, 1962; Buss, 1961; Rule & Nesdale, 1976). However, there appear to be additional problems associated with the construction of the test that may also be of concern to investigators. These problems include reports of low reliability, lack of systematic and empirical methods for item selection, and reports of possible distortions in responding due to social desirability for certain populations. Researchers attempting to learn the Rosenzweig system may also be overwhelmed by the author's tendency toward overinclusivensss in his labeling and scoring of aggressive phenomenon.

Some positive features of the P-F Study include a particularly rich background of theoretical and empirical literature and the fact that it has spawned the development of additional measures of anger and hostility (e.g., the HDHQ, Gottschalk-Gleser Content Analysis Scales). The P-F Study's game-like format may be particularly appealing in evaluating children and adolescents, an age group for which it has demonstrated some construct validity. Investigators whose focus is the assessment of anger, hostility, and aggression may be interested in the specific use of extrapunitive and intrapunitive scores as they are theoretically relevant to the anger phenomenon and seem to have some validity.

BEHAVIORAL MEASURES OF ANGER AROUSAL

Most of the research to date on the behavioral expression of anger and hostility has focused on overt acts of aggression within a social-psychological or criminological framework. As such, the emphasis has been on situational, cultural, and epidemiological factors associated with overt aggression. Little attention has been paid to the relationship between these behaviors and their emotional concomitants. Although it is clear that anger and hostility may not always be antecedent conditions for overt aggression (Bandura, 1973; Geen & Berkowitz, 1967), they often are concomitants and mediators of it (Rule & Nesdale, 1976). Further, the behavioral expression of anger and hostility may take a variety of forms, many of which are more subtle than the behaviors that are typically labeled as acts of aggression.

"Aggression Machine" Measures

The "aggression machine," a device originated by Buss (1961), has been widely employed in experimental studies of aggression. It is typically used in a laboratory setting where the subject is instructed to act as a for a learning experiment and to deliver shocks to a "learner" as a form of feedback when errors are made. Depending on the design of the experiment, differences in the amount of shock delivered are interpreted as behavioral manifestations of personality states or traits, the result of situational variables such as the type or context of a particular provocation, or attributional factors.

Numerous indices have been used to assess the level of aggression for aggression machine devices: shock intensity (Buss, 1961, 1963); number of shocks (Berkowitz, 1965); duration of shock delivery (Geen & Berkowitz, 1967); response latency (Knott, 1970); and amount of physical pressure applied to the shock lever (Hokanson, 1961). Although these measures appear to have been used interchangeably by various investigators, there are reports of differential sensitivity and lack of significant correlations between the indices. For example, Geen, Rabosky, and O'Neal (1968) measured both the number and intensity of shocks delivered by subjects who had been experimentally provoked by being given repeated shocks themselves. They found that a subject's self-reported anger was significantly correlated with the number of shocks delivered but unrealted to their intensity. This finding was replicated in a later study (Geen & O'Neal, 1969) and the authors concluded that the number of shocks may provide a more concrete and reliable index of a subject's retaliatory feelings and behavior. This notion has received additional support from a psychophysiological investigation that found number of shocks to be more closely related to changes in diastolic blood pressure than intensity of shock (Gentry, 1970). Knott (1970), however, has suggested that the particular index used is less important as demonstrated levels of anger and hostility increase to significant levels.

While some studies have provided data to support the idea that shock machine indices are related to independent observer-based ratings of aggression (Shemberg, Leventhal, & Allman, 1968), levels of provocation and anger (Geen et al., 1968; Geen & O'Neal, 1969; Knott, 1970), and observed sex differences in the overt expression of anger and hostility (Buss, 1961; Knott & Drost, 1970), the scope and focus of many investigations of such devices have been limited. Although such research paradigms have often employed various types of frustrating, attacking, and provoking stimuli to elicit the expression of aggression, surprisingly few have systematically explored the relationship between shock delivery and various cognitive and physiological indices of anger and hostility. In those cases where no significant relationship has been observed, it is not clear whether significant levels of anger were provoked. Moreover, in such studies little appreciation is demonstrated for the possible interaction of social desirability factors in suppressing reports of such affect—especially since the experiments often involve college students being evaluated, directly or indirectly, by their professors.

The aggression machine has a number of advantages: It ostensibly involves the delivery of a noxious stimuli, which is in keeping with theoretical definitions of hostility and aggression; it is an objective and easily quantifiable index; and there is a large body of theoretically relevant literature employing this research paradigm. Disadvantages of the shock machine method include the need for special equipment; problems relating to the use of shock with human subjects; the necessity of bogus and deceptive manipulations; its narrow focus on one manifestation of aggressive behavior; and questions regarding the assessment of aggression versus obedience (cf. Milgram, 1963). Some more recent researchers, in consideration of some of the above problems, have employed a modified version of the aggression machine, involving the delivery of noxious noise rather than shock, and suggest that it may still provide a reliable and valid measure of some aspects of behavioral expression of aggression or hostility (Check & Malamuth, 1983).

The Gottschalk-Gleser Content Analysis Scales for Hostility

The Gottschalk-Gleser Content Analysis Scales provide a qualitative and quantitative analysis of thematic verbal content and associated psychological states (Gottschalk, Winget, & Gleser, 1969). Although the theoretical basis for this method is ecletic and has its underpinnings in psychoanalytic, linguistic, and learning theories, the specific scales are largely derived from an empirical psychodynamic (ego analytic) frame of reference. The authors acknowledge the difficulty of assessing the multifaceted anger-hostility-aggression complex and define hostility as a ''transient affective state'' characterized by symbolic representations of ''physical or verbal aggression, self-reported dislike or suspicion,'' as well as the ''disposition or potential to become aroused'' in such a manner (pp. 26–27). Drawing on existing psychodynamic theory related to the assessment of hostility (Elizur, 1949; Rosenzweig, Flemming, & Clarke, 1947) and their own clinical and empirical work (Gottschalk, Gleser, & Springer, 1963), the authors developed three hostility scales that could be derived from samples of a subject's spoken or written verbal reports. The scales are keyed to the direction of the hostile impulse and include a Hostility Directed Outward scale, which may be further subdivided into overt and covert dimensions; a Hostility Directed Inward scale; and an Ambivalent Hostility scale, which taps content that simultaneously includes references to both self and others.

The verbal sample for the Gottschalk-Gleser scales is obtained in a relatively unstructured interview by simply asking the subject to speak for 5 minutes, with as little interruption as possible, about any interesting or dramatic personal life experiences. This sample is generally tape recorded, transcribed verbatim, and then broken down into scoreable segments (grammatical clauses). Specific types of hostile affect are identified and differentially weighted on a variety of factors, including manifest content, the degree to which it directly describes hostile acts (e.g., wanting to kill or injure someone versus mere disapproval of another), and its relative frequency of usage. The authors claim that a 5 minute verbal sample allows for a sensitive and valid assessment of transient state hostility and that repeated samples (three to five are recommended) across time and situation can provide a trait hostility measure.

Inter-rater reliability coefficients are reported by the authors for three different clinical samples (Gottschalk & Gleser, 1969) and range from .65 to .66 for Overt Hostility Outward, .82 to .96 for Covert Hostility Outward, .78 to .87 for Total Hostility Outward, .78 to .89 for Hostility Inward, and .76 to .91 for Ambivalent Hostility. The authors specifically recommend caution with respect to the interpretation of Overt Hostility Outward and encourage the use of an average score derived from two raters to insure reliable assessment across all scales.

Gottschalk and Gleser (1969) present an impressive array of validation studies for the Content Analysis Scales. In a preliminary investigation 10 schizophrenic patients identified by clinical observers as belligerent and hostile were compared to a demographically matched sample identified as autistic. The hostile sample scored significantly higher on the Hostility Outward scales. Larger psychiatric samples were subsequently used to assess construct validity for all scales. In the most definitive study, hostility scale scores were compared to a variety of theoretically related measures for a sample of 50 psychiatric patients. Findings indicated significant and positive relationships between the Hostility Outward scale and behavioral ratings of anger and hostility on the Oken Scale (Oken, 1960) ($r=.36$ for the overall sample, .50 for males); self-reported hostile affect on an adjective checklist developed by Gleser (Gottschalk, Gleser, & Springer, 1963) ($r=.30$ for the overall sample, .57 for males); and selected subscales of the Buss-Durkee Hostility Inventory (Buss & Durkee, 1957) (for Assault $r=.32$, for Negativism $r=.42$). Ambivalent Hostility and Hostility Inward were both found to be related to Beck Depression Scale (Beck, Ward, Mendelson, Mock, & Erbaugh, 1961) scores ($r=.37$ and .52 respectively). As might be expected, correlations between the various indices of hostility were significantly higher for males on Hostility Outward and higher for females on Ambivalent Hostility and Hostility Inward. Addational support for construct validity is provided by a study of 16 male adolescents and 25 antisocial offenders in which the hostility scales were found to correlate with scores on an adjective checklist and behavioral ratings on the Oken Scale. Similar results were obtained in another investigation (Ross, Adsett, Gleser, Joyce, Kaplan, & Tieger, 1963) utilizing a sample of 80 medical students; low but significant correlations were found between Hostility Outward and extrapunitive scores and also between Hostility Inward and intropunitive scores on the Rosenzweig Picture-Frustration Test (Rosenzweig, 1950).

In keeping with their interdisciplinary focus, the authors have studied some psychophysiological correlates of anger and hostility for the Content Analysis Scales. They report significant positive correlations between Hostility Inward and diastolic blood pressure and significant negative correlations between Hostility Outward and systolic blood pressure among a sample of nine hypertensives, suggesting that the scales are sensitive and related to known physiological corre-lates of anger/hostility responses (Gottschalk, Gleser, D'Zmura, & Hanenson, 1964). Data from a double blind study of 45 male delinquent adolescents also indicates that the scales may be sensitive to the effects of known psychophar-macological agents (Gleser, Gottschalk, Fox, & Lippert, 1965). In this study, subjects receiving chloriazepoxide (a minor tranquilizer) showed significant de-creases on Hostility Outward and Ambivalent Hostility scales that did not occur for a placebo group and were not attributable to overall lowered volume of speech or verbal content.

Although a number of the Gottschalk and Gleser validation studies can be challenged on the grounds of sample size and a priori psychodynamic assump-tions regarding the weighting and selection of scoreable content, they provide a preponderance of data to support the validity of the method and scales. The data does provide better support for the Total Hostility Outward and Hostility Inward scales than for the Overt, Covert, and Ambivalent Hostility scales. Given the authors' sophisticated melding of clinical/logical and statistical methods, as well as longstanding and prolific involvement in the area of verbal content analysis, it is surprising that other investigators have not used these measures to corroborate or extend their utility. This may, in part, be due to the decreased popularity of projective and psychodynamically derived methods in clinical psychology in past years (Garfield & Kurtz, 1974, 1976). Further, investigators may be reluctant to use such an unstructured measure out of concern over obtaining inadequate compliance, few verbalizations, and thus unscoreable data. Advantages of the Gottschalk-Gleser Scales include the availability of normative data for white adult males and both black and white children (Gottschalk, 1982; Gottschalk & Gleser, 1969); the provision of a detailed and clearly written administration and scoring manual (Gottschalk, Winget, & Gleser, 1969); a reportedly decreased likelihood of distorted assessments due to social desirability factors inherent in more objective and structured scales; and the fact that it does not require the subject to read or write. The authors have also published data that indicate the same verbal sample may be used to provide assessments of anxiety, social alienation, personal disorganization, achievement striving, human relations, feelings of hope, and cognitive impairment, making the verbal content analysis method a potentially rich and valuable one for clinicians and researchers (Got-tschalk, 1982; Gottschalk & Gleser, 1969).

The Oken Rating Scale for Anger

Although a number of behavioral rating scales for anger and hostility have been developed for research and clinical purposes (cf. Hargreaves, 1968; Schacter, 1957), Oken's (1960) Rating Scale for Anger is probably the most detailed and comprehensive measure of its kind currently available. The scale was developed in a study of suppressed anger in a heterogeneous sample of psychiatric inpatients. Three general categories of behavioral anger expression were chosen on the basis of clinical and logical criteria and were defined as: (1)overt behavioral or motoric expression such as facial expressions, clenched fists, pounding, gesturing, and pointing; (2)directly verbalized subjective feelings of anger such as reports of dislike, irritation, and being "mad;" and (3)qualitative aspects of verbal and vocal behavior (paralanguage) such as strident pitch, loud volume, depreciatory tone, tight or explosive rhythm and cadence, and profanity.

The author developed a manual with behaviorally referenced descriptors of various levels of anger intensity and extensity (i.e., the degree to which anger dominates the process of communication or disrupts it) to aid the rater in assigning quantitative values to the type of anger expressed in each category. Each category is scored on a 0–3 scale yielding a total score of 0–9, which provides an estimate of the general level of anger experienced by the subject. The author also suggests that the categories tapping overt motoric and paralanguage expressions can be summed and compared to the category assessing directly verbalized feelings to yield an estimate of the level of expressed versus suppressed anger in the subject. A statistical regression method is recommended to separate potential subjects in a given sample into "expresser" and "suppressor" groups on the basis of mean difference scores. In the original study, ratings were made in relation to an experimentally induced affective state elicited by a 25 minute "stress interview." The stress interview method was previously developed by the author's associates and is described as an interpersonal process in which the interviewer probes and confronts conflictual areas identified in the patient's history and makes provocative interpretations and assumptions while allowing the subject to respond in a transactional manner (Grinker, Sabshin, Hamburg, Board, Basowitz, Korchin, Persky, & Chevalier, 1957). During the interview the subject is observed through a one-way mirror and rated on both verbal and nonverbal expressions of anger.

Inter-rater reliability of the Oken Scale was assessed for a sample of seven subjects in the original study. Correlations coefficients of .81, .87, and .80 were reported for overt motoric, verbalized subjective feelings, and paralanguage categories respectively, with complete agreement observed for raters across all categories approximately 50% of the time and only one unit of difference for the categories approximately 80% of the time. As expected, the three categories of expression intercorrelated significantly, with coefficients ranging from .71 to .89.

Since few investigators have actually made use of the Oken Scale, validation data is sparse. In the original study, Oken (1960) reported relatively high correlations between the ratings assigned for the three categories of anger expression ($r=.73$, .87, and .78) and a less refined and global rating scale previously developed by his colleagues (Hamburg, Sabshin, Board, Grinker, Korchin, Basowitz, Health, & Persky, 1958). It is unclear, however, whether the same raters were used to arrive at both sets of observations, raising questions as to whether the two measures were administered independently. Differences between expresser and suppressor subjects, as defined by the Oken Scales and a number of psychophysiological indices, were also examined in this study. As predicted on the basis of previous studies of anger and blood pressure (Ax, 1953; Funkenstein, King, & Drolette, 1954), the expresser group had lower diastolic and higher systolic blood pressure whereas the suppressor group had higher diastolic and lower systolic levels despite equal overall ratings of anger for the groups. Given the existing data and theory in the field, these findings were interpreted as providng evidence of construct validity for the Oken Scales.

Gottschalk and Gleser (1969) report a number of studies in which the Oken Scale was used in conjunction with their Content Analysis Scales for hostility. In a study of 25 individuals charged with antisocial acts, the Oken Scale was found to be significantly and positively correlated ($r=.52$) with the level of externally directed hostility as assessed by the Content Analysis Scales. In another study of 50 psychiatric outpatients (Gottschalk & Gleser, 1969), significant and positive correlations were obtained between the Oken Scale, the Gleser adjective checklist for hostility ($r=.39$), and the Buss-Durkee Hostility Inventory ($r=.27$). The authors also found the Oken Scale to be negatively but not significantly correlated with social desirability as assessed by the MMPI lie scale ($r=.21$).

The Oken Scale currently has a rather limited data base in support of its reliability and validity. Although the rationally derived content of the scale appears to have adequate face validity, there is a need for comparative studies of different emotional states to establish divergent validity of the scale. Nonetheless, given further use and development, the scale may have good potential as a measure of anger-related behaviors. Unlike other scales, it appears to be sensitive to a broad range of verbal and nonverbal behaviors characteristic of anger, hostility, and aggression. While some investigators might be uncomfortable with the relatively nonstandardized stimulus characteristics of the stress interview, it has the accompanying advantages of being quite naturalistic because it is interpersonal and transactional in nature. Moreover, the scale could conceivably be employed with a variety of structured or unstructured behavior sampling techniques, depending on the needs of the investigator. The possibility of deriving expresser and suppressor subsamples with the Oken Scale should be of particular interest to those involved in the study of behavioral medicine, hypertension, and coronary heart disease.

PSYCHOPHYSIOLOGICAL CORRELATES OF ANGER

Current laboratory technology permits the assessment of an increasing number and array of physiological processes. The discussion here is limited to those psychophysiological indices that have shown some potential for differentiating anger from other emotional states. Thus, overviews of the research on the emotional correlates of blood pressure, catecholamine excretion, and muscle action potentials are presented.

Throughout the larger part of this century, most investigators in psychophysiology adopted Cannon's (1936) unidimensional model of a basic "fight or flight" reaction as the underlying biological substrate of emotion. This view persisted until the 1950s when Ax (1953) conducted what is now a classic study comparing physiological reactions to both anger and fear. In this study a sample of normal men and women were subjected to laboratory induced fear and anger. Fourteen different physiological measures were taken and analyzed in terms of frequency. Results indicated that seven of the measures significantly differentiated anger from fear. Specifically, anger was characterized by more diastolic blood pressure rises, heart rate falls, galvanic skin responses, and muscle tension increases. In contrast, fear was associated with more skin conductance increases, muscle tension peaks, and respiration increases.

Schachter (1957) was able to replicate Ax's (1953) findings in a similar experiment with both normal and hypertensive subjects. In this study, amplitude rather than frequency of physiological variables was assessed. Expanding on Ax's notions and the existing knowledge regarding the differential effects of epinephrine and norepinephrine secretion in the body, Schachter suggested that fear could be considered an epinephrine mediated response while anger was the result of both epinephrine and norepinephrine, with norepinephrine playing the dominant role. The most notable differences between an epinephrine and norepinephrine response occur in the cardiovascular system because norepinephrine results in general vasoconstriction and a relative increase in peripheral or diastolic blood pressure attended by no increase or a drop in heart rate. In contrast, epinephrine tends to result in a generalized increase on most measures accompanied by no change or a relative decrease in diastolic pressure. Thus, Schachter contended that anger could potentially be differentiated from fear and on the basis of catecholamine secretion (epinephrine and norepinephrine) and changes in blood pressure.

In another key study, Funkenstein, King, and Drolette (1954) attempted to refine Ax's theory regarding differential psychophysiological correlates of anger. Stress was induced in a sample of male college students who were then interviewed in detail regarding their resulting emotional state. Feelings of anger and anxiety were differentiated on the basis of objective criteria and then types of anger were further discriminated. Specifically, subjects were identified as either having anger directed inward or outward and compared and contrased with an anxiety group on the same psychophysiological measures employed by Ax (1953). The findings were generally similar to those obtained by Ax and were interpreted as confirming a norepinephrine like response pattern for anger, particularly for anger directed outward. Anger-inward subjects were found to have psychophysiological patterns more similar to those observed in the anxiety group.

Anger and Blood Pressure

Recent research has tended to confirm the notion that anger is differentially associated with cardiovascular response. In a series of studies by Harburg and his associates (Harburg, Erfurt, Havenstein, Chape, Schull, & Schork, 1973; Harburg, Blakelock, & Roeper, 1979) the relationship of suppressed anger to blood pressure levels and the incidence of hypertension was examined. In one study (Harburg et al., 1973) approximately 6000 white and 6000 black males were asked to respond to hypothetical injustice situations; the samples were subdivided according to whether they suppressed anger, expressed anger, and/or felt guilt about either experiencing or expressing anger. Higher diastolic blood pressures were observed in those subjects who suppressed anger. Moreover, a greater percentage of the hypertensives in the sample were found in the suppressed anger group as compared to the anger expressive or anger suppressive without guilt groups. The investigators concluded that certain subtypes of anger, specifically suppressed anger, have greater effects upon the cardiovascular system than others. Harburg et al. (1979) extended and replicated these findings for a large sample of black and white males and females and suggested that anger in the form of resentment is associated with relatively higher diastolic blood pressure readings than freely expressed anger or reflective thinking about perceived injustice or attack. Using a somewhat different method of assessing anger with a similar population, Gentry, Chesney, Gary, Hall, and Harburg (1982) replicated the findings of Harburg et al. (1973, 1979). Esler, Julius, Zweifler, Randall, Harburg, Gardiner, and DeQuattro (1977) also demonstrated the same relationship between suppressed hostility and high diastolic blood pressure in a clinical sample using a more formal psychometric measure (Buss-Durkee Hostility Inventory). Moreover, the relationship was selectively observed for anger and hostility but not for anxiety.

While the above studies are generally conclusive with respect to the association between trait anger and blood pressure readings, the utility of such physiological measures of anger is somewhat limited. Given current research guidelines for human subjects, it is difficult to employ experimental anger induction methods such as those used in the earlier studies by Ax, Schachter, and Funkenstein et al. However, there have been a few recent studies of this type that confirm the notion that blood pressure indices can be used to selectively assess anger responses. In a study of 64 male college students Gentry (1970) used a shock machine design whereby subjects were verbally insulted and then given an opportunity to shock a confederate learner as a form of feedback for errors in performance. As would be predicted from earlier studies, the insulted subjects demonstrated differential increases in diastolic blood pressure. Analysis of results further indicated a significant and positive correlation between number of shocks delivered and diastolic blood pressure readings. No psychometric assessments of anger level or type were conducted in this study.

In a carefully performed study, Schwartz, Weinberger, and Singer (1981) examined cardiovascular patterns in paid volunteers following the learning and practice of anger, happiness, fear, relaxation, and control imagery. A validity check of the affective imagery procedure found it to be effective in inducing reliable patterns of psychophysiological response. Anger produced the greatest overall increase in cardiovascular response and was distinctly opposite to the pattern observed for relaxation. As reported in previous studies, anger was associated with greater increases in diastolic blood pressure than any of the other emotional states. Although anger did produce the highest mean increase on the systolic measure, it was not significantly different from increases observed for fear or happiness.

In a seminal study of the application of cognitive-behavioral therapy methods for anger reduction, Novaco (1975) employed psychometric as well as physiological measures in the form of systolic and diastolic blood pressure readings. After treatment, a group of 35 individuals labeled as having significant anger control problems showed significant decreases on both systolic and diastolic indices concomitant to decreases in anger inventory ratings and self-reported anger. These decreases occurred in both imaginal and role-play provocations and there was no difference between diastolic and systolic readings. The presence of a main effect for blood pressure and the absence of differential reductions for systolic and diastolic indices may reflect differences in psychophysiological patterns of decreased versus increases blood pressure, the specific type of anger studied (e.g., undercontrolled as opposed to overcontrolled), as well as the general arousal-reducing properties of the treatment program. These explanations receive some support from the lack of significant correlations reported between the blood pressure indices and the psychometric measures of anger, as well as the concomitantly observed decreases in galvanic skin response, a measure more closely tied to general arousal than anger per se.

Anger and Catecholamines

Following the suggestion that epinephrine and norepinephrine secretion might vary across emotional states, a number of investigators have examined the relationship between such neurohormones and anger, hostility, and aggression. Although epinephrine and norepinephrine are known to disappear rapidly from the blood (Lund, 1951) a fairly constant proportion of an infused dose is excreted in an unchanged state in the urine (Elmadjian, Lamson, & Neri, 1956). Thus, investigators have made use of urine samples to estimate the amount of catecholamines secreted by the subject.

In a representative study, Elmadjian, Hope, and Lamson (1957) studied emotional states and the differential excretion of epinephrine and norepinephrine for normal and psychotic subjects. Using a bioassay procedure and psychiatric ratings of ward behavior, they found that patients exhibiting aggressive and hostile behavior excreted higher levels of norepinephrine whereas those exhibiting self-effacing or fearful displays excreted higher levels of epinephrine. In a similar study, Silverman, Cohen, Shmavonian, and Kirshner (1981) categorized subjects as either anxious or angry on the basis of an apparently unstandardized "focused projective test" and psychiatric interviews, and found the mean level of epinephrine to be higher in the anxious subjects and the mean level of norepinephrine to be higher in angry subjects. Moreover, these results could not be attributed to general activity levels. Estimates of relative mixtures of anxiety and anger in subjects were also found to be positively correlated with the relative rates of epinephrine and norepinephrine secreted.

Although there are thus some data to suggest such assays might be useful as indicators of anger and aggression, more work is needed in this area. The bulk of the available research on neurohormonal assays has focused more on anxiety than anger (Breggin, 1964). Moreover, the interpretation of catecholamine assays involves more than a simple readout of biochemical levels because levels can vary widely as a result of the particular assay technique used, the intensity of affective arousal, the general vascular status of the subject, and the general level of motoric activity of the subject. A study by Fine and Sweeney (1968) also indicates that such measures are subject to the influence of socioeconomic factors in that lower educational and occupational status is associated with higher norepinephrine levels regardless of demonstrated differences in affective status.

Anger and Electromyography

In Ax's (1953) original study the absolute number of muscle tension increases was reportedly higher for anger than fear, though the number of muscle tension peaks was higher for fear, suggesting that both states are associated with electromyographic (EMG) activity. In a representative study of personality correlates of muscle tension, Heath, Oken, and Shipman (1967) selected psychiatric outpatients who scored high and low on six personality variables and then took EMG readings for seven muscle groups. Apart from finding some muscle tone differences in depressives (more muscle tension), no strong or consistent patterns were observed. The authors concluded that the relationship between muscle tension and personality or emotional factors is very complex and that individuals are probably highly variable in these reactions. Other investigators have reported similar findings for the relationship between EMG and emotion, with some differences for depressed samples (Goldstein, 1965; Hardyck, 1966; Rimon, Steinbeck, & Huhmar, 1966).

More recently, Schwartz, Fair, Salt, Mandel, and Klerman (1976) performed a series of EMG studies to examine facial muscle patterning in response to specific types of affective imagery. Drawing on the cross-cultural work of Ekman, Friesen, and Ellsworth (1972) and Izard (1972) on facial recognition of mood states, the authors attempted to evoke feelings of anger, happiness, and sadness in a sample of female subjects. A covert imagery procedure was employed to selectively evoke differential affective states and the validity check was provided by Izard's Differential Emotions Scale (1972). Given the speed and sensitivity with which the facial muscles respond (Basmajian, 1967) the authors reasoned that it would only be possible to electronically record discrete patterns of low level muscle activity during the generation of affective imagery because these movements might not be visually detectable by the average observer. Surface electrodes were placed at four locations: the right side of the face over the corrugator of the eyebrow; the frontalis of the forehead; the depressor anguli oris of the mouth; and the masseter muscle of the jaw. Comparisons of the imagery-evoked emotional states indicated differential EMG correlates for the specific emotions. Anger was noteworthy in that it was characterized by significant muscle potential increases over all four electrode placements with particularly high increases noted in the depressor region of the mouth. In contrast, happiness was associated with significantly decreased corrugator, increased masseter, and increased depressor activity. Sadness was associated with increased corrugator and depressor potential. Comparisons across all three emotional states for each muscle group further clarify the differential EMG effects, indicating that the corrugator and frontalis can each differentiate happinesss from both sadness and anger whereas the masseter and depressor each differentiate sadness from anger expression. The authors condlude that facial EMGs can reliably differentiate emotional states and provide a sensitive and objective procedure for assessing normal and clinical mood states.

Comments on Psychophysiological Measures of Anger

This partial review of psychophysiological findings suggest that some physiological variables may be used to help differentiate the presence or absence of anger. Little data supports the use of such measures to determine the type or degree of anger experienced by any given individual. The possible exception to this may be blood pressure because suppressed hostility, suppressed anger, and resentment have been repeatedly associated with differential diastolic elevations despite the use of numerous and varied methods of assessing these types of anger. While quite fascinating and potentially promising, the use of facial EMGs for anger assessment requires corroborative study on larger and more varied subject samples before any conclusions can be reliably drawn.

Given the variability associated with individual response specificity, subjects are often used as their own controls in psychophysiological studies. Some assessments (e.g., biological assays) are best performed as a series blocked over time and stringently controlled for extraneous stimulus input to insure accurate and reliable assessment. The risk for subject, environment, and equipment/technique-induced artifact is still relatively high with such procedures and results must be interpreted with caution. The psychophysiological measures here reviewed are clearly best used in conjunction with cognitive labeling processes during states of physiological arousal (Schachter, 1964; Schachter & Singer, 1962) and should be considered supplemental measures rather than substitutes for cognitive measures of anger arousal. Depending on the particular interests, laboratory facilities, and technical expertise of the reader, such indices may indeed provide valuable adjunctive measures. Those readers interested in employing such measures for clinical or research purposes will obviously require more technical and detailed discussion of the specialized procedures and equipment (See Greenfield & Sternbach, 1972; Martin & Venables, 1980).

CONCLUSIONS

Issues in the Assessment of Emotion

Emotions are generally conceptualized as multifaceted phenomena. Izard (1977) notes that emotions are complex phenomena with neural, expressive, and experiential components. According to Eysenck (1975) emotions are characterized by three distinct and measurable parameters: physiological concomitants, introspective (verbal) aspects, and behavioral observations. It is not difficult to accept the view that the emotional experience is comprised of distinct components and, indeed, numerous common sense and investigative examples bear this out. Researchers studying particular emotions typically adhere to this framework. For example, Novaco (1977) conceptualizes anger as an emotional response to provocation that is determined by three modalities of person variables: cognitive, somatic-affective, and behavioral.

Researchers generally concede that arriving at an adequate means to measure emotion is a difficult task. Of course, it would seem desirable to employ assessment of all three parameters of the emtion in question. Unfortunately, the three parameters have not been found to intercorrelate to the extent that might be expected (Eysenck, 1975; Martin, 1972). Upon considering the complexity of the emotional experience, this state of affairs is somewhat understandable. For example, the well known "poker face" phenomenon makes it clear that emotions can be hidden (i.e., behavioral expressions may be controlled). Similarly, it is often possible to act contrary to the dictates of one's emotional state, as when an individual suffering from stagefright successfully manages an apparently calm appearance. On the other hand, as can be illustrated by the acting profession, emotions can be feigned (i.e., behavioral expression can be approximated without the accompanying physiologic or subjective experience).

Eysenck (1975) also makes the point that correlations between the three parameters of emotion have typically been obtained in the laboratory, where the amount of emotion evoked is small and the circumstances admittedly artifical. This may very well be an important consideration in laboratory measurement of emotion, as is illustrated by one recent study (Biaggio et al., 1981). In this study, validation of four objective measures of anger arousal was undertaken, employing self-reports of anger arousal and behavior, and indices of physiological reaction as criterion measures. Although many of the correlations obtained between the measures of anger arousal and self-report were significant, correlations between the measures and physiological indices were generally low and insignificant. It was concluded that there had been insufficient physiological arousal during the experimental conditions. This particular study employed blood pressure and galvanic skin response, which previous researchers had found to accompany anger arousal (Ax, 1953; Novaco, 1975; Schachter, 1957).

Even given the use of physiological indices that have been shown to accompany anger arousal and sufficient experimental manipulation of emotional arousal, there may be problems interpreting physiological arousal. According to the response specificity concept (Lacey & Lacey, 1979), each individual responds to a given stimulus event in an idiosyncratic manner. That is, one subject may show cardiovascular changes while another may exhibit skin potential variations. Kallman and Feuerstein present a corollary: The "response specificity concept leads to the conclusion that there is no single biological system or group of systems that responds to only one psychological event" (1977, pp. 349-350). Land also warns that "nearly all physiological responses can be generated by a great variety of internal and external stimuli and it seems unlikely that any physiological event could be used in an exact substitutive way as an index of a psychological state." (1971, p. 99). Further, researchers have been unable to profile a certain set of physiological indicators that reliably accompany particular emtional states. Given all the drawbacks of using solely physiological indicators of emtion, Eysenck concludes "the evidence suggests that verbal report. . . is in many ways the preferred method of measuring and indexing states of emotional arousal" (1975, p. 441). Indeed, if we consider the common-sense illustrations of the poker face and feigned emotion phenomena, we might conclude that verbal report is the single most valid (i.e., phenomenologically accurate) measure of emtional experience.

However, prospective researchers in this area must consider the nature of the phenomenon they wish to assess as well as the advantages and disadvantages of various assessment strategies. For instance, there are significant problems with assessment via self report. In fact, the recognition of these difficulties has probably helped spur the development of alternate measurement strategies. For instance, need for social approval has been demonstrated to affect an individual's report of hostile feelings (Conn & Crowne, 1964; Novaco, 1975; Young, 1976). And self-report will not satisfactorily reveal more subtle or unconscious aspects of anger, for instance, the tendency to suppress anger. For these reasons, researchers employing self-report measures might also consider assessing anger suppression and test-taking attitude. Also, in selecting a self-report measure, the content of the scale must be considered. Since anger is a multifaceted phenomenon, a measure that assesses a broader sample of the experience/cognition/expression of anger is obviously desirable. This principle also holds for the various assessment strategies. It must be recognized that each strategy has merit since it assesses some aspect of the emotional experience of anger; examining a broad range of facets will result in a more reliable and valid assessment.

Delineation of the Constructs

Though there is an extensive literature on the general topics of anger, hostility, and aggression, these constructs have not always been clearly differentiated. This state of affairs has resulted in some confusion as to the meaning of individual constructs and their relationship to one another. This confusion has impeded communication among investigators and made it difficult to compare findings of research on the various constructs.

A clarification of the constructs and their relationship to one another thus seems desirable. Such a delineation would permit more accurate categorization of the behaviors/emotions involved and would facilitate communication among professionals. Toward this end, the following definitions and differentiations are offered for anger, hostility, and aggression.

Anger has generally been considered an emotion, though the emotional experience obviously connotes not only the cognition of emotion but the possibility of physiological arousal and behavioral manifestation. Anger can then be defined as a strong emotion or experiential state that occurs in response to a real or imagined frustration, threat, or injustice and is accompanied by cognitions related to the desire to terminate the negative stimulus. Thus, anger is a reactive emotion that has a clear antecedent. For more intense emotional experiences, physiological arousal is likely to accompany the anger experience, although such arousal may be slight or nonexistent in mild experiences. It is possible that some behavior will be precipitated by the emotional experience but this is not necessary to define the presence of anger. In fact, it seems best to differentiate between the emotional experience of anger and anger expression, which may involve a simple statement of one's experience (i.e., "That makes me angry") and other manifestations that are more properly defined as aggression, assertion, passive aggression, etc.

Hostility, on the other hand, is best defined as a psychological trait characterized by an enduring attitude of anger and/or resentment and a behavioral predisposition to act out aggression. Spielberger et al. (1983, p. 160), making a similar distinction between anger and hostility, notes that "although hostility usually involves angry feelings, this concept has the connotations of a complex set of attitudes that motivate aggressive behaviors." Since hostility appears to be positively reinforced by injurious consequences, expressions of hostility tend to be instrumental while expressions of anger are more reactive in nature. Hostility is likely to be associated with other similar traits in the individual, for instance suspicion and resentment, and, like these traits, is likely to be a fairly stable part of the personality.

It has generally been agreed that aggression is a behavior which specifically involves the delivery of noxious, damaging, or violent stimuli for offensive or defensive purposes. Aggression may be precipitated by a variety of stimuli and forms of aggression can be categorized with respect to their antecedents. That is, angry aggression would involve a reactive response to some frustration or threat that aroused anger in the individual. Hostile aggression would be a manifestation of a more generalized attitude of resentment or anger and thus would be a more active than reactive event. Instrumental aggression can be defined as aggression that is motivated by a specific goal and that is not accompanied by anger or hostility (i.e., some instances of criminal theft would be classified as instrumental aggression). Also, aggression may take many forms, from subtle verbal insult to obvious physical injury. Thus, aggression may also be categorized according to its form of manifestation, that is, verbal, physical, or passive (i.e., characterized by covert forms of expression).

These definitions are offered as a point of departure for prospective researchers in the field. If research can proceed from a clearly formulated model of the constructs of anger, hostility, and aggression, comparison of individual studies and categorization of forms of emotional experience and behavior will be facilitated.

REFERENCES

Albee, G. W., & Goldman, R. (1950). The Picture-Frustration Study as a predictor of overt aggression. *Journal of Projective Techniques, 14,* 303–308.

Arnaud, S. H. (1959). A system for deriving quantitative Rorschach measures of certain psychological variables for group comparisons. *Journal of Projective Techniques, 23,* 403–411.

Ax, A. F. (1953). The physiological differentiation between fear and anger in humans. *Psychosomatic Medicine, 15* 433–442.

Bandura, A. (1973). *Aggression: A social learning analysis.* Englewood Cliffs, NJ: Prentice-Hall.

Basmajian, J. B. (1967). *Muscles alive.* Baltimore, MD.: Williams & Wilkins.

Beck, A. T., Ward, C. H., Mendelson, M., Mock, J. E., Erbaugh, J. K. (1961). An inventory for measuring depression. *Archives of General Psychiatry, 4,* 561–571.

Bem, D. J., & Allen, A. (1974). On predicting some of the people some of the time: The search for cross-situational consistencies in behavior. *Psychological Review, 81,* 506–520.

Berkowitz, L. (1962). *Aggression: A social psychological analysis.* New York: McGraw-Hill.

Berkowitz, L. (1965). Some aspects of observed aggression. *Journal of Personality and Social Psychology, 2,* 359–369.

Bernard, J. (1949). The Rosenzweig Picture-Frustration Study: I. Norms, reliability and statistical evaluation. II. Interpretation. *Journal of Psychology, 28,* 325–343.

Biaggio, M. K. (1980). Assessment of anger arousal. *Journal of Personality Assessment, 44,* 289–298.

Biaggio, M. K., Supplee, K., & Curtis, N. (1981). Reliability and validity of four anger scales. *Journal of Personality Assessment, 45,* 639–648.

Blackburn, I. M., Lykelsos, G., & Tsiantis, J. (1979). *British Journal of Social and Clinical Psychology, 18,* 227–235.

Breggin, P. R. (1964). The psypchophysiology of anxiety with a review of the literature concerning adrenaline. *Journal of Nervous and Mental Diseases, 139,* 558–568.

Buss, A. H. (1961). *The psychology of aggression.* New York: Wiley.

Buss, A. H. (1963). Physical aggression in relation to different frustrations. *Journal of Abnormal Psychology, 67,* 1–7.

Buss, A. H., & Durkee, A. (1957). An inventory for assessing different kinds of hostility. *Journal of Consulting Psychology, 21,* 343–349.

Buss, A. H., Fischer, H., & Simmons, A. J. (1962). Aggression and hostility in psychiatric patients. *Journal of Consulting Psychology, 26,* 84–89.

Caine, T. M., Foulds, G. A., & Hope, K. (1967). *Manual of the hostility and direction of hostility questionnaire.* London: University of London.

Campbell, D. T., & Fiske, D. W. (1959). Convergent and discriminant validation by the multitrait-multimethod matrix. *Psychological Bulletin, 56,* 81–105.

Cannon, W. B. (1936). *Bodily changes in pain, hunger, fear, and rage* (2nd Ed). New York: Appleton, Century & Crofts.

Check, J. V. P., & Malamuth, N. N. (1983, June). *The hostility toward women scale.* Paper presented at The International Society for Research on Aggression, Victoria, British Columbia.

Clarke, H. J., Rosenzweig, S., & Fleming, E. E. (1947). The reliability of the scoring of the Rosenzweig Picture-Frustration Study. *Journal of Clinical Psychology, 3,* 364–370.

Cleveland, S. E., & Fisher, S. (1956). Psychological factors in the neurodermatoses. *Psychosomatic Medicine, 18,* 209–220.

Cleveland, S. E., & Johnson, D. C. (1962). Personality patterns in young males with coronary diseases. *Psychosomatic Medicine, 24,* 600–610.

Conn, L., & Crowne, D. P. (1964). Instigation to aggression, emotional arousal, and defensive emulation. *Journal of Personality, 32,* 163–179.

Cook, W. W., & Medley, D. M. (1954). Proposed hostility and pharisiac-virtue scales for the MMPI. *Journal of Applied Psychology, 38,* 414–418.

Crane, R. (1981). *The role of anger, hostility and aggression in essential hypertension.* Unpublished doctoral dissertation, University of South Florida.

Crowne, D. P., & Marlowe, D. (1960). A new scale of social desirability independent of psychopathology. *Journal of Consulting Psychology, 24,* 349–354.

Cummings, C. P. (1954). *The role of various psychological variables in children's nailbiting behavior.* Unpublished doctoral dissertation, Pennsylvania State University, University Park, PA.

Deiker, T. E. (1974). A cross-validation of MMPI scales of aggression on male criminal criterion groups. *Journal of Consulting and Clinical Psychology, 42,* 196–202.

Edmunds, G. (1976). The predictive validity of the Buss-Durkee Inventory. *Journal of Clinical Psychology, 32,* 818–820.

Edwards, A. L. (1953). The relationship between the judged desirability of a trait and the probability that the trait will be endorsed. *Journal of Applied Psychology, 37,* 90–93.

Ekman, P., Friesen, W. V., Ellsworth, P. (1972). *Emotion in the human face.* New York: Pergamon.

Elizur, A. (1949). Content analysis of the Rorschach with regard to anxiety and hostility. *Rorschach Research Exchange and Journal of Projective Techniques, 13,* 247–284.

Elmadjian, F., Hope, J. M., & Lamson, E. T. (1957). Excretion of epinephrine and norepinephrine in various emotional states. *Journal of Clinical Endocrinology, 17,* 608–620.

Elmadjian, F., Lamson, E. T., & Neri, R. (1956). Excretion of adrenaline and noradrenaline in human subjects. *Journal of Clinical Endocrinology, 16,* 222–234.

Endicott, J., & Spitzer, R. L. (1972). What! Another rating scale? The psychiatric evaluation form. *Journal of Nervous and Mental Disorders, 154,* 88–104.

Epstein, S., Nelson, J. V., & Tonofsky, R. (1957). Responses to inkblots as measures of individual differences. *Journal of Consulting Psychology, 21,* 211–215.

Esler, M., Julius, S., Zweifler, A., Randall, O. R., Harburg, E., Gardiner, H., & DeQuattro, V. (1977). Mild high-renin essential hypertension. *New England Journal of Medicine, 296,* 405–411.

Evans, D. R. (1970). Specific aggression, arousal, and reciprocal inhibition therapy. *Western Psychologist, 1,* 125–130.

Evans, D. R., & Stangeland, M. (1971). Development of the Reaction Inventory to measure anger. *Psychological Reports, 29,* 412–414.

Eysenck, H. J. (1975). The measurement of emotion: Psychological parameters and methods. In L. Levi (Ed.) *Emotions: Their parameters and measurement* (pp. 439–467). New York: Raven.

Eysenck, H. J., & Eysenck, S. B. G. (1965). *The Eysenck Personality Inventory.* London, University of London.

Feshbach, S. (1955). The drive-reducing function of fantasy behavior. *Journal of Abnormal and Social Psychology, 50,* 3–11.

Fine, B. J., & Sweeney, D. R. (1968). Personality traits, situational factors, and catecholamine excretion. *Journal of Experimental Research in Personality, 3,* 15–27.

Finney, B. C. (1955). Rorschach test correlates of assaultive behavior. *Journal of Projective Techniques, 19,* 6–16.

Forsyth, R. P. (1959). The influences of color, shading and Welch anxiety level on Elizur Rorschach content test analyses of anxiety and hostility. *Journal of Projective Techniques, 23,* 207–213.

Foulds, G. A. (1965). *Personality and personal illness.* London: Tavistock.

Foulds, G. A., & Caine, T. M. (1959). The assessment of some symptoms and signs of depression in women. *Journal of Mental Science, 105,* 182–189.

Foulds, G. A., Caine, T. M., & Creasy, M. A. (1960). Aspects of extra- and intro-punitive expression in mental illness. *Journal of Mental Science, 106,* 599–610.

Franklin, J. C., & Brozek, J. (1949). THe Rosenzweig Picture-Frustration test as a measure of frustration response in semistarvation. *Journal of Consulting Psychology, 13,* 293–301.

Funkenstein, P. H., King, S. H., & Drolette, M. (1954). The direction of anger during a laboratory stress-inducing situation. *Psychosomatic Medicine, 16,* 404–413.

Garfield, S. L., & Kurtz, R. (1974). A survey of clinical psychologists: Characteristics, activities and orientations. *The Clinical Psychologist, 28,* 7–10.

Garfield, S. L., & Kurtz, R. (1976). Clinical psychologists in the 1970s. *American Psychologist, 31,* 1–9.

Gaylord, R. H. (1969). Estimating test reliability from the item-test correlations. *Educational and Psychological Measurement, 29,* 303–304.

Geen, R. G., & Berkowitz, (1967). Some conditions facilitating the occurrence of aggression after the observation of violence. *Journal of Personality, 35,* 666–676.

Geen, R. G., & O'Neal, E. C. (1969). Activation of cue-elicited aggression by general arousal. *Journal of Personality and Social Psychology, 11,* 289–292.

Geen, R. G., Rabosky, J. J., & O'Neal, E. C. (1968). Methodological study of measurement of aggression. *Psychological Reports, 23,* 59–62.

Gentry, W. D. (1970). Effects of frustration, attack, and prior aggressive training on overt aggression and vascular processes. *Journal of Personality and Social Psychology, 16,* 718–725.

Gentry, W. D., Chesney, A. P., Gary, H. E., Hall, R. P., & Harburg, E. (1982). Habitual anger-coping styles: I. Effect on mean blood pressure and risk for essential hypertension. *Psychosomatic Medicine, 44,* 195–202.

Gleser, G. C., Gottschalk, L. A., Fox, R., & Lippert, W. (1965). Immediate changes in affect with chlordiazepoxide in juvenile delinquent boys. *Archives of General Psychiatry, 13,* 291–295.

Goldfried, M. R., Stricker, G., & Weiner, I. B. (1971). *Rorschach handbook of clinical and research applications.* Englewood Cliffs, NJ: Prentice-Hall.

Goldstein, I. B. (1965). The relationship of muscle tension and autonomic activity to psychiatric disorders. *Psychosomatic Medicine, 17,* 39–52.

Gorlow, L., Zimet, C., & Fine, H. J. (1952). The validity of anxiety and hostility Rorschach content scores among adolescents. *Journal of Consulting Psychology, 16,* 73–75.

Gottschalk, L. A. (1982). Manual of uses and applications of the Gottschalk-Gleser Verbal Behavior Scales. Research Communications in Psychology, Psychiatry, and Behavior, 7, 273–329.

Gottschalk, L. A., & Gleser, G. C. (1969). *The measurement of psychological states through the Content Analysis of Verbal Behavior.* Berkeley, CA: University of California.

Gottschalk, L. A., Gleser, G. C., & Springer, K. J. (1963). Three hostility scales applicable to verbal samples. *Archives of General Psychiatry, 9,* 254–279.

Gottschalk, L. A., & Gleser, G. C., D'Zmura, T., & Hanenson, I. (1964). Some psychophysiological relationships in hypertensive women: The effect of Hydrochlorothiazide on the relation of affect to blood pressure. Psychosomatic Medicine, 26, 610–617.

Gottschalk, L. A., Winget, C. N., & Gleser, G. C. (1969). *Manual of instructions for using the Gottschalk-Gleser Content Analyis Scales: Anxiety, hostility, and social alienation-personal disorganization.* Berkeley, CA.:University of California.

Greenfield, N. S., & Sternbach, R. A. (1972). *Handbook of psychophysiology.* New York: Holt, Rinehart & Winston.

Grinker, R. R., Sabshin, M., Hamburg, D. A., Board, F. A., Basowitz, H., Korchin, S. J., Persky, H., & Chevalier, J. A. (1957). The use of an anxiety-producing interview and its meaning to the subject. *A.M.A. Archives of Neurology and Psychiatry, 77,* 406–419.

Hafner, A. J., & Kaplan, A. M. (1960). Hostility content analysis of the Rorschach and TAT. *Journal of Projective Techniques, 24,* 137–143.

Hamburg, D. A., Sabshin, M., Board, F. A., Grinker, R. R., Korchin, S. J., Basowitz, H., Heath, H., & Persky, H. (1958). Classification and rating of emotional experiences. *A.M.A. Archives of Neurology and Psychiatry, 79,* 415–426.

Harburg, E., Blakelock, E. H., & Roeper, P. J. (1979). Resentful and reflective coping with arbitrary authority and blood pressure: Detroit. *Psychosomatic Medicine, 41,* 189–202.

Harburg, E., Erfurt, B. A., Havenstein, L. S., Chape, C., Schull, W. J., & Schork, M. A. (1973). Socio-ecological stress, suppressed hostility, skin color, and Black-White male blood pressure: Detroit: *Psychosomatic Medicine, 35,* 276–296.

Hardyk, C. D. (1966). Personality characteristics and motor activity: Some empirical evidence. *Journal of Personality and Social Psychology, 4,* 181–188.

Hargreaves, W. (1968). Systematic nursing observation of psychopathology. *Archives of General Psychiatry, 18,* 518–531.

Haskell, R. J. (1961). Relationship between aggressive behavior and psychological tests. *Journal of Projective Techniques, 25,* 431–440.

Haven, H. (1969). Racial differences on the MMPI O-H scale. *ECI Research Reports, 1(6),* 1–18.

Heath, H., Oken, D., & Shipman, W. G. (1967). Muscle tension and personality. *Archives of General Psychiatry, 16,* 720–726.

Heyman, S. R. (1977). Dogmatism, aggression, and gender roles. *Journal of Clinical Psychology, 33,* 694–698.

Hokanson, J. E. (1961). The effects of frustration and anxiety on overt aggression. *Journal of Abnormal and Social Psychology, 62,* 346–351.

Holt, R. R. (1970). On the interpersonal and intrapersonal consequences of expressing or not expressing anger. *Journal of Consulting and Clinical Psychology, 35,* 8–12.

Holzberg, J. D., & Posner, R. (1951). The relationship of extrapunitiveness on the Rosenzweig Picture-Frustration Study to aggression in overt behavior and fantasy. *American Journal of Orthopspychiatry, 21,* 767–779.

Izard, C. E. (1972). *Patterns of emotions.* New York: Academic.

Izard, C. E. (1977). *Human emotions.* New York: Plenum.

Kallman, W. M., & Feuerstein, M. (1977). Psychophysiological procedures. In A. R. Ciminero, K. S. Calhoun, & H. E. Adams (Eds.), *Handbook of behavioral assessment* (pp. 329–364). New York: Wiley

Kane, P. (1955). *Availability of hostile fantasy related to overt behavior.* Unpublished doctoral dissertation. University of Chicago, Chicago, IL.

Kaswan, J., Wasman, M., & Freedman, L. Z. (1960). Aggression and the Picture-Frustration Study. *Journal of Consulting Psychology, 24,* 446–452.

Knott, P. D. (1970). A further methodological study of the measurement of interpersonal aggression. *Psychological Reports, 26,* 807–809.

Knott, P. D., & Drost, B. A. (1970). Sex-role identification, interpersonal aggression and anger. *Psychological Reports, 27,* 154.

Konecni, V. J. (1975). Annoyance, type and duration of postannoyance activity, and aggression: The "Cathartic Effect." *Journal of Experimental Psychology: General, 104,* 76–102.

Lacey, J. I., & Lacey, B. C. (1970). Some autonomic-CNS interrelationships. In P. Black (Ed.), *Physiological correlates of emotion* (pp. 205–226). New York: Academic.

Lane, P. J., & Kling, J. S. (1979). Construct validation of the Overcontrolled Hostility Scale of the MMPI. *Journal of Consulting and Clinical Psychology, 47,* 781–782.

Lang, P. J. (1971). The application of psychophysiological methods to the study of pschotherapy and behavior modification. In A. E. Bergin & S. L. Garfield (Eds.), *Handbook of psychotherapy and behavior change: An empirical analysis* (pp. 75–125). New York: Wiley.

Leibowitz, G. (1968). Comparison of self-report and behavioral techniques of assessing aggression. *Journal of Consulting and Clinical Psychology, 32,* 21–25.

Lindzey, G. (1950). An experimental test of the validity of the Rosenzweig Picture-Frustration Study. *Journal of Personality, 18,* 315–320.

Lindzey, G., & Goldwyn, R. M. (1954). Validity of the Rosenzweig Picture-Frustration Study. *Journal of Personality, 22,* 519–547.

Lipetz, M. E., & Ossorio, P. G. (1967). Authoritarianism, aggression, and status. *Journal of Personality and Social Psychology, 5,* 468–472.

Lit, J. (1956). *Formal and content factors of projective tests in relation to academic achievement.* Unpublished doctoral dissertation, Temple University, Philadelphia, PA.

Loveland, N. T., & Singer, M. J. (1959). Projective test assessment of the effects of sleep deprivation. *Journal of Projective Techniques, 23,* 323–334.

Lucas, W. B. (1961). The effects of frustration on the Rorschach responses of nine year-old children. *Journal of Projective Techniques, 25,* 199–204.

Lund, A. (1951). Elimination of adrenaline and noradrenaline from the organism. *Acta Pharmacological et Toxicologica, 7,* 297–308.

Maiuro, R. D., Hall, G. C. N., Patterson, C. M., & Vitaliano, P. P. (1983, April). *The relationship between anger and depression in a male clinical population.* Paper presented at the meeting of the Western Psychological Association, San Francisco, CA.

Martin, I., & Venables, P. (1980). *Techniques in psychophysiology. New York: Wiley.*

Martin, J. (1972). *Somatic reactivity. In H. J. Eysenck (ed.), Handbook of abnormal psychology* (pp. 309–361). London: Pitman.

Megargee, E. I. (1973). Recent research on overcontrolled and undercontrolled personality patterns among violent offenders. *Sociological Symposium,* (No. 9), 37–50.

Megargee, E. I., Cook, P. E., & Mendelsohn, G. A. (1967). Development and validation of an

MMPI scale of assaultiveness in overcontrolled individuals. *Journal of Abnormal Psychology, 72,* 519–528.

Megargee, E. I., & Mendelsohn, G. A. (1962). A cross-validation of twelve MMPI indices of hostility and control. *Journal of Abnormal and Social Psychology, 65,* 431–438.

Mercer, M., & Kyriazis, C. (1962). Results of the Rosenzweig Picture-Frustration Study for physically assaultive prisoner mental patients. *Journal of Consulting Psychology, 26,* 490.

Milgram, S. (1963). Behavioral study of obedience. *Journal of Abnormal and Social Psychology, 67,* 371–377.

Miller, L., Spilka, B., & Pratt, S. (1960). Manifest anxiety and hostility in "clinically insane" patients. *Journal of Clinical and Experimental Psychopathology, 21,* 41–48.

Mischel, W. (1968). *Personality and assessment.* New York: Wiley.

Murstein, B. I. (1958). Some determinants of the perception of hostility. *Journal of Consulting Psychology, 22,* 65–69.

Nisenson, R. A. (1972). Aggressive reactions to frustration in relation to the individual level of extrapunitiveness. *Journal of Personality Assessment, 36,* 50–54.

Novaco, R. W. (1974). *The effect of disposition for anger and degree of provocation on self-report and physiological measures of anger in various modes of provocation.* Unpublished manuscript, Indiana University, Bloomington, IN.

Novaco, R. W. (1975). *Anger control: The development of an experimental treatment.* Lexington, MA.: Lexington.

Novaco, R. W. (1977). Stress inoculation: A cognitive therapy for anger and its application to a case of depression. *Journal of Consulting and Clinical Psychology, 45,* 600–608.

Oken, D. (1960). An experimental study of suppressed anger and blood pressure. *Archives of General Psychiatry, 2.* 441–456.

Philip, A. E. (1968). The constancy of structure of a hostility questionnaire. *British Journal of Social and Clinical Psychology, 7,* 16–18.

Philip, A. E. (1969). The development and use of the Hostility and Direction of Hostility Questionnaire. *Journal of Psychosomatic Research, 13,* 283–287.

Rader, G. E. (1957). The prediction of overt aggressive verbal behavior from Rorschach content. *Journal of Projective Techniques, 21,* 294–306.

Rimon, R., Steinback, A., & Huhmar, E. (1966). Electromyographic findings in depressive patients. *Journal of Psychosomatic Research, 10,* 159–170.

Rorschach, H. (1942). *Psychodiagnostics* (P. Lemkau & B. Kronenberg, Trans.). Berne, Switzerland: Verlag Hans Huber. (Originally published, 1921)

Rose, D., & Bitter, E. J. (1980). The Palo Alto Destructive Content Scale as a predictor of physical assaultiveness in men. *Journal of Personality Assessment, 44,* 228–233.

Rosenzweig, S. (1934). Types of reaction to frustration. *Journal of Abnormal and Social Psychology, 29,* 298–300.

Rosenzweig, S. (1945). The picture-association method and its application in a study of reactions to frustration. *Journal of Personality, 14,* 3–23.

Rosenzweig, S. (1950). Revised norms for the adult form of the Rosenzweig Picture-Frustration Study. *Journal of Personality, 3,* 344–346.

Rosenzweig, S. (1963). Validity of the Rosenzweig Picture-Frustration Study with felons and delinquents. *Journal of Consulting Psychology, 27,* 535–536.

Rosenzweig, S. (1976). *Manual for the Rosenzweig Picture-Frustration Study.* St. Louis: S. Rosenzweig.

Rosenzweig, S. (1977). *Manual for the children's form of the Picture-Frustration Study.* St. Louis: Rana House.

Rosenzweig, S. (1978a). *Aggressive behavior and the Rosenzweig Picture-Frustration Study.* New York: Praeger.

Rosenzweig, S. (1978b). *The Rosenzweig Picture-Frustration Study: Basic manual.* St. Louis: Rana House.

Rosenzweig, S. (1978c). *Adult form supplement to the basic manual of the Rosenzweig Picture-Frustration Study.* St. Louis: Rana House.

Rosenzweig, S., & Adelman, S. (1977). Construct validity of the Rosenzweig Picture-Frustration Study. *Journal of Personality Assessment, 41,* 578–588.

Rosenzweig, S., & Braun, S. H. (1970). Adolescent sex differences in reactions to frustration as explored by the Rosenzweig Picture-Frustration Study. *Journal of Genetic Psychology, 116,* 53–61.

Rosenzweig, S., Fleming, E. E., & Clarke, H. J. (1947). Revised scoring manual for the Rosenzweig Picture-Frustration Study. *Journal of Psychology, 24,* 165–208.

Rosenzweig, S., Fleming, E. E., & Rosenzweig, L. (1948). The children's form of the Rosenzweig Picture-Frustration Study. *Journal of Psychology, 26,* 141–191.

Rosenzweig, S., Ludwig, D. J., & Adelman, S. (1975). Retest reliability of the Rosenzweig Picture-Frustration Study and similar semi-projective techniques. *Journal of Personality Assessment, 39,* 3–12.

Rosenzweig, S., & Rosenzweig, L. (1952). Aggression in problem children and normals as evaluated by the Rosenzweig Picture-Frustration Study. *Journal of Abnormal and Social Psychology, 47,* 683–687.

Ross, W. D., Adsett, N., Gleser, G. C., Joyce, C. R. B., Kaplan, S. M., & Tieger, M. E. (1963). *Journal of Projective Techniques, 27,* 223–225.

Rothenberg, A. (1971). On anger. *American Journal of Psychiatry, 128,* 454–460.

Rule, B. G., & Nesdale, A. R. (1976). Emotional arousal and aggressive behavior. *Psychological Bulletin, 83,* 851–863.

Russell, G. W. (1981). A comparison of hostility measures. *The Journal of Social Psychology, 113,* 45–55.

Sanders, R., & Cleveland, S. E. (1953). The relationship between certain examiner personality variables and subjects' Rorschach scores. *Journal of Projective Techniques, 17,* 34–50.

Sarason, I. G. (1961). Intercorrelations among measures of hostility. *Journal of Clinical Psychology, 17,* 192–195.

Schachter, J. (1957). Pain, fear, and anger in hypertensives and normatensives: A psychophysiological study. *Psychosomatic Medicine, 29,* 17–29.

Schachter, S. (1964). The interaction of cognitive and physiological determinants of emotional states. In L. Berkowitz (ed.), *Advances in experimental social psychology. Vol. I.* (pp. 49–80). New York: Academic.

Schachter, S., & Singer, J. E. (1962). Cognitive, social and physiological determinants of emotional state. *Psuchological Review. 69,* 379–399.

Schultz, S. D. (1954). A differentiation of several forms of hostility by scales empirically constructed from significant items on the MMPI. *Dissertation Abstracts, 17,* 717–720.

Schwartz, G. E., Fair, P. S., Salt, P., Mandel, M. R., & Klerman, G. L. (1976). Facial muscle patterning to affective imagery in depressed and non-depressed subjects. *Science, 192,* 489–491.

Schwartz, G. E., Weinberger, D. B., & Singer, J. A. (1981). Cardiovascular differentiation of happiness, sadness, anger, and fear following imagery and exercise. *Psychosomatic Medicine, 4,* 343–364.

Shemberg, K. M., Leventhal, D. B., & Allman, L. (1968). Aggression machine performance and rated aggression. *Journal of Experimental Research and Personality, 3,* 117–119.

Silverman, A. J., Cohen, S. I., Shmavonian, B. M., Kirshner, N. (1981). Catecholamines in psychophysiologic studies. *Recent Advances in Biological Psychiatry, 3,* 104–118.

Sommer, R., & Sommer, D. T. (1958). Assaultiveness and two types of Rorschach color responses. *Journal of Consulting Psychology, 22,* 57–62.

Spielberger, C. D., Gorsuch, S. L., & Lushene, R. E. (1970). *Manual for the State-Trait Anxiety Inventory (Self-Evaluation Questionnaire)*. Palo Alto, CA.: Consulting Psychologists Press.

Spielberger, C. D., Jacobs, G., Russell, S., & Crane, R. S. (1983). Assessment of anger: The State-Trait Anger Scale. In J. N. Butcher & C. D. Spielberger, C. D. (Eds.), *Advances in personality assessment: Vol. 2* (pp. 159–187). Hillsdale, NJ: Lawrence Erlbaum Associates.

Storment, C. T., & Finney, B. C. (1953). Projection and behavior: A Rorschach study of assaultive mental hospital patients. *Journal of Projective Techniques, 17,* 349–360.

Sutcliffe, J. P. (1955). An appraisal of the Rosenzweig Picture-Frustration Study. *Australian Journal of Psychology, 7,* 97–107.

Taylor, M. V., Jr. (1952). Internal consistency of the scoring categories of the Rosenzweig Picture-Frustration Study. *Journal of Consulting Psychology, 16,* 149–153.

Taylor, M. V., Jr., & Taylor, O. M. (1951). Internal consistency of the Group Conformity Rating of the Rosenzweig Picture-Frustration Study. *Journal of Consulting Psychology, 15,* 250–252.

Vernallis, F. F. (1955). Teeth-grinding: Some relationships to anxiety, hostility, and hyperactivity. *Journal of Clinical Psychology, 11,* 389–391.

Walker, R. G. (1951). A comparison of clinical manifestations of hostility with Rorschach and MAPS test performances. *Journal of Projective Techniques, 15,* 444–460.

Walters, G. D., Greene, R. L., & Solomon, G. S. (1982). Empirical correlates of the Over-controlled-Hostility Scale and the MMPI 4-3 high-point pair. *Journal of Consulting and Clinical Psychology, 50,* 213–218.

White, W. C. (1975). Validity of the Overcontrolled-Hostility (O-H) Scale: A brief report. *Journal of Personality Assessment, 39,* 587–590.

White, W. C., McAdoo, W. G., & Megargee, E. I. (1973). Personality factors associated with over and undercontrolled offenders. *Journal of Personality Assessment, 37,* 473–477.

Wolf, I. (1957). Hostile acting out and Rorschach test content. *Journal of Projective Techniques, 21,* 414–419.

Young, I. L. (1976). Personality characteristics of high and low aggressive adolescents in residential treatment. *Journal of Clinical Psychology, 32,* 814–818.

Zelin, M. L., Adler, G., & Myerson, P. G. (1972). Anger Self-Report: An objective questionnaire for the measurement of aggression. *Journal of Consulting and Clinical Psychology, 39,* 340.

Zillman, D. (1978). Attribution and misattribution of excitatory reactions. In J. H. Harvey, W. J. Ickes, & R. F. Kidd (Eds.), *New directions in attribution research: Vol. 2* (pp. 335–368). Hillsdale, NJ: Lawrence Erlbaum Associates.

4 Impulsiveness Defined Within a Systems Model of Personality

Ernest S. Barratt
University of Texas Medical Branch

INTRODUCTION

The purposes of this chapter are: to discuss briefly, within the framework of current research, the need and rationale for a systems theory model of personality; to review the theory and research related to defining impulsiveness within a systems theory model; to review our current research on the biological bases of timing and rhythm performance related to defining personality traits. Personality traits including impulsiveness are defined within our research by profiles of biological, social, and psychological measures, the latter including both cognitive and behavioral measures (Barratt & Patton, 1983; Barratt, in press).

Our evolving personality model is primarily of heuristic value at this time. A brief overview of our model is presented to indicate the link between our past and current research. The model attempts to cope with the circularities and shortcomings of defining personality traits exclusively by questionnaire responses (Nicholls, Licht, & Pearl, 1982). The circularity arises primarily when one seeks to ascribe the etiological bases of personality traits by correlating questionnaire scores with other behavioral or psychophysiological data. For example, one might observe that a person is impulsive if he scores high on an impulsiveness questionnaire; impulsive persons so defined and selected are visual evoked potential augmentors, ergo, visual evoked potential augmentors will score high on impulsiveness tests. Actually, augmenting/reducing of visual cortical evoked potentials has been significantly related to a number of other personality traits including sensation seeking and hypomania. Then, are impulsive persons also sensation seekers or hypomanic?

Much of our research has involved the study of impulsiveness among "normal" persons. One pervasive problem for personality theorists is the relative difficulty of getting insight into "normal" compared to persons with florid psychopathology. This problem involves not only the question of whether the symptoms of psychopathology are a matter of degree, (i.e., are they on a continuum of severity from normal to pathological?) but, further, can personality theory add significantly to our understanding of everyday life-coping processes? For example, what role does impulsiveness play in everyday life situations? In a recent editorial labeled "Panpsychiatry: Psychiatry as Ideology", Wortis (1983) noted that "when the notion becomes widespread that psychiatric symptoms and mechanisms are all pervasive, it is easy to succmb to the idea that psychiatry makes the world go around" (p. 1). His thesis is similar to that of Hebb (1974) who advised that "it is to the literary world, not to psychological science, that you go to learn how to live with people, how to make love, how to make enemies—as a supplement to William James, read Henry James, and Jane Austin, and Mark Twain" (p. 74). Wortis in a earlier editorial (1982) noted that "it is not surprising that the major disorders with their grosser pathology are easier to define than, say, neurotic or personality disorders, which involve patterns of motivation, nuance, overlap and emphasis. The problem with the categories of neuroses, personality disorders, antisocial behavior, and the like points up another difficulty—the scope of psychiatry. The further one moves from the major psychoses and gross pathology into the realm of character development and the common anxieties, the more difficult and questionable does the nosological task become" (p. 1363). Difficult, yes. But also challenging and possible. In my opinion, the most challenging part of the task is addressing the need for a personality model. Wortis and Hebb viewed personality from a biological orientation. It is obvious to me that if personality theory is to provide convincing evidence of its value in describing and predicting behavior beyond those persons with extreme psychopathologies, personality research will have to be based on an eclectic model that interrelates biological, social, and psychological data. This approach will also enhance understanding of the possible continuum of "symptoms" from normal to the psychopathological states.

Toward a Systems Theory Personality Model

Although technical advances in psychology and related disciplines have made the study of personality more sophisticated, yesteryear's basic controversies still persist. Some current problems in personality research are older than psychology itself. The revival of a more general interest in cognition during the last decade, especially the research relating cognition to brain functions, has its historical roots in the age old mind–body dichotomy. Hebb (1974), for example, viewed psychology as a biological science and stated that "introspectionism is a dead duck" (p. 73). Yet, many of the items on personality questionnaires require introspective analyses. For example, the Eysenck's research indicates that the questionnaire item with the highest relationship to "impulsiveness narrow" is "Do you generally do and say things without stopping to think?" (Eysenck & Eysenck, 1977). Although it is possible to study cognition within personality research without using introspective reports or subjective data, to rule out these techniques by fiat will, in our opinion, result in a less useful understanding of individual differences in personality research. Another contemporary debate involving the relative influence of genetic inheritance versus the social milieu on personality development merely continues the longstanding nature–nurture problem in personality research. In contrast to the two old debates, speculations about the relative roles of neural transmitters in the expression of personality traits reflect a more recent explosion of information within the neural sciences. To resolve both the longstanding and more recent controversies, a personality model that allows us to assess the relative influences of a wide range of biological, social, and psychological measures is necessary.

Anyone familiar with the history of personality research realizes that an integrated personality model has been called for for many years (Kluckhon & Murray, 1949; Murphy, 1947, 1958; Miller, Galanter, & Pribram, 1960; Thorpe & Schmuller, 1958). There have been circumscribed attempts to integrate biological and psychological concepts; for example, Pribram and Gill's (1976) reformulation of Freud's psychoanalytic theory in the light of both Freud's "project" and more modern neuropsychological concepts, or of Eysenck's (1967) personality model based in part on neural and conditioning concepts. Models employing factor analytic individual difference measures (Guilford, 1975; Cattell, 1979), cognitive-social learning concepts (Rotter, 1966; Mischel, 1973), or social interaction concepts (Endler & Magnusson, 1976) have also been proposed. These have resulted in debates about many specific facets of personality, such as the constancy or consistency in the expression of traits in a wide variety of situations (Olweus, 1979; Mischel & Peake, 1982). Researchers who have studied global or more circumscribed measures of personality occasionally must have experienced some futility with the inadequacy of their measures in the light of the always-global debates. That malaise about our impulsiveness research led us, about 5 or 6 years ago, to search for a model that would allow us to integrate our research with these many different approaches to personality measurement.

What questions should this integrative model help us to answer? We started with a simple question about the range of measurements involved in personality research: What is the basic or minimal number of categories of measurements with which we work in our impulsiveness research? Once this question was answered, we then asked how the measurements within and between these categories could be interrelated in a systems model. The answer to the first question was fairly straightforward and certainly not unique. There were four categories of measurements: (1) biological measures; (2) behavioral measures; (3) cognitive measures; (4) external stimuli or environmental measures. Within each category there is a wide range of measurements involving varying levels of complexity and of interaction. For example, external stimuli range from measurements of physical characteristics of stimuli (e.g., photon or wave measurements of light) to the symbols imbedded in social and cultural systems. It occurred to us to start with a clear delineation of measurements within each of these four categories and then to search for a way to interrelate the four categories into a system. Viewing personality as exclusively within any one or two categories provides a biased view. Lazare (1973) noted, in his discussion of hidden conceptual models in psychiatry, how these four categories provide the primary emphases for the four major models of diagnostics and therapeutics within psychiatry. That is, the medical model is primarily biologically oriented; the psychological model is cognitively oriented; the social model is oriented to roles and interpersonal relationships; behavioral models are focused primarily on overt behaviors. As Lazare illustrates, viewing the same patient with varying degrees of emphasis on each of the four categories results in a very different diagnostic and therapeutic approach. For us, it was important that our research be inclusive enough to define impulsiveness using all four categories of measurements and that it lend itself to conceptualization in a systems model. That led, next, to addressing the second question, "How can these four categories of measurements be interrelated in a systems model?"

Before answering this question, let us digress briefly to consider Rorer and Widiger's recent discussion of personality assessment in the 1983 *Annual Review of Psychology*. They suggest that personality assessment has plateaued in its usefulness to predict behavior because it uses "assessment (individual difference) models that are inappropriate to the task, which is more complicated than has been realized." They note further that "the complications are conceptual, and understanding them requires a significant change in orientation" (p. 433). Rorer and Widiger provide an excellent overview of the conceptual and methodologial problems with which modern personality theorists must cope. Their critique of logical positivism and their discussion of the philosophical underpinnings of personality theory furnish recommended reading. They discuss selected methodological innovations which "deal with hypothetical constructs (open sets) in nonexperimental settings" (p. 452) including causal modeling. But such approaches also have their limitations. Cliff (1983) recently outlined some cautions that need to be observed in the use of causal modeling; he noted that "ex post facto analyses are not tests of models" (p. 115). Our choice has been to continue laboratory research which Rorer and Widiger prioritize at a lower level than "everyday life experience" research. In an earlier report on our impulsiveness research (Barratt, 1972), we outlined our attempts to bridge the "laboratory-everyday life experience" gap by observing the same subjects in both settings. In a more recent review of our impulsiveness research (Barratt & Patton, 1983) we noted a further shift to the use of a general systems model, which we discussed briefly. We agree that most relationships of independent variables with behavior are "probabilistic and multiply determined" (p. 439) as Rorer and Widiger indicate. Conceptually, we start with a systems model to interrelate the four categories of data enumerated above. We then progress to multivariate analyses within the system to obtain broad relationships that provide suggestions of independent and dependent variables that can be studied in the laboratory using more traditional research designs. The results of the latter experiments along with the results of the multivariate analyses are then used to modify the theoretical model as findings dictate. We have begun following these procedures only recently but the results have been rewarding. For example, specific biological markers (e.g., visual augmenting/reducing measurements) are often not trait specific but, within a matrix of other markers, do fit into a unique profile for some traits. This research approach requires concatenated experiments and research progresses slowly. However, to the extent that this procedure or alternative ones suggested by Rorer and Widiger are used, the research results from different laboratories will be more easily compared and integrated into a personality theory.

As we discussed recently (Barratt & Patton, 1983), we were influenced in our development of a model by Ashby's (1960) cybernetic model and the discussion of Ashby by (Diamond, Balvin, & Diamond, 1963). Ashby proposed a four category systems model for understanding learning and "behavoral" coping (Fig. 4.1). Since Ashby worked within a framework of cybernetics and was concerned with only "observable" phenomena, cognition was obviously not part of his system. The loop through the motivation box from the environment was a "reward" subsystem which carried with it "control" information for continuing or discontinuing a specific behavior. In its control function, Ashby's loop is somewhat analagous to the Miller et al. (1960) concept of a TOTE unit (test-operate, test-exist) for resolving incongruities between the "state of the organism and the state being tested for" in adaptation.

Diamond et al. (1963) noted that the feedback within Ashby's model was essentially negative and directed at limiting the activity of the system. Further, they remarked "this does not exclude the possibility that positive, response-enhancing feedback may also come to play an important part in adaptive behavior, but it does mean that any system which relies exclusively upon positive feedback—and this is the kind of system which is explicit in a great deal of S-R theorizing—is headed for a catastrophic breakdown" (pp. 108–109). For Miller et al. the TOTE unit has a hierarchical relationship to a "Plan"; they also present various alternatives for what the arrows represent within a system. In addition to representing energy or information, they note that the arrows can represent "control" which is clearly Ashby's intent. But how does cognition fit into Ashby's model? Taking liberty with Ashby's cybernetic (mechanistic) interpretation, we propose that his motivation box encompasses cognitive functions as well as drives or incentives. To the extent that motivation is involved in processing

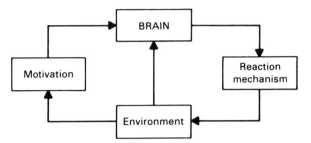

FIG. 4.1.   Double Feedback: Ashby's minimal requirements for an adaptive nervous system (from Diamond et al., 1962, p. 108).

"reward" information, working memory (at a minimum) has to be involved. Ashby in his *Introduction to Cybernetics* (1956) considered memory functions in stating that "possession of memory is not a wholly objective property of a system—it is a relationship between a system and an observer, ... Thus, to involve *memory* in a system as an explanation of its behavior is equivalent to saying that we cannot observe the system completely" (p. 116). That dictum may be accurate from a completely cybernetic, mechanistic viewpoint but we propose that we can include memory and other conscious and unconscious cognitive functions as part of the system in the box that Ashby labels motivation. One might argue further that cognition is really inherent in brain functions and that the cognitive box is misplaced in our version of Ashby's ultrastable system model, especially conscious cognitive processes. Representing cognition and brain functions as separate categories (really the mind/body problem) has been approached many ways. For example, McGeer, Eccles, and McGeer (1978) described "three worlds" to account for varying levels of cognitive processing (Fig. 4.2). The conscious self is World 2 and memory functions are World 3. We shall not belabor the many possible models that we and others have devised for interrelating our four basic categories of concepts; we do suggest as noted earlier that it is imperative to keep these four categories of concepts and data clearly separated in personality models—for heuristic purposes if for no other reason. We also feel that a closed system such as Ashby's model is more workable than an open system. Many models, for example, have the environment as an open ended input–output part of the system (e.g., the World 1 of McGeer et al.). We propose that one's life space (Lewin, 1935) is relatively circumscribed at any one point in time and can be considered as part of a closed system. Our current reinterpretation of Ashby's model (Fig. 4.3) provides the basis for our impulsiveness and related personality research. The model as presented in Fig. 4.3 is not complete for it contains only examples of subsystems within each of the four categories. The complexity and inclusiveness of other concepts in the model is easily achieved. For example, the cognition subsystems could be elaborated to include Sternberg's (1977) cognitive model. The brain subsystems can include

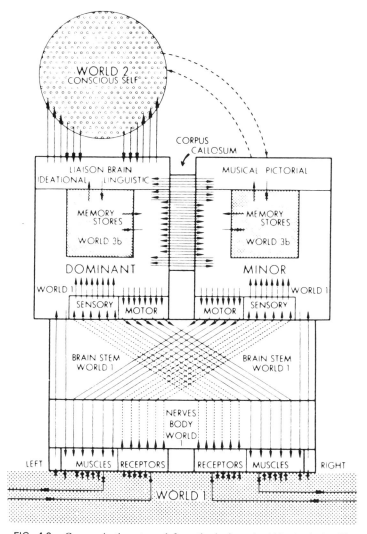

FIG. 4.2. Communications to and from the brain and within the brain. The diagram shows the principal lines of communication from peripheral receptors to the sensory cortices and so to the cerebral hemispheres. Similarly, the diagram shows the output from the cerebral hemispheres via the motor cortex and so to muscles. Both these systems of pathways are largely crossed as illustrated, but minor uncrossed pathways are also shown by the vertical lines in the brainstem. The dominant left hemisphere and minor right hemisphere are labeled, together with some of the properties of these hemispheres that are found displayed in Figure 16.8. The corpus callosum is shown as a powerful cross linking of the two hemispheres, and, in addition, the diagram displays the modes of interaction between Worlds 1, 2, and 3, as described in the text, and also illustrated in Figure 16.10 (from McGeer et al., 1978, p. 559).

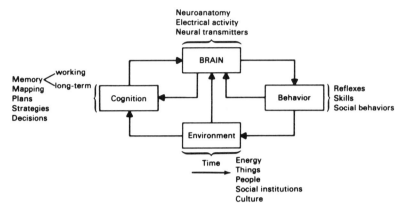

FIG. 4.3.   Reformulation of Ashby's model as a *basic* personality model.

not only neuroanatomical but also biochemical and hormonal pathways. The behavior category includes all forms of behavior including responding to personality questionnaires. The environmental subsystems include social and cultural measures as outlined in a number of models of social systems (e.g., Kuhn, 1974), other individuals, and in general, a person's life space. As we indicated earlier, Ashby interpreted his own model very differently because his cybernetic approach was more mechanistic and was restricted to observable phenomena and cognition was not part of his system. Rorer and Widiger's (1983) critique of logical positivism is consonant with our attempt to change the direction of our personality research.

How does this systems model relate to personality theory and, more specifically, to impulsiveness? The system can be viewed from an organizational or structural viewpoint and also from a process viewpoint with correlative functions. Different personality traits can be more related in our measurement of them to one category or focus within the system, but personality traits are fully defined or described only by a profile including all four categories. For example, in contrasting the traits of impulsiveness and anxiety, one might ask where the main focus is within the system for each trait. If one compares the items on impulsiveness and anxiety questionnaires, it is obvious that impulsiveness questionnaires include more behavior items while anxiety questionnaires include more "feeling" items. One acts impulsively. One feels anxious, although anxiety obviously affects behavior. Thus, from the conscious experiences of the person taking the tests, there are differences in the loci of their introspective analyses while answering the questionnaire. However, as noted earlier, attention to all four categories of measurements is necessary to define the personality traits within personality theory.

Before leaving this section, some selected comments might clarify the above brief overview of our model.

1. It is possible to devise a wide variety of systems models. The one that we have presented is primarily a negative feedback, closed system. Eysenck (1967), in contrast, uses primarily a hierarchical model in his personality research.

2. Models are developed at a conceptual level and have primarily heuristic value. Models are not necessarily isomorphic with, or substitutes for, reality.

3. One's philosophical or professional orientation will influence both one's choice of a model and one's interpretation of models. For example, in presenting our model to different professional groups, the location of a cognitive box outside the brain is more readily accepted in general by psychoanalytically oriented professionals than by biologically oriented professionals. The inferential nature of cognition is less readily accepted by biologically than psychoanalytically oriented professionals.

4. It should be reemphasized that measurements of selected variables may be read high or low in several personality profiles. Cortical arousal, MAO, or augmenting/reducing of visual evoked potentials may be high on several profiles. Alternatively, their relative role in each profile may be different.

5. Temporal relationships are important. Some profiles are more enduring over time and reflect personality traits while other profiles are less enduring and represent state conditions.

Our ultimate goal is to advance personality measurement by using techniques other than questionnaires per se. However, this goal is far from being realized at this time and much of what is discussed in the next section relies almost exclusively on questionnaire definitions of impulsiveness.

Impulsiveness within a System Model

We shall briefly review impulsiveness research within each of the four basic categories of our system, elaborating upon selected facets of the profile of impulsiveness within the system. We recently presented a general overview of our impulsiveness research (Barratt & Patton, 1983) and do not repeat that deeper review of the data here. Rather we shall extend and clarify selected aspects of our research not covered in that review. We also relate our research results to the more general problems in current personality research as discussed by Rorer and Widiger (1983).

Since most of our past research identified impulsiveness by questionnaires, when we refer to high and low impulsive persons, these distinctions are based on questionnaires (primarily the Barratt Impulsiveness Scale; Barratt, 1959; Barratt & Patton, 1983). We have alluded to the potential pitfalls of this approach in the previous section and in our recent review (Barratt & Patton, 1983). We shall supplement our laboratory research data with clinical and everyday life experience observations in order to roundout this presentation of our conceptual model of impulsiveness.

Because impulsiveness and anxiety were orthogonal personality traits in our earlier multivariate analyses of responses to personality questionnaires (Barratt, 1965), we often selected subjects for research for their varying levels of both anxiety and impulsiveness. This combined impulsiveness-anxiety quest was partly responsible for our becoming interested in a systems model of personality. Interaction effects of these two personality traits were obvious and we became interested in the characteristics of a system that would exhibit varying levels of both anxiety and impulsiveness.

Behavior Category

Laboratory Studies.   We have related impulsiveness to a wide range of psychomotor and perceptual-motor tasks (Barratt, 1959, 1967, 1971, 1972; Barratt, Patton, Olsson, & Zuker, 1981; Barratt & Patton, 1983). Our initial interest was in both speed of response and intraindividual variability of behavior. Since high-impulsive subjects appeared to respond "without thinking", we hypothesized that their reaction times would be faster. Our data did not confirm this hypothesis and, as noted below, the true relationship is much more complex. Further, some of our earlier exploratory research indicated that high-impulsive subjects had higher levels of intraindividual variability in performing psychomotor tasks. Selected results of these laboratory studies will be briefly summarized by considering the tasks presented to the subjects.

1. High-impulsive subjects perform less efficiently on a pursuit rotor task than do low-impulsive subjects. The faster the rotor speed, the less the time on target by the high-impulsive subjects in comparison to the low impulsive.
2. In reaction time tasks, the difference between high- and low-impulsive subjects depends on the task requirements of a warning signal, the warning signal-imperative signal interval, and level of information to be discriminated when the imperative signal is presented. We extensively studied reaction time related to both impulsiveness and anxiety and the results have been consistent over the years.

a. In discrimination reaction time tasks involving a variable warning signal-imperative signal interval (3 to 9 seconds), high-impulsive subjects have slower release reaction times than do low-impulsive subjects; the higher the level of information associated with the discrimination at the imperative signal, the greater the discrepancy between the two groups.

b. In reaction time tasks involving no warning or briefer warning signals (20 to 1000 ms) than those described above, high-impulsive subjects respond more slowly than low-impulsive subjects if the warning signal-imperative signal interval is 600 ms to 800 ms or longer; if the interval is 600 ms or less, the high-impulsive subjects respond faster than low-impulsive subjects.

In most of these reaction time experiments, we used a paradigm in which a flashing light signaled an intertrial interval. When the light stopped flashing, the subject was instructed to place his forefinger on a "home key" (latency reaction time), wait for the warning signal (S1), prepare to respond to the imperative stimulus, release the home key as quickly as possible when the imperative stimulus (S2) appeared (release reaction time), and then depress a second switch (jump reaction time). The latency reaction time, which we interpret as a more "natural" or characteristic level of responding, was not related to impulsiveness but was related to anxiety in most experiments. The jump reaction time was significantly positively correlated with the release time and with impulsiveness.

c. High impulsiveness subjects make significantly more errors than do low impulsiveness subjects in apparatus maze tasks (e.g., Snoddy Maze) and on paper-and-pencil mazes (e.g., Porteus mazes).

d. In vigilance tasks (30 minutes to 90 minutes), involving monitoring a visual stimulus on a screen, high-impulsive subjects make more errors of commission (false responses) but not more errors of omission than do low-impulsive subjects; that is, during vigilance tasks of 30 to 90 minute duration, high-impulsive subjects will respond more often when they should not respond (no stimulus present), but do not differ from low-impulsive subjects in the number of times that they correctly respond to the presentation of a stimulus.

e. In visual tracking tasks, high-impulsive subjects are more variable in following a dot which has a "random" path on the screen.

f. In a paced tapping task, high impulsiveness subjects tapped faster than the pacing time and had greater intraindividual variability of tapping than low impulsiveness subjects. In this experiment, the absolute error of tapping did not relate to impulsiveness. Moreover, anxiety too was not significantly related to tapping in this experiment.

g. In general, in all of the above tasks, high-impulsive subjects had greater intraindividual variability of their performance than did low-impulsive subjects.

Everyday Life Behavior and Clinical Observations

How does impulsiveness affect behavior in everyday life? Most of our studies involving subjects in everyday life also involved measures of anxiety and other personality traits including socialization. As noted previously, because anxiety and impulsiveness as measured by personality questionnaires are orthogonal (or at most have a very low correlation), persons with varying levels of both traits can be selected from the four quadrants of a scatter diagram (i.e., high impulsive, low anxiety, etc.). Although we found interaction effects of anxiety and impulsiveness on the performance of laboratory tasks, interaction effects were more obvious in everyday life situations. A brief overview of our everyday life and clinical observations indicates that: (1) High-impulsive, low-anxiety subjects were more unreliable in keeping appointments; they more often were late for a research session than were members of the other three groups; they made good 'first appearances'' but among individuals who interacted with them on a sustained basis, they had difficulties in interpersonal relationships. For example, in a study of medical students (Barratt & White, 1969), professors often were impressed with the high-impulsive low-anxiety students. In contrast, these students were not well integrated into their social fraternities and the officers of the fraternities considered them to be "trouble makers." The ones who were married had marital problems. The same observations with interpersonal relationships were observed in a study of Catholic priests living in a closely-knit community. (2) High-impulsive, high-anxiety subjects tend to develop more severe psychiatric symptoms than do the other three groups; in the study of medical students, the high-impulsive, high-anxiety students all sought psychiatric help in their first 3 years of medical school. (3) The low-impulsive, low-anxiety persons appear, in general, to be less highly motivated toward social mobility than are the other three groups. They have very few problems in interpersonal relationships and report few psychiatric problems. (4) The high-anxiety, low-impulsive persons are highly motivated, prone to worry, and often have difficulty with performance in everyday life because of their anxiety. Among medical students, they often had difficulty on test performance because of test anxiety.

Results of our recent research on everyday behavior of impulsive subjects are preliminary because they are so new. Over the past two years, as part of a psychodiagnostic service, we have been looking more systematically at impulsiveness, anxiety, and sociability in a wide range of psychiatric disorders. The preliminary analyses of these data show consistent conformation of our laboratory findings. However, the interactions are obviously complex. When one considers that one "personality system" can be characterized by many "trait interactions", the necessity for a systems model is clear. Impulsiveness as a personality trait obviously interacts with anxiety. How many more "traits" does it interact with? Perhaps, higher order personality factors may be more fruitful to research than more specific, lower order personality factors (Barratt & Patton, 1983). In this context, the Eysencks' (1969, 1976) three broad dimensions of Neuroticism, Extroversion, and Psychoticism or some similar approach may be the best initial way to study personality within a systems model, especially in beginning the search for biological correlates. We return to this point later.

Cognition Category

Our inclusion of formal experiments involving cognition in our impulsiveness research is rather recent (Barratt & Patton, 1983). This work has concentrated primarily on time judgements, "time zone" research, and cognitive tempo or rate of information processing (Barratt, 1977, 1981; Barratt, Adams, & White,

1977). These, added to some earlier data, primarily using paper and pencil cognitive tasks, are relevant to understanding cognitive functions related to impulsiveness. A brief overview of these results follows:

1. In general, among adults, cognitive ability as measured by standardized intelligence tests such as the WAIS is not significantly related to impulsiveness. However, among adolescents significant negative relationships of impulsiveness with the WISC-R verbal IQ were found.

2. Impulsiveness is significantly negatively related to the time to perform the Stroop Test but not to errors.

3. Impulsiveness is significantly negatively related to time to perform Trails B.

4. High-impulsive subjects underproduce time judgments in comparison to low-impulsive subjects. That is, when asked to judge a 1 minute time interval, for example, high-impulsive subjects report a much shorter time interval than do low-impulsive subjects. Thus, experientially, time passes much more slowly for high-impulsive subjects since their subjective experience has a faster cognitive tempo.

5. On selected tests of "creativity" high-impulsive subjects perform better than low-impulsive subjects. These tests primarily involve ideational fluency and calling up spontaneously "original" responses to stimuli, whether verbal or pictorial.

6. In "time zone" research using a modification of Cottle's techniques (1976), high-impulsive subjects were more willing to predict the future than were low impulsives. This is consistent with earlier "risk-taking" experiments (Barratt, 1966) in which high impulsive subjects demonstrated a tendency to take more risks in a "gambling" experiment than did low-impulsiveness subjects.

We have not systematically studied cognitive functions in everyday life situations. However, extrapolating from items on impulsiveness questionnaires, we derive some insight into cognitive functions related to impulsiveness in everyday life experiences (despite the limitations of circularity in this approach). The Eysencks (1977) made a distinction between impulsiveness narrow and impulsiveness broad. Our use of impulsiveness is primarily impulsiveness broad, a more inclusive concept (Barratt & Patton, 1983; Barratt, in press). High-impulsiveness subjects in comparison to low-impulsiveness subjects in our research often act and speak without thinking, make up their minds quickly, take greater risks, and do not plan ahead.

Brain Category

In this section we report only a summary of our main psychophysiological findings with human subjects. We have for many years done lower primate research, trying to understand the biological underpinnings of what we consider to be neural circuits mediating impulsive behavior at the human level. We shall not discuss the lower animal research here, however significant its impact on the direction of our current research. Let us next list some of the more consistent psychophysiological findings with human subjects.

1. The psychophysiological measures of high-impulsiveness subjects are more variable than are those of low-impulsiveness subjects. That variability is seen in measures of cortical activity (evoked potentials and event related potentials) as well as of autonomic function.

2. High-impulsive subjects in comparison to low-impulsive subjects are visual evoked potential augmentors.

3. During a resting state, the EEG of high-impulsive subjects contains less low voltage fast activity, a higher level of alpha frequency rhythm, which, in our opinion, suggests a less aroused cortical state and diminished brain-stem reticular activation.

4. High-impulsive subjects do not produce contingent negative variation (CNV) responses to selected stimuli that will result in a CNV among low-impulsiveness subjects. For example, high-impulsive subjects in visual discrimination tasks including geometric stimulus patterns did not produce a CNV while low-impulsive subjects did. However, to "more sensational stimuli," "pornographic" stimuli, the high-impulsive subjects did produce a CNV, although the CNVs were still significantly lower in amplitude than those of the low-impulsive subjects.

5. High-impulsive subjects produce significantly more spontaneous eye-blinks in a resting state and while performing tasks than do low-impulsive subjects. This became obvious to us while doing a conditioned eye-blink experiment (Barratt, 1971) and also when recording visual evoked potentials. In the visual evoked potential experiments, we have a computer program that monitors both eye-movements and eye-blinks in order to control for artifacts in our evoked potentials. High-impulsive subjects have a much higher percentage of "blink artifacts" than do low-impulsive subjects.

Environment Category

The main question here is related to the current controversy in personality research about the constancy of the expression of personality traits across different laboratory or "real-world" environmental stimuli (Rorer & Widiger, 1983; Mischel, 1973; Olweus, 1979). Within the laboratory, the relationship of impulsiveness to performance on behavioral and cognitive tasks has been consistent. For example we have replicated the reaction time tasks many times with the same results. These results suggest that when there is a warning signal and an imperative signal with a distinct interval of 600 to 800 ms, or more, high-impulsive subjects respond more slowly. Further, if the task requirements involve increasing the level of information to be processed, the high-impulsive subjects are less efficient at responding than low-impulsive subjects. Where the task requirements involve a more spontaneous responding, high-impulsive subjects respond with a higher level of output, as in the creativity tasks, and faster reaction time.

Whether stimuli have a "sensational" quality in terms of social definitions appears also to relate to impulsiveness. High-impulsive subjects give less of a CNV to stimuli in general than do low-impulsive subjects, although more sensational stimuli do produce a CNV in high-impulsive subjects.

In everyday life, high-impulsive subjects, especially high-impulsive, low-anxiety subjects, have more difficulties in maintaining good, sustained, interpersonal relationships. In contrast, they make a good "first impression" and appear to impress people when the interactions involved are more brief. Related to these observations, Kipnis (1971) found that high-impulsive subjects chose college majors and vocational fields with less emphasis on rigorous, detailed, cognitive processing than the sciences or mathematics.

Interrelating the Four Categories

How do the above observations interrelate in our personality model? First, we have to reiterate that impulsiveness is only one trait among many that characterize the system. Although we have selectively studied anxiety and socialization in relationship to impulsiveness in our research (Barratt & Patton, 1983), there are obviously many other state and trait personality measures that we have not measured that could have a potential influence on our results. However, our results on impulsiveness to date do appear to suggest some consistencies across the four categories in our model that can be studied in the laboratory. Let us briefly, then, interrelate the results to arrive at a systems concept of impulsiveness.

High-impulsive persons are more variable in perceptual-motor tasks; have more difficulty responding efficiently to tasks involving the establishment of a "set", and this inefficiency becomes more obvious if the information to be processed is increased, either in terms of level or increased timing requirements; and high-impulsive subjects have a fast cognitive tempo. Further, the psychophysiological responses of high impulsives are more variable and they appear to have a lower level of cortical arousal related to reticular brain-stem activity. The latter could be interpreted as a moderate level of arousal and selective responding rather than reflecting a low level of arousal per se. Looking at a system with these traits, we concluded that the main characteristics of the impulsive system related to its temporal characteristics in information processing during task performance. We proposed that a high-impulsive person's cognitive tempo, or rate of information processing, is out of synchrony with the task demands. This is more obvious in laboratory experiments where the task demands are much more circumscribed than many everyday life demands. However, the more everyday life tasks demand rigorous attention to detail or a sustained, consistent effort over time, the more difficult and less attractive are these pursuits to the high-impulsive person. One key, then, to a better understanding of impulsiveness is to learn more about the biological bases of performance on timing and rhythm tasks and their related cognitive functions.

Biological Bases of the Performance of Timing and Rhythm Tasks Related to Impulsiveness

Our current research is aimed at a better description, within the systems model, of the interrelationship of cognitive tempo or rate of information processing; brain functions; performance on cognitive and behavioral tasks with varying timing and rhythm demands; and selected personality traits, including impulsiveness. We are not limiting our inquiry to impulsiveness for two reasons: (1) As noted in previous sections, impulsiveness exists in the system, not in a vacuum; to understand the role of the system in impulsiveness requires some insight into the role of these system characteristics in other personality profiles; (2) There are indications that the characteristics of the system that we have identified for our current research efforts are related to other personality traits. As one example, Melges in his book, *Time and The Inner Future* (1982), has presented an indepth overview of time judgments and "time zone" concepts related to different personality traits and psychopathologies.

Because of its multivariate interdisciplinary nature, our current research involves the use of concepts and techniques from several research traditions. Apposite threads are:

1. Research in Information Processing and Motor Control.   Two general models of information processing and motor control are in vogue. One model involves a "motor programming" paradigm (Gunilla, Oberg, & Divac, 1981; McGeer & McGeer, 1980), giving a cognitive explanation of the *preprogramming* of the motor cortex prior to making a response. The second model is based more upon the classical physiological theories of motor functioning (Granit, 1970; Marsden, 1980). Our research encompasses both models. As noted below, we shall be relating topographical maps of voltage changes in the cortex to cognitive tempo and the preprogramming of movement control, and timing and rhythm requirements of the tasks among subjects with different personality profiles.

2. Individual Differences in the Performance of Psychomotor Tasks.   This area of research has a long history and includes the general goal of arriving at a taxonomy of psychomotor tasks (e.g., Fleishman, 1954; Gagne & Fleishman, 1959; Irion, 1966; Pawlik, 1966). If one examines all of the attempts to arrive at a taxonomy of psychomotor tasks, it is clear that there is always common variance among the tasks that relates to either timing or rhythm requirements. We propose that this common variance is related primarily to cognitive tempo or the rate and intraindividual variability of information processing.

3. Psychophysiological Correlates of Both Cognition and Motor Perfor-mance. Our primary interest here is in changes in the topographical maps of voltage levels of the cortex as subjects perform tasks with varying timing and rhythm demands. The research associating event-related cortical potentials (e.g., P300) with cognition (Donchin, 1979; Naatanen & Michie, 1979) and the cor-relation of event-related cortical potentials to motor functions (Kornhuber & Deecke, 1980) is pertinent to our current inquiry. Our psychophysiological mea-sures will include recording maps of electrical cortical activity as individuals perform cognitive and behavioral tasks (Buchsbaum, Rigal, Coppola, Cappellet-ti, King, & Johnson, 1982).

Using the techniques and concepts that have evolved in these research areas and combining them with the more traditional personality techniques, we are studying both selected patient groups and "normal" control groups. Patient populations chosen are those that commonly exhibit impulsive behavior. For example, we are currently sutdying head injury patients who are participating in a cognitive rehabilition program. Manic patients and matched controls for each patient will be studied.

Preliminary data from our current research with normal controls is consistent with the hypothesis that shifts in major cortical dipoles prior to making a re-sponse are related to cognitive tempo as measured by time judgments and to questionnaire measures of impulsiveness. The cognitive-behavioral tasks used in this research require the subjects to make a visual discrimination in a go, no-go reaction time paradigm. The imperative stimuli that signal making a discrimina-tion are preceded by a warning signal and are presented randomly at varying rates in the left and right (uncrossed) visual fields.

We are also developing artificial intelligence techniques for analyzing both the psychophysiological and behavioral data together. (Jagannathon, Bourne, Jansen & Ward, in press). We are extending beyond these EEG data to include combined analyses of the psychophysiological and behavioral data.

This brief overview of our current research indicates the value of using a system model in personality research. Impulsiveness appears to relate to the inherent brain processes that control performance in timing and rhythm for cognitive and behavioral tasks. The rate of cognitive processing preceding a response appears to be out of synchrony with the task demands. Thus, we would expect topographical maps of cortical voltage levels, recorded during the cognitive processing of information just prior to making a response, to differ between high- and low-impulsive subjects.

ACKNOWLEDGMENTS

This research was supported by the Office of Naval Research and by The Moody Foundation, Galveston, TX.

REFERENCES

Ashby, W. (1956). *An introduction to cybernetics*. New York: Wiley.
Ashby, W. (1960). *Design for a brain*. New York: Wiley.
Barratt, E. (1959). Anxiety and impulsiveness related to psychomotor efficiency. *Perceptual and Motor Skills, 9*, 191–198.
Barratt, E. (1965). Factor analysis of some psychometric measures of impulsiveness and anxiety. *Psychological Reports, 16*, 547–554.
Barratt, E. (1966). *Psychophysiological correlates of impulsiveness and risk taking: Cross sectional and longitudinal studies*. Annual Report, Office of Naval Research, Washington, D.C.
Barratt, E. (1967). Perceptual-motor performance related to impulsiveness and anxiety. *Perceptual and Motor Skills, 25*, 485–492.
Barratt, E. (1971). Psychophysiological correlates of classical differential eyelid conditioning among subjects selected on the basis of impulsiveness and anxiety. *Biological Psychiatry, 1971, 3*, 339–346.
Barratt, E. (1972). Anxiety and impulsiveness: Toward a neuropsychological model. In C. Spielberger (Ed.), *Anxiety: Current trends in theory and research* (Vol. 1). New York. Academic.
Barratt, E. (1977). Time estimation related to measures of distraction and impulsivity among adolescent psychiatry patients. Paper presented at International Neuropsychology Society, Santa Fe, New Mexico.
Barratt, E. (1981). Time perception, cortical evoked potentials and impulsiveness among three groups of adolescents. In J. Hays, T. Roberts, & K. Soloway (Eds.), *Violence and the violent individual*. New York: SP Medical Scientific Books.
Barratt, E. (in press). The biological basis of impulsiveness: The significance of timing and rhythm disorders. *Personality and Individual Differences*.
Barratt, E., Adams, P., & White, J. (1977). The relationship of evoked potential characteristics to time perception judgment. Paper presented at Society for Neuroscience, Anaheim, CA.
Barratt, E. & Patton, J. (1983). Impulsivity: Cognitive, behavioral, and psychophysiological correlates. In M. Zuckerman (Ed.), *Biological bases of sensation seeking, impulsivity, and anxiety*. Hillsdale, NJ: Lawrence Erlbaum, Associates.
Barratt, E., Patton, J., Olsson, N., & Zuker, G. (1981). Impulsivity and paced tapping. *Journal of Motor Behavior, 13*, 286–300.
Barratt, E. & White, R. (1969). Impulsiveness and anxiety related to medical student's performance and attitudes. *Journal of Medical Education, 44*, 604–607.
Buchsbaum, M., Rigal, F., Coppola, R., Cappelletti, J., King, C., & Johnson, J. (1982). A new system for gray-level surface distribution maps of electrical activity. *Electroencephalography and Clinical Neurophysiology, 53*, 237–242.
Cattell, R., (1979). *The structure of personality in its environment*. New York: Springer.

Cliff, N. (1983). Some cautions concerning the application of causel modeling methods. *Multivariate Behavioral Research, 18*, 115–126.

Cottle, T. (1976). *Perceiving time*. New York: Wiley.

Diamond, S., Balvin, R., & Diamond, F. (1963). *Inhibition and choice*. New York: Harper & Row.

Donchin, E. (1979). Event-related brain potentials: A tool in the study of human information processing. In H. Begleiter (Ed.), *Evoked brain potentials and behavior*. New York: Plenum.

Endler, N. & Magnusson, D. (1976). Toward an interactional psychology of personality. *Psychological Bulletin, 83*, 956–974.

Eysenck, H. (1967). *The biological basis of personality*. Springfield, Ill: Thomas Co.

Eysenck, H. & Eysenck, S. (1969). *Personality structure and measurement*. San Diego: Knapp.

Eysenck, H. & Eysenck, S. (1976). *Psychoticism as a dimension of personality*. London: Hodder & Stoughton.

Eysenck, S. & Eysenck, H. (1977). The place of impulsiveness in a dimensional system of personality description. *British Journal of Clinical Psychology, 16*, 57–68.

Fleishman, E. (1954). Dimensional analysis of psychomotor abilities. *Journal of Experimental Psychology, 54*, 437–454.

Gagne, R. & Fleishman, E. (1959). *Psychology and human performance*. New York: Holt.

Granit, R. (1970). *The basis of motor control*. New York: Academic.

Guilford, J. (1975). Factors and factors of personality. *Psychological Bulletin, 82*, 802–814.

Gunilla, R., Oberg, E., & Divac, I. (1981). Levels of motor planning: Cognition and the control of movement. *Trends in Neural Science, 4*, 122–124.

Hebb, D. (1974). What psychology is about. *American Psychologist, 29*, 71–79.

Irion, A. (1966). A brief history of research on the acquisition of skill. In E. Bilodeau (Ed.), *Acquisition of skill*. New York: Academic.

Jagannathon, V., Bourne, J., Jansen, B., & Ward, J. (in press). Artificial intelligence methods in quantitative electroencephalogram analysis. *Computer Programs in Biomedicine*.

Kipnis, D. (1971). *Character structure and impulsiveness*. New York: Academic.

Kluckhon, C. & Murray, H. (1949). *Personality in nature, society, and culture*. New York: Knopf.

Kornhuber, H. & Deecke, L. (Eds.). (1980) *Motivation, motor and sensory processes of the brain: Electrical potentials, behavior, and clinical use*. New York: Elsevier/North-Holland.

Kuhn, A. (1974). *The logic of social systems*. San Francisco: Jossey-Bass.

Lazare, A. (1973). Hidden conceptual models in clinical psychiatry. *New England Journal of Medicine, 288*, 345–350.

Lewin, K. (1935). *A dynamic theory of personality*. New York: McGraw Hill.

Marsden, C. (1980). The basal ganglia and the programming of behavior. *Trends in Neural Science, 3*, 284–287.

McGeer, P., Eccles, J. & McGeer, E. (1978). *Molecular neurobiology of the mammalian brain*. New York: Plenum.

McGeer, P. & McGeer, E. (1980). The control of movement by the brain. *Trends in Neural Science, 3*, 29–30.

Melges, F. (1982). *Time and the inner future*. New York: Wiley.

Miller, G., Galanter, E., & Pribram, K. (1960). *Plans and the structure of behavior*. New York: Holt.

Mischel, W. (1973). Toward a cognitive social learning reconception of personality. *Psychological Review, 80*, 252–283.

Mischel, W. & Peake, P. (1982). Beyond deja vu in the search for cross-situational consistency. *Psychological Review, 89*, 730–755.

Murphy, G. (1947). *Personality. A biosocial approach to origins and structure*. New York: Harper & Brothers.

Murphy, G. (1958). *Human potentialities*. New York: Basic Books.

Naatanen, R. & Michie, P. (1979). Different variants of endogenous negative brain potentials in performance situations: A review and classification. In D. Lehmann & E. Callaway (Eds.), *Human evoked potentials: Applications and problems.* New York: Plenum.

Nicholls, J., Licht, B., & Pearl, R. (1982). Some dangers of using personality questionnaires to study personality. *Psychological Bulletin, 92,* 572–580.

Olweus, D. (1979). The stability of aggressive reaction patterns in human males: A review. *Psychological Bulletin, 86,* 852–875.

Pawlik, K. (1966). Concepts in human cognition and aptitudes. In R. Cattell (Ed.), *Handbook of multivariate experimental psychology.* Chicago: Rand McNally.

Pribram, K. & Gill, M. (1976). *Freud's 'project' reassessed.* New York: Basic Books.

Rorer, L. & Widiger, T. (1983). Personality structure and assessment. *Annual Review of Psychology, 34,* 431–463.

Rotter, J. (1966). Generalized expectancies for internal versus external control of reinforcement. *Psychological Monographs, 80.* (Whole)

Sternberg, R. (1977). *Intelligence, information processing, and analogical reasoning: The componential analysis of human abilities.* Hillsdale, NJ: Lawrence Erlbaum Associates.

Wortis, J. (1982). DSM III: The big debate. *Biological Psychiatry, 17,* 1363–1365.

Wortis, J. (1983). Panpsychiatry: Psychiatry as ideology. *Biological Psychiatry, 18,* 1–2.

5 The Assessment of Trait-State Anxiety and Musical Performance

Donald L. Hamann
University of Northern Colorado

Musicians tend to agree that performing in public stimulates performer anxiety. How musicians respond to anxiety in musical performance can vary. This chapter discusses anxiety assessment in musical performance and includes: (a) Statements and discussion concerning musicians' performances while experiencing heightened states of anxiety, based on literature from nonresearch orientated publications; (b) a review of anxiety theories based on studies from the psychological and psychiatric literature; (c) a review of research studies dealing with anxiety and musical performance, which did not utilize the trait-state distinction in anxiety assessment; and (d) a review of research literature that utilized the trait-state distinction in the assessment of anxiety in musical performance.

Anxiety is an integral part of an everyday requirement for human growth and development (Spielberger, 1979). Every individual has a "normal" level of anxiety that can be considered to be a personality characteristic. This normal level of anxiety is referred to as trait anxiety. However, when musicians discuss anxiety and performance they are usually referring to state anxiety.

State anxiety is a deviation from the "normal" or trait level of anxiety and may fluctuate from situation to situation. Spielberger (1979) reports, "state anxiety . . . [is] an emotional reaction that consists of subjective feelings of tension, apprehension, nervousness and worry, and heightened activity of the autonomic nervous system" (p. 17). Perhaps a majority of musicians consider anxiety, both state and trait, to have only negative effects on performance ability and outcomes, but there is disagreement among them.

MUSICIANS AND ANXIETY

Authors, such as Grindea (1978) and Havas (1976), tend to agree that anxiety can help or hinder performance skills of musicians, thus affecting the quality of the performance. Havas (1978) states:

As all performers know, nobody plays the same in public as he does alone. One plays either much better or much worse. When the audience acts as a stimulus to the performer, so that he can release his inborn anxiety through his playing, the performance usually becomes sparkling and exciting. But when the anxieties are exaggerated before an audience and the player knows that he is unable to communicate the music, it is then that neuroses set in. If this becomes a regular occurrence the player sometimes ends up with a nervous breakdown. (p. 13)

Grindea (1978)

states that "the slightest hesitation or emotional anxiety during the performance creates inner nervous tension . . . which is almost simultaneously transmitted to various parts of the body—usually to the weaker parts of the playing apparatus—causing muscular tension" (p. 104). Muscular tension can inhibit the musician in a performance and may lead to decreased performance quality.

Negative Performance-Generated Anxiety Conditions

It is possible that negative performance-generated anxiety conditions can be produced or result from a variety of inhibitory factors. Waite (1977) categorized inhibitory factors into four areas: (1) Heightened awareness and concern with the motor activity and mental processes; (2) Self-consciousness from a threatened ego; (3) General bodily tension; (4) Recurring conditioned anxiety.

Performers who are negatively affected by anxiety may, in a performance situation, become overly concerned with technical inabilities on the instrument. They may feel threatened by the type or composition of an audience, especially an audience composed of peers. A "poor" performance in front of such an audience may pose an ego threat to performers; thinking that an "inferior" performance reflects their quality as individuals. Present concern over past poor performance situations can also cause performers to produce excess muscle tension or momentarily loose mental concentration, which can result in "memory slips" or temporary technical difficulties.

Positive Performance-Generated Anxiety Conditions

Anxious performance situations are viewed by some musicians to be beneficial and desired. Performers who benefit from anxious performing situations may gain physical endurance and improve tonal production and pitch control. Rapid or technically difficult passages become readily and easily playable. Heightened awareness of mental and physical capacities can enable performers to enhance performances through tonal, dynamic, technical, and musical improvement. When musicians benefit from anxious situations, they feel that direct communication with body, mind, and instrument has occurred. This is conveyed to the audience, and in effect becomes part of the music and part of an aesthetic experience.

ANXIETY THEORIES

Many of the articles that are written concerning the effects of anxiety in musical performance are not research based, but are speculative in nature. A study of the literature in the areas of psychiatric and psychological research reveals that anxiety theories in learning behavior have been formulated based on performance factors. Three such theories that provide insight into research on anxiety are Drive Theory, Spielberger's extension of Drive Theory, and Spielberger's Trait-State Anxiety Theory. The study of such theories can provide valuable information on which research in the assessment of anxiety in musical performance can be based.

Drive Theory

Hull (1943) believed that excitatory potential (E), which has the effect of determining the strength of a response (R), is a multiplicative function of the total effective drive state (D) and habit strength (H). Therefore, $R = f(E) = f(D \times H)$. Drive Theory (Spence, 1958; Taylor, 1956) is an extension of Hullian Learning Theory. Spielberger (1971) reports the following concerning Drive Theory:

> While Drive Theory does not explicitly differentiate between trait and state anxiety, this distinction is implicit in Spence's Reactive Hypothesis [1958] which may be restated as follows: Ss [Subjects] high in A-Trait [Trait Anxiety] will respond with greater elevations in A-State [State Anxiety] than low A-Trait Ss in situations involving some form of stress. It follows that the concept of D is logically more closely associated with A-State than with A-Trait, and that the assumption that Ss with high scores on A-Trait measures will be higher in D than Ss with low A-Trait scores is questionable. (p. 273)

When applying Hullian Learning Theory to Drive Theory the following predictive assumptions on levels of learning are reported by Heinrich and Spielberger (1982, p. 146).

1. For simple or easy learning tasks, in which correct responses are dominant and competing error tendencies are minimal, the performance of high-anxious subjects will be superior to that of low-anxious subjects.

2. For difficult learning tasks, in which competing error tendencies are strong relative to correct responses, high drive will activate these error tendencies and the performance of high-anxious subjects will be inferior to that of low-anxious subjects.

3. For tasks of intermediate difficulty, the stage of learning is taken into account. High anxiety will be detrimental to performance early in learning when the strength of correct responses is weak relative to competing error tendencies. Later in learning, high anxiety will begin to facilitate performance as correct responses are strengthened and error tendencies are extinguished.

Spielberger's Extension of Drive Theory

Spielberger's extension of Drive Theory contains predictive statements concerning the effects of anxiety and intelligence on performance in learning tasks that vary in difficulty. Predictions relating to Spielberger's extension of Drive Theory are summarized by Heinrich and Spielberger (1982, pp. 147).

1. For subjects with superior intelligence, high anxiety will facilitate performance on most learning tasks. While high anxiety may initially cause performance decrements on very difficult tasks, it will eventually facilitate the performance of bright subjects as they progress through the task and correct responses become dominant.

2. For subjects of average intelligence, high anxiety will facilitate performance on simple tasks and, later in learning, on tasks of moderate difficulty. On very difficult tasks, high anxiety will generally lead to performance decrements.

3. For low-intelligence subjects, high anxiety may facilitate performance on simple tasks that have been mastered. However, performance decrements will generally be associated with high anxiety on difficult tasks, especially, in the early stages of learning.

Mastery of a task (habit strength) and anxiety are related in both Drive Theory and Spielberger's extension of Drive Theory. Drive Theory does not differentiate between trait and state anxiety, but a study of research literature reveals that high A-Trait subjects tend to show performance changes attributable to higher D in situations characterized by psychological stress (Spielberger, 1971). Drive can be associated with differences in A-State. Spielberger reports the following concerning drive level and elevations in A-State:

> Assuming that elevations in A-State reflect drive level, drive theory delineates the complex effects of differences in A-State (D) on performance. According to the theory, the effects of A-State on performance in a learning task will depend upon the relative strengths of the correct habits (responses) and the competing error

tendencies evoked by the task. On simple tasks, in which correct responses are stronger than error tendencies, high A-State would be expected to facilitate performance. On complex or difficult tasks, in which error tendencies are stronger than correct responses, it would be anticipated that high A-State would interfere with performance, at least in the initial stages of learning. (p. 274)

Trait-State Anxiety Theory

In Trait-State Anxiety Theory, Spielberger (1966, 1972) supplemented Drive Theory in order to specify the conditions under which subjects differing in A-Trait would be expected to show differences in A-State (D). By using both A-Trait and A-State measures, both the predictive information regarding the "probability" of A-State arousal and actual A-State arousal can be determined. Spielberger (1971, p. 277) reports the following assumptions of Trait-State Anxiety Theory:

1. In situations that are appraised by an S as threatening, an A-State reaction will be evoked. Through sensory and cognitive feedback mechanisms, high levels of A-State will be experienced as unpleasant.

2. The intensity of an A-State reaction will be proportional to the amount of threat that the situation poses for S. The duration of an A-State reaction will depend upon the persistence of S's interpretation or appraisal of the situation as threatening.

3. High A-Trait Ss will perceive situations or circumstances that involve threats to self-esteem, such as failure or negative evaluation of performance, as more threatening than Ss who are low in A-Trait, and will respond to such situations with greater elevations in A-State.

4. Elevations in A-State have motivational or drive properties that may directly influence behavior, or serve to initiate psychological defenses that have been effective in reducing A-States in the past.

Anxiety Theories and Musical Performance

Based on the anxiety theories, it can be stated that A-State can have motivational or drive properties and that anxiety can enhance performance level, based on the amount of task mastery and correct habit strength or training and ability of subjects. It can also be stated that musicians may perceive performance situations, which involve perceived negative evaluation or threats to ego, as threatening and that such situations would cause increased levels of A-State proportional to A-Trait. This type of information can be valuable in assessing the possible "outcomes" of musicians' performances in anxious situations.

Under anxious performance situations, subjects with many years of formal musical training or high task mastery, and high A-Trait would be expected to achieve increased performance ability as a result of increased A-State or drive, according to anxiety theory predictive statements. Conversely, subjects with little formal training or low task mastery, and high A-Trait would be expected to experience decrements in performance ability. Further, musicians performing in situations that are perceived to involve negative evaluation or threats to ego, would be expected to experience increased anxiety states. It would appear that information from anxiety theories would be essential in the formation of research questions in the assessment of anxiety and musical performance.

Anxiety Research in Music Not Utilizing The Trait-State Distinction

Given the predictive statements from anxiety theories based on a large body of research in the area of psychological and psychiatric literature, it would seem appropriate to assess anxiety in musical performance based on assumptions from these sources. Unfortunately, most of the research in music does not address findings in the area of psychological or psychiatric literature, nor anxiety theories formulated from the same. Given this vast oversight on the part of music researchers, the majority of research studies published on anxiety and musical performance have been conducted in the area of anxiety reduction. The general assumption made by these researchers tends to be that anxiety diminishes the quality of performances for all or for some performers. The remainder of the research studies of anxiety and musical performance deal with anxiety assessment and analyses of possible variables affecting performance quality, either negatively or positively, under anxious performance conditions, without regard to anxiety theories.

Research on anxiety in musical performances can be grouped into three categories: (a) Anxiety reduction and control through behavior modification techniques; (b) anxiety reduction through beta-blockage agents; and (c) assessment of anxiety in stressful situations without reference to anxiety theories.

Anxiety Reduction in Musical Performance Through Behavior Modification

Techniques such as Biofeedback, behavior modification procedures, Autogenic Training, and Progressive Relaxation have been used to reduce or control anxiety in individuals without the use of beta-blockage agents. In studies and programs by Appel (1976), Bryson (1980), Lund (1972), Nagel, Himle, and Papsdorf (1981), McCune (1982), Nideffer and Hessler (1978), Reynolds and Morasky (1981), Terwilliger (1972), Wardle (1975), and Wolfe (1977), in which anxiety reduction techniques were used, it was reported by researchers that either anxiety reduction did not diminish the quality of a performance or that anxiety reduction improved the quality of a performance.

Many of these researchers assumed that anxiety diminished performance quality for all subjects and based their research questions on this premise. Others selected only subjects who reportedly experienced performance decrements under anxious situations and based research questions and data collection on the premise that anxiety reduction techniques could be valuable for particular performers. Although research on anxiety reduction may be useful for those performers who may experience a type of anxiety often referred to as "neurotic" anxiety (an extremely heightened state which may result in physical incapacitation or loss of control) such research seems premature without a stronger base in anxiety assessment in musical performance. Without a thorough study of all related anxiety research, including anxiety theories, a complete understanding of anxiety effects on musicians may be lacking and research questions and hypotheses may be questionable.

Bryson (1980), one of the researchers who did not assume that anxiety diminished performance quality for all performers, appeared to question the premise of anxiety reduction research. Bryson (1980) stated: "Performance anxiety in itself does not always adversely affect the quality of a performance. There are some musicians who believe that they must experience some performance anxiety, or they will not perform at their best levels. Anxiety can bring about increased endurance and sensibility" (p. 2). Anxiety reduction research in musical performance continues to be a popular area for study. It would seem however, that the question of how anxiety affects all musicians in performance situations is not addressed. Some research in anxiety reduction for musicians who may be neurotic anxious has been conducted. These studies generally utilize beta-blockage agents to control neurotic anxiety effects.

Beta-Blockage Agents and Anxiety Research in Music

Brantigan, Joseph, and Brantigan (1978, 1979), James, Griffith, Pearson, and Newbury (1977), and Liden and Gottfries (1974) also conducted anxiety reduction research, but utilized beta-blockage agents for reduction of anxiety in musical performance. The drugs that were employed in their research were oxprenolol, alprenolol chloride, and propranolol. With the exception of Brantigan, Joseph, and Brantigan (1978, 1979), researchers did not assume that anxiety deterred performance quality for all musicians. Subject selection criteria for the studies of James et al. (1977) and Liden and Gottfries (1974) were performed by determining which subjects "needed" to reduce anxiety in performance because of tendencies toward neurotic anxious symptoms. Although subject selection criteria differed in these studies, all researchers reported that anxiety was reduced in subjects and that performance quality decrements decreased under the influence of the beta-blockage agents. This would seem to indicate that neurotic anxiety can be altered or controlled for those musicians who experience these symptoms through use of certain drugs.

Published empirical research in the assessment of anxiety in music is minimal. Even though most of the researchers dealing with anxiety and musical performance tend to research the effects of anxiety reduction on subjects, a few studies have been completed by individuals who have attempted to assess the effects of anxiety on musicians without stating a premise that anxiety reduction techniques may or should be utilized.

Anxiety Assessment in Music Not Utilizing The Trait-State Distinction

Although few in number, some researchers have attempted to assess the effects of anxiety on musicians in performance situations without preconceived expectations of outcomes based on research premises. In these studies, researchers tended to "overlook" the literature in areas outside of their discipline, nor did they address anxiety theory predictions or trait-state distinctions. It is interesting to note however that these researchers' findings did not tend to support findings in anxiety reduction research.

Leglar (1979) found that removal of musical scores and the size and nature of the audience were significant factors in increased subject anxiety. Although indicating that a majority of performers did not perform as well in a public versus a studio situation, because of increased anxiety states, this researcher did state that some performers did perform "better" in situations of increased anxiety states.

Hutter (1980) generated descriptive data through the use of an original questionnaire and two standard psychological scales, which were reported to measure perceived autonomy and control over one's life. Hutter reported that highly anxious performers indicated that anxiety impeded excellence in performing, but that some musicians felt a certain degree of anxiety was necessary for excellence in performance.

In studies by Bartosch, Groll-Knapp, Haider, Piperek, and Schulz (1981) it was reported that subjects in group performance situations experienced significantly less anxiety increase than when performing in solo situations. It was also reported that subjects performing in group situations did not perform significantly better than subjects performing in solo situations.

Spencer (1970) investigated the relationship of situational anxiety to the vocal performances of students. Spencer reported that all students experienced more significant increases in anxiety in jury situations than in voice lessons and that all subjects performed significantly better in jury situations than in voice lessons.

Although there appears to be a "folk wisdom" among researchers in anxiety reduction techniques that to reduce is to better performance outcomes, it would appear that such assumptions need a foundation for empirical support. Researchers of anxiety assessment report that some or all musicians tend to benefit from the effects or drive of anxiety states. In this maze of conflicting reports, these researchers tended to overlook the literature in other areas of anxiety research and anxiety theories. A study of this literature reveals that anxiety theory predictive statements have been formulated and that performance increments and decrements for subjects with varying levels of training, ability, and anxiety may be expected (Carron, 1971; Heinrich & Spielberger, 1982; Spence, 1958; Spence & Spence, 1966; Spielberger, 1966, 1971, 1972).

Trait-State Anxiety Assessment and Musical Performance

The following research studies were conducted to attempt to address the problems of anxiety assessment in music, utilizing the trait-state distinction. Based on psychiatric and psychological literature, and the subsequent anxiety theories, research questions were formulated to assess anxiety in musical performance. The following five studies in anxiety assessment and musical performance were based on four different samples of musicians; three university samples and one secondary sample.

Since method, procedure, and analyses of results in these studies were basically consistent and longitudinal in nature, they will be reported in such a nature. Measures of anxiety and rationale for the same are presented before the findings of the studies are reported.

METHOD

In the studies by Hamann (1982, 1983, 1984), Hamann and Herlong (1980), and Hamann and Sobaje (1983) state and trait anxiety were measured by the *State-Trait Anxiety Inventory* (STAI) (Spielberger, Gorsuch, & Lushene, 1970). The *State-Trait Personality Inventory* (STPI) (Spielberger, Barker, Russell, Silva De Crane, & Westberry, Knight & Marks, 1979) was also administered, along with the STAI in studies by Hamann (1982) and Hamann and Sobaje (1983). The STPI was used as an exploratory variable in these two studies because it was not commercially available at the time research was initiated and reliability and validity data were still being compiled. The STPI provided additional measures of anxiety, both state and trait, as well as measures of curiosity and anger.

The STAI and STPI in Anxiety Assessment

The STAI and STPI were not used in conjunction with physiological measures or projective tests on the advisement of leading authorities in the area of anxiety assessment and testing procedures. A study of research literature in the area of anxiety assessment and testing revealed that many anxiety inventories have greater reliability than do physiological measures or projective tests, specifically the STAI, because they are less affected by extraneous factors. In addition, an inventory requires no special training for administration or scoring (Goldfried, 1966; Levitt, 1967; Martens, 1971; Neuringer, 1962).

In addition to having high test–retest reliability, the STAI does not induce unrelated situational anxiety due to equipment attachment requirements that physiological tests may produce when assessing musical performance and anxiety of subjects. Further, when musicians perform they should not be impeded or restricted by wires, discs, or other equipment that may be needed to assess physiological anxiety measures. Due to the activity and physical demands of musical performance, especially in instrumental performance, unrelated physiological data may be produced that could affect anxiety assessment interpretation. The anxiety inventory was therefore chosen for measurement of anxiety because of high reliability, ease of use and administration, and ease of interpretation.

Data Questionnaire

Objective and subjective measures of subjects' performance experience, readiness, and confidence were determined using a pilot-tested data questionnaire. The 16 item questionnaire contained inquiries pertaining to subjects' sex, years of formal training and nonformal training (i.e., private instruction or study of an instrument without the aid of private instruction), years of ensemble experience, assessment of solo performance experience, years and experience performing on other instruments or voice other than the one performed for the study, and subjective "forced item" responses on subjects' mental, technical, and confidence levels for performance of works in studies completed.

The data questionnaire was constructed based on information received from numerous student and professional musicians. Based on their responses, items that were thought to affect performance levels or outcomes in anxious situations were included in the questionnaire. It is interesting to note that the only variable that consistently appeared to affect performance outcomes in these studies was years of formal training or "task mastery on an instrument."

Sample

Samples for the studies ranged from 18 to 90 subjects. Subjects in the studies by Hamann (1982, 1984), Hamann and Herlong (1980), and Hamann and Sobaje (1983) were drawn from university populations of musicians in North Carolina and Colorado. The subjects in the study by Hamann (1983) were selected from secondary music students participating in the Weld (County, CO) 1981 State Solo and Ensemble Contest.

PROCEDURE

Performance Situations

In the university sample studies, subjects performed one work, within a 5-day span, in both reduced and an enhanced performance situation. The reduced performance situation consisted of performing and recording a work in a room with only the accompanist present (if applicable) and recording equipment. In the enhanced anxious situations, the university subjects performed either for a critical audience of peers and faculty or in a jury situation. In both enhanced performance situations, evaluations of subjects' ability were concurrently being administered to determine either grade and/or level advancement.

In the secondary sample testing situation, subjects performed only once for an audience of adjudicators. The adjudicators were rating subjects on performance ability for possible award classification.

In all performance situations, subjects were administered the STAI or the STAI and STPI inventories after each performance. All subjects were administered the data questionnaire after the first performance.

Adjudication of Musical Performances

Three to five adjudicators were employed for the evaluation of live performances (secondary sample study) or recorded performances (university sample studies). In the secondary sample, subjects performed only once for judges and these performances were rated for musical quality. In the university studies, adjudicators rated performances that were tape recorded from both the reduced and the enhanced performance situations. All judges were professional instructors and performers. The adjudicators were unaware of the nature of the study (secondary sample study) or the nature of the study and the conditions under which performances were recorded (all university sample studies).

Adjudicators were instructed to evaluate performances in the context of their "ideal" performance concept. Adjudicators utilized a seven item/category evaluation form. Each category had one Likert scale ranging from 1 (Excellent) to 5 (Fair). The adjudicator evaluation form was developed using a model by Fiske (1979) and was pilot tested by Hamann (1979).

RESULTS

Interjudge reliability for studies was determined by computing quotient of agreement statistics and Pearson product-moment correlations. Mean quotient of agreement among judges ranged from .75 to .79. Pearson product-moment mean correlation coefficients, computed by utilizing Fisher's z-transformation formula, ranged from .74 to .79.

Data from the STAI, the STAI and STPI, adjudicator rating forms, and the data questionnaire were analyzed utilizing two-way analyses of variance (ANOVAs), split-plot designs, with either equalized or nonequalized subgroups, and chi-squares. Tukey's studentized-range statistic was also computed to compare means for significant differences found in the ANOVAs.

Results From Trait-State Anxiety Assessment Studies and Musical Performance

The university research studies dealing with anxiety assessment and musical performance were conducted in a longitudinal manner and are therefore discussed in order of their completion. Four such studies were completed, the first referred to as Study #1 and the last referred to as Study #4. The study pertaining to the secondary anxiety and musical performance research was conducted somewhat independently of the university sample studies. Since procedures differed from university samples and subjects were of a different age group, the secondary sample is reported independently of other studies.

Secondary Musical Performance and Anxiety Assessment

Research in the area of anxiety assessment and musical performance among subjects at the secondary level (grades 7 to 12) is virtually nonexistent. Hamann (1983) completed a study in which 87 secondary music students served as subjects. There were 48 solo and 39 ensemble performers in the study.

Subjects were administered the STAI and data questionnaire. Musical performances were evaluated and rated by adjudicators for musical quality.

It was reported that subjects reported significantly ($p < .05$) higher state anxiety levels before performances than during performances. Subjects with high A-Trait (trait anxiety) experienced significantly ($p < .01$) greater increases in A-State (state anxiety) than subjects classified as medium or low A-Trait. Subjects performing in solo situations as compared with subjects performing in ensemble situations reported significantly ($p < .05$) greater increases in A-State. Although significant differences in A-State due to A-Trait, performance situation, and performance medium were reported, Hamann (1983, p. 9) stated:

> Perhaps most interesting . . . may be the findings that all other variables including: Playing from memory or music; performance experience in ensembles; formal and non-formal training; student self confidence (technical and mental readiness) and confidence with accompanists; medication; sex; instrument; performance on another instrument; or solo performance experience had no significant effect on the outcome of the performances of students in relation to anxiety and playing quality.

Results from this study tend to support the findings of Bartosch et al. (1981) that subjects performing in solo situations, as compared to performance in ensemble situations, will experience significantly greater increases in A-State. Although Leglar (1979) reported that score removal was a significant factor in increased subject anxiety, results from this study do not support such findings.

Although no significant differences in performance level due to anxiety and "variables" were reported in the study of secondary subjects and musical performance, studies of university musicians and anxiety assessment research do reveal such differences. The following four studies, also utilizing the trait-state distinction in the evaluation of anxiety assessment and musical performance in university musicians' performances, reveal strong relationships to anxiety theory predictions.

University Musical Performance and Anxiety Assessment: Study 1

In a study by Hamann and Herlong (1980), an initial university sample pilot study in anxiety assessment and musical performance utilizing the trait-state distinction, 18 classical guitarists served as subjects. Subjects performed in a reduced and an enhanced performance situation. Based on subjects' A-Trait scores, they were grouped into one of three categories: low, medium, or high A-Trait. Subjects were also grouped into one of three categories according to the number of years of playing experience or five categories based on years of formal study.

It was reported that siginficant differences ($p<.05$) were found among subjects performing under reduced and enhanced anxious performance situations. All subjects' A-State levels significantly increased in the enhanced performance situation. It was also observed, although not found to be significantly different, that subjects with more years of formal study performed in a superior manner in enhanced performance situations than in reduced anxious situations. All of these subjects experienced significant A-State increases between situations.

From this initial pilot study, two hypotheses were formulated on which future research was based: (1) That a reduced and an enhanced anxious performance situation could be established and (2) that a tendency toward task mastery (high formal years of study), high A-Trait, and increased performance ability may be found among musical performers. According to anxiety theory predictive statements, increased A-State due to A-Trait could facilitate increments in performance levels for subjects with high task mastery skills. The tendency of subjects in this study towards this predictive statement prompted further research.

University Musical Performance and Anxiety Assessment: Study 2

In a second study by Hamann (1982) 90 university musicians served as subjects. Subjects were administered both the STAI and STPI as well as the data questionnaire form. Procedures, methods, and so forth were performed as previously discussed.

Subjects were grouped by levels of trait anxiety according to STAI percentile ranks for college undergraduates reported in the *Manual for State–Trait Anxiety Inventory* (Spielberger et al., 1970). The three category groupings were high, medium, and low. Subjects were also grouped into one of three categories (high, medium, or low) based on STPI trait anxiety, curiosity, and anger scores.

Significant ($p < .05$) differences were found between STAI and STPI state anxiety mean scores of subjects performing under reduced and enhanced performance conditions and between STPI state anger and curiosity mean scores under both situations. It was also reported that performance condition and years of formal study were significantly ($p < .05$) related in their effect on judged performance quality. The following was reported by Hamann (1982, p. 88).

Based on results from this study, it was found that subjects with high years of formal study (training) performed in a superior manner under conditions of significantly increased anxiety states. Musicians in this sample respond . . . according to Spielberger's extension of Drive Theory. Therefore, anxiety can have motivational or drive properties . . . .

Other results from this study, which are consistent with anxiety theory, specifically the Trait–State Theory, are that subjects with high trait anxiety will experience significantly greater state increase in anxiety level than will subjects with medium or low trait anxiety. Further, it was found that subjects with high trait curiosity had significantly higher state increases in state curiosity than did medium or low trait subjects. Although no theory specifically indicates such outcomes in relation to curiosity levels, such results are consistent with anxiety theory statements . . . .

From analyses of results, it was also found that subjects experienced significantly greater increases in state anxiety and anger between [enhanced and reduced anxious performance] situations.

In the 1982 study by Hamann, two similar findings to the 1980 study are discussed: (1) That musicians experienced increased state anxiety from reduced to enhanced performance situations and (2) that subjects with high years of formal study (task mastery) performed significantly "better" in the enhanced anxious performance situations than did subjects with medium or low years of formal training (YFT). Although not conforming directly to anxiety theory predictive statements that high levels of anxiety will facilitate performance levels for subjects with high task mastery and that the converse will occur for subjects with low task mastery, a tendency can be seen in both studies toward subjects' responses to anxiety.

Of additional interest in this study was the finding that both the STAI and STPI Anxiety scales correlated very highly in the measurement of the same. This finding would tend to substantiate the reliability and validity statement of the STAI and provide additional criteria for the STPI scale.

Also found in this study were the significant differences in curiosity and anger levels between performance situations among subjects. Similiar results were also reported in the 1983 study by Hamann and Sobaje.

University Musical Performance and Anxiety Assessment: Study 3

The study by Hamann and Sobaje (1983) employed 60 subjects. As in the previous study (See study 2), subjects were administered both the STAI and STPI along with the data questionnaire. Subjects were again grouped in categories of high, medium, and low based upon trait scores from the STAI and STPI and on YFS.

Significant main effect differences were found in ANOVAs comparing subjects' mean STAI and STPI state anxiety, curiosity, and anger scores by STAI and STPI trait levels under performance situations. Subjects categorized as high trait anxious, curious, or angry had significantly higher state anxiety mean score differences than did subjects with low anxiety, low curiosity, or medium or low anger. Subjects with medium curiosity had significantly higher state scores than did subjects categorized in the low curiosity group.

Significant main effect differences were also found in ANOVAs comparing subjects' trait anxiety, curiosity, and anger with subjects' state scores and performance scores under performance situations. It was also reported that subjects received significantly "better" performance ratings from adjudicators when performing in enhanced anxious situations and experiencing significantly higher state anxiety and anger levels.

A significant interaction between trait anger and performance condition was found. In Fig. 5.1 it can be seen that subjects with high trait anger as compared with subjects of medium trait anger and medium trait subjects as compared with subjects of low trait anger, experienced significantly greater state increases in anger due to performance condition.

A significant ordinal interaction was reported between performance conditions and YFS. As is shown in Fig. 5.2, subjects with high YFS had a higher mean score point total (indicating a poorer performance rating because the judges' scales were labeled 1 [Excellent] and 5 [Fair]) in the reduced anxious performance situation than in the enhanced anxious situation. It can also be seen that subjects with high YFS had a significantly lower mean score performance rating, indicating superior performance, under the enhanced anxious performance situation than did subjects with low or medium YFS. Hamann and Sobaje (1983, p. 48) reported the following:

> The implications of this study . . . are that anxiety will facilitate performance ability for subjects performing under stressful situations, especially for those subjects with heightened task mastery skills . . . and [that] performers may experience

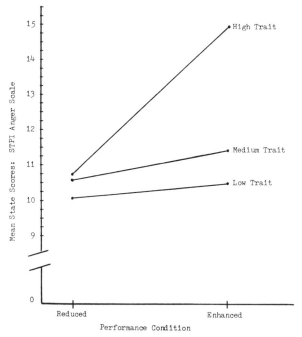

FIG. 5.1.   STPI mean state anger scores for high, medium and low trait-anger groups in the reduced and enhanced performance conditions.

increased state anxiety, curiosity, or anger levels due to either performance condition, trait levels of these measures, or situation.

In this study, it was again reported that a situational performance condition can affect state anxiety, curiosity, and anger levels, and that subjects with High trait levels of these measures experienced significantly higher levels of state increases of the same. Consistent with the findings in studies 1 and 2, subjects with high YFS performed better in enhanced anxious situations than did other subjects. It was also noted that a direct relationship between findings in this study and anxiety theory predictive statements was found.

University Musical Performance and Anxiety Assessment: Study 4

In the study by Hamann (1984) data that were gathered previously were analyzed in view of the categorical distinctions discussed in the Trait–State Anxiety Theory. Instead of three levels (high, medium, and low) of A-Trait, only two levels (high and low) were established. The same categorical distinction was established for subjects' YFS.

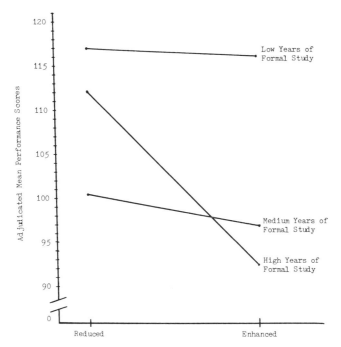

FIG. 5.2.   Adjudicated mean performance scores for low, medium and high years of formal study groups in the reduced and enhanced performance conditions.

A significant main effect difference ($p<.025$) was found in the ANOVA comparing subjects' mean A-State with A-Trait levels under performance conditions. Subjects categorized as high A-Trait reported significantly higher A-State score between performance conditions than did subjects categorized as low A-Trait.

Significant main effect differences ($p<.0001$) were also found in ANOVAs comparing subjects' A-Trait with A-State, A-Trait with performance rating/adjudicators' scores, YFS and performance rating, and A-Trait and YFS with performance rating. Two significant ordinal interactions were also reported ($p<.0001$) in ANOVAs comparing subjects' YFS with performance rating/adjudicators' scores.

In Fig. 5.3 comparing subjects YFS with adjudicators' ratings, it can be seen that subjects with high YFS received poorer adjudicator ratings than did subjects with low YFS in the reduced anxious situation. However in the enhanced anxious situation, subjects with high YFS received significantly ''superior'' performance scores than did subjects with low YFS. Additionally, subjects with low YFS received poorer ratings in the enhanced performances than in the reduced situation. (Note: Higher adjudicator scores indicate ''lower or poorer'' performance levels.)

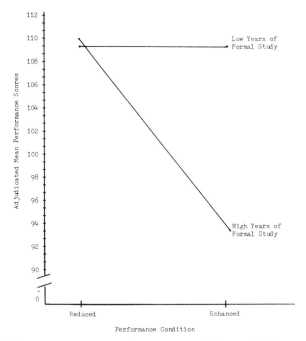

FIG. 5.3.   Adjudicated mean performance scores for low and high years of formal study groups in the reduced and enhanced performance conditions.

In Fig. 5.4 a second interaction is shown in which A-Trait and YFS with adjucicators' ratings were compared. Subjects with high YFS and either high or low A-Trait performed significantly better in enhanced anxious situations, than did other subjects. Subjects with high YFS and high A-Trait, as compared to subjects with high YFS and low A-Trait received poorer ratings in the reduced anxious situation but received superior ratings in the enhanced anxious situations. Subjects with low YFS and high A-Trait received poorer ratings in both reduced and enhanced anxious situations when compared to subjects in other groupings.

Hamann (1984) stated, ''Based on the findings in this study, there appears to be a strong, direct relation between Trait–State Anxiety Theory predictive statements and musicians' performance outcomes'' (p. 44). Anxiety does appear to have drive properties for those musicians with high task mastery and A-Trait.

SUMMARY

Based on reported findings in the research of assessment of anxiety and musical performance, it would appear that there is a relationship between anxiety theory predictive statements and performance effects on musicians. One anxiety theory

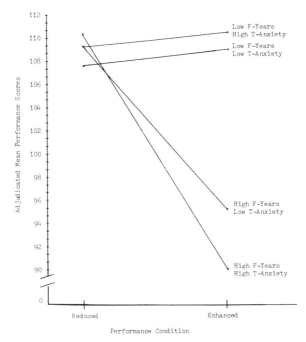

FIG. 5.4. Adjudicated mean performance scores for low and high STAI trait-anxiety groups and low and high years of formal study groups in the reduced and enhanced performance conditions.

emerges as being relevant and highly applicable in anxiety assessment in music research—the Trait–State Anxiety Theory.

The Trait–State Anxiety Theory (Spielberger 1966, 1972) is an extension of other anxiety theories and further delineates and defines the conditions under which subjects differing in A-Trait would be expected to show differences in A-State. Subjects with high A-Trait would be expected to experience significantly higher A-State increases than subjects with low A-Trait in stressful situations.

In all of the studies assessing musical performance that utilized the trait–state distinction, it was reported that subjects with high A-Trait experienced significantly greater increases in A-State than subjects categorized as low A-Trait, from reduced to enhanced anxious performance situations. It can be stated that musicians with high A-Trait can be expected to experience significantly greater A-State increases in performance situations that are viewed as threatening or that involve evaluation of ability and performance skills for grade or level advancement than will subjects with medium or low A-Trait. These findings tend to support those of Leglar (1979) and Spencer (1970). Additionally, subjects with high trait curiosity and/or anger will respond in a similiar manner as subjects with high A-Trait.

Spielberger states that anxiety can produce drive, or motivational properties, for certain individuals. Subjects with high A-Trait who have acquired high task mastery in any given area would be expected to display superior performance skills when experiencing significant A-State arousal than would subjects with low A-Trait and equal task mastery. For subjects with high A-Trait but low task mastery, high A-State arousal would inhibit task performance ability as the task difficulty increases. Thus, according to the Trait–State Anxiety Theory, subjects with high A-Trait and high task mastery can be expected to achieve greater task achievement than would subjects with low A-Trait and high task mastery because anxiety would produce a greater drive effect for individuals possessing high A-Trait. Conversely, subjects with high A-Trait but low task mastery would not perform as well as subjects with low A-Trait and low task mastery, given that the tasks were of sufficient difficulty, as anxiety would tend to deter performance skills because of low task mastery and the effects of anxiety arousal.

Although a relationship between A-Trait and task mastery in performance situations was not found in the study of secondary music students, the studies assessing university music subjects did reveal a positive and direct relationship. When comparing university musicians' years of formal study or task mastery with levels of A-Trait, it was reported that subjects with high task mastery and high A-Trait not only exhibited the greater increases in A-State, but also performed significantly better in enhanced anxious situations than did other subjects. Thus, it can be stated that for subjects with high A-Trait and task mastery, a high drive effect was produced, which resulted in superior performance. A high drive effect was also produced for subjects with high task mastery and low A-Trait, but not as great as for subjects with high task mastery and high A-Trait.

Conversely, for those musicians with low task mastery and high A-Trait, increased A-State tended to deter performance level. These subjects experienced even greater decrements in performance level than did subjects with low A-Trait and low task mastery in enhanced anxious performance situations, as would be expected from Trait–State Anxiety Theory predictive statements.

DISCUSSION

The implications of the studies dealing with the trait–state distinction and musical performance are many, but perhaps of greatest importance is that a direct relationship between anxiety theory statements and musical performance outcomes was found. It would therefore seem imperative that further research in the assessment of anxiety in musical performance address the trait–state distinction. It would appear that musicians do benefit from the properties of drive and do respond to anxiety according to Trait–State Anxiety Theory predictive statements.

Musicians who are categorized as high trait anxious, curious, or angry can expect to experience significant increases in state levels of these measures in stressful performance situations. The effects of anxiety on performance outcomes have been discussed at length here, but the effects of curiosity and anger have not.

It can be hypothesized that musicians experiencing increased curiosity states in performance situations tend to focus on the aural sense, that is, when musicians are curious they tend to "listen more carefully" because of their extensive training in this area. When musicians in a performance situation acquire a heightened sense of aural awareness due to state curiosity arousal, they may tend to be increasingly aware of "performance flaws" not previously perceived. Upon the "hearing" of these flaws in a performance situation, these musicians may experience increased anger states as they may believe that the performance is not being performed "as rehearsed." Although hypothetical in nature, there may be a relationship between curiosity and anger states in musical performance as discussed, but research is needed to support any such assumption.

In general, it was reported that most all musicians experienced significant A-State increases from reduced to enhanced performance situations. It should then be expected that when musicians perform in a situation that involves evaluation procedures or that may be perceived to be threatening to ego, significant A-State arousal will be experienced.

How musicians respond to anxiety in performance situations may not have fully been answered, but definite trends have been revealed. Contrary to reported findings of researchers dealing with anxiety reduction techniques, anxiety assessment research findings do not support conclusions that anxiety reduction improves performance quality for all musicians. Based on anxiety assessment research findings, anxiety reduction may actually decrease performance effectiveness because it may reduce drive properties. Although it was found that some musicians with low task mastery skills did not perform as well in situations that produced increased anxiety states, it would seem that more years of formal study are needed to benefit from anxious arousal states.

It would appear that musicians do respond according to anxiety theory predictive statements and that anxiety can have drive properties for musicians. Future research in anxiety assessment of musicians and performance must address these findings and the literature outside of music research. The trait–state distinction in the assessment of music appears to have important implications for researchers in the area of anxiety assessment. It would seem imperative that future anxiety assessment research in musical performance deal with the trait–state distinction in relation to Trait–State Anxiety Theory statements.

REFERENCES

Appel, S. A. (1976). Modifying solo performance anxiety in adult pianists. *Journal of Music Therapy, 1,* 2–16.

Bartosch, J., Groll-Knapp, E., Haider, M., Piperek, M., & Schulz, W. (1981). *Stress and music.* Vienna: Wilhem Braumuller.

Brantigan, T. A., Joseph, N. H., & Brantigan, C. O. (1978). Beta-blockade and musical performance. *The Lancet, 2,* 986.

Brantigan, T. A., Joseph, N. H., & Brantigan, C. O. (1979). Stage fright revisited. *The American Organist, 13,* 20–21.

Bryson, E. (1980). *Reducing performance anxiety in pianists and vocalists.* Unpublished master's thesis, Appalachian State University.

Carron, A. V. (1971). Reactions to "anxiety and motor behavior." *Journal of Motor Behavior, 2,* 181–188.

Fiske, H. (1979). Musical performance evaluation ability: Toward a model of specificity. *Council of Research in Music Education, 59,* 27–31.

Goldfried, M. R. (1966). The assessment of anxiety by means of the Rorschach. *Journal of Projective Techniques, 30,* 364–380.

Grindea, E. (Ed.). (1978). *Tensions in the performance of music.* London: Kahn & Averill.

Hamann, D. L. (1979). *The development of a musical performance evaluation instrument.* Unpublished manuscript, University of Northern Colorado, Greeley, CO.

Hamann, D. L. (1982). An assessment of anxiety in instrumental and vocal performance. *Journal of Research in Music Education, 30,* 77–90.

Hamann, D. L. (1983). Anxiety and musical performance: How will it effect your students? *UPDATE, 2*(1), 7–9.

Hamann, D. L. (1984). Musician anxiety and performance ability. *Dialogue in Instrumental Music Education, 8*(2).

Hamann, D. L. & Herlong, S. (1980). Response to anxiety in musical performance. *String Vibrations, 9*(2), 13–15.

Hamann, D. L. & Sobaje, M. (1983). Anxiety and the college musician: A study of performance conditions and subject variables. *Psychology of Music, 11*(1), 37–50.

Havas, K. (1976). *Stage fright* (3rd ed.). London: Bosworth.

Havas, K. (1978). The release from tension and anxiety in string playing. In C. Grindea (Ed.), *Tensions in the performance of music* (pp. 13–27). London: Kahn & Averill.

Heinrich, D. L. & Spielberger, C. D. (1982). Anxiety and complex learning. In H. W. Krohne & L. Laux (Eds.), *Achievement, stress, and anxiety* (pp. 145–165). Hemisphere/McGraw-Hill.

Hull, C. L. (1943). *Principles of behavior.* New York: Appleton.

Hutter, J. (1980). A structural analysis of the performance anxiety syndrome as experienced among solo musicians. (Doctoral dissertation, City University of New York). (University Microfilms No. 8014968)

James, I. M., Griffith, D. N. W., Pearson, R. M., & Newbury, P. (1977). Effect of oxprenolol on stage-fright in musicians. *The Lancet, 2,* 952–954.

Leglar, M. A. (1979). Measurement of indicators of anxiety levels under varying conditions of musical performance. *Dissertation Abstracts International, 39,* 5201A–5202A. (University Microfilms No. 7906734)

Levitt, E. E. (1967). *The psychology of anxiety.* Indianapolis: Bobbs-Merrill.

Liden, S. & Gottfries, C. G. (1974). Beta-blocking agents in the treatment of catecholamine-induced symptoms in musicians. *The Lancet, 2,* 529.

Lund, D. R. (1972). A comparative study of three therapeutic techniques in the modification of anxiety behavior in instrumental music performance. *Dissertation Abstracts International, 33,* 1189A. (University Microfilms No. 72023, 026)

McCune, B. A. (1982). Functional performance anxiety modification in adult pianists (Doctoral dissertation, Columbia University Teachers College). (University Microfilms No. 8304030)

Martens, R. (1971). Anxiety and motor behavior: A review. *Journal of Motor Behavior, 22,* 151–179.

Nagel, J., Himle, D., & Papsdorf, J. (1981). Coping with performance anxiety. *NATS Bulletin, 37*(4), 26–27; 31–33.

Neuringer, C. (1962). Manifestations of anxiety on the Rorschach test. *Journal of Projective Techniques, 26,* 318–326.

Nideffer, R. M. & Hessler, N. D. (1978). Controlling performance anxiety. *College Music Symposium, 18,* 146–153.

Reynolds, C. & Morasky, R. (1981). Intensity without tension: Biofeedback. *Music Educators Journal, 67*(9), 52–55.

Spence, D. W. (1958). A theory of emotionally based drive (d) and its relation to performance in simple learning situations. *American Psychologist, 13,* 131–141.

Spence, J. T. & Spence, D. W. (1966). The motivational components of manifest anxiety: Drive and drive stimuli. In C. D. Spielberger (Ed.), *Anxiety and behavior* (pp. 291–326). New York: Academic.

Spencer, R. L. (1970). A study of the relationship of situational anxiety to vocal solo performances of college freshmen voice students (Doctoral dissertation, North Texas State University, 1969). *Dissertation Abstracts International, 31,* 138A. (University Microfilms No. 70–9158)

Spielberger, C. D. (1966). Theory and research on anxiety. In C. D. Spielberger (Ed.), *Anxiety and behavior* (pp. 3–20). New York: Academic.

Spielberger, C. D. (1971). Trait-state anxiety and motor behavior. *Journal of Motor Behavior, 3,* 256–279.

Spielberger, C. D. (1972). Anxiety as an emotional state. In C. D. Spielberger (Ed.), *Anxiety: Current trends in theory and research* (Vol. 1, pp. 24–49). New York: Academic.

Spielberger, C. D. (1979). *Understanding stress and anxiety.* New York: Harper & Row.

Spielberger, C. D., Barker, L., Russell, S., Silva De Crane, R., Westberry, L., Knight, J., & Marks, E. (1979). *Preliminary manual for the State-Trait Personality Inventory.* Unpublished manuscript, University of South Florida.

Spielberger, C. D., Gorsuch, R. L., & Lushene, R. E. (1970). *Manual for the State-Trait Anxiety Inventory.* Palo Alto, CA: Consulting Psychologists Press.

Taylor, J. A. (1956). Drive theory and manifest anxiety. *Psychological Bulletin, 53,* 303–320.

Terwilliger, R. D. (1972). The effect of group counseling on the vocal recital performance of undergraduate education vocal music majors. *Dissertation Abstracts International, 33,* 577A. (University Microfilms No. 72–22, 715)

Waite, J. R. (1977). Reducing musical performance anxiety: A review of literature and a self-help manual. *Dissertation Abstracts International, 38A,* 114A. (University Microfilms No. 77–19, 359)

Wardle, A. (1975). Behavior modification by reciprocal inhibition of instrumental music performance anxiety. In C. K. Madsen, R. D. Greer, & C. H. Madsen, Jr. (Eds.), *Research in music beahvior* (pp. 191–205). New York: Teacher's College Press.

Wolfe, R. L. (1977). A comparison of self-versus therapist-administered biofeedback relaxation training and desensitization (Doctoral dissertation, University of Rochester, 1976). *Dissertation Abstracts International, 38B,* 923B–924B. (University Microfilms No. 77–16, 258)

6

Behn-Rorschach Measures of Psychologists, Psychiatrists and Social Workers Accepted for Training in Psychoanalytic Therapy

Theodora M. Abel
Samuel Roll
University of New Mexico

Vega A. Lalire
Lehigh Valley Guidance Clinic

The goal of this study was to compare personality differences as measured by the Behn-Rorschach, for psychologists, psychiatrists, and social workers who applied for training at the Postgraduate Center for Mental Health in New York City. Comparisons of the three major mental health professions have been made in terms of income (the difference between the income of psychologists and psychiatrists in the U.S. is about $20,000 a year.), training ("The psychologist has no M.D.", or conversely, "The psychiatrist has no Ph.D."), and job descriptions ("The psychologist doesn't prescribe drugs, the psychiatrist doesn't give tests, and the social worker doesn't do either."). We have not been able, however, to find any empirical investigations of personality differences between practitioners of the three mental health disciplines.

Previous research has typically involved only one profession, and has focused on the success or failure of training. Holt and Luborsky (1958a,b), for example, studied psychiatric residents in training. In their famous study of clinical psychology trainees, Kelly and Fiske (1951) found that the Rorschach was a weaker predictor of success than the Miller Analogies Test and the Strong Vocational Interest Blank. Carlson (1969) refined the work of Kelly and Fiske, finding that the Rorschach equaled the Miller Analogies Test in predicting success and was better in predicting failure. Kelly and Fiske had had the protocols interpreted by the experts' own unarticulated system. Carlson based her work on theoretically explicit formulations of how specific Rorschach measures (M, FC, CF, and C) were related to personality.

In one study done at the Postgraduate Center (Abel, Oppenheim & Sager, 1956), the focus was on success or failure (defined as admission to the postgraduate training). The "preferred" Rorschach scores were high M and H; more Fc

157

than CF or C; M twice as high as C; high F% and high R. The candidates were psychiatrists, social workers, and psychologists but they were grouped together and there were no differences across profession comparisons. Of the cases judged as good risks by the Rorschach measures, 76% were accepted for training after a series of independent interviews. Of the 25 judged as poor risks by the Rorschach measures, 76% were rejected for training by the same interviewers. The interviewers did not have access to the Rorschach protocols.

The present study is not focused on success or failure, but rather on differences across the professions in candidates who had already been successful in being accepted for psychoanalytic training. The predictions for the present study were as follows:

Prediction	*Rationale*
1. Penetration to Barrier Ratio: MD > MSW > PhD	MDs are trained in medical model of assessing physical health and prescribing drugs as well as studying the interior of the body. MSWs are trained in looking into situational and environmental factors.
2. W%: PhD > MD > MSW	We thought that high W% would show greater theoretical interests, more abstract attitude, and ability to make a broad survey of presented material.
3. Large D%: MSW > MD > PhD	A large D demonstrates a more realistic approach to life.
4. A%: MSW > PhD > MD	We thought this because of a relatively greater likelihood to accept popular frame of reference by MSWs.
5. FC: MSW > PhD and MD	MSWs readiness to master feelings out of consideration for others.
6. CF: MSW > PhD > MD	MSWs are most emotional although the MDs would have the most control over emotional reactions.
7. M: PhD > MD > MSW	This we felt due to the relationship of M to relatively greater theoretical interests of psychologists.

METHODS

The subjects were all cadidates for training at the Postgraduate Center for Mental Health. Psychiatrists had finished a residency, the psychologists had a PhD, an internship, and some further clinical experiences, and the social workers all had several years of experience. There were 30 psychologists, 30 social workers, and 22 psychiatrists. Some psychiatrists were excluded from the study because they were over 50 and thus exceeded the age range of the other groups. Both males and females were included although there were more female social workers and more male psychologists and psychiatrists.

All the candidates were given an interview and tests prior to admission. This study includes only those who were accepted on the basis of their application and interviews. The interviews were done independently of the tests. The tests were originally scored by the person administering the test. However, for the purposes of this study, the tests were rescored by persons who did not see the candidates and who did not know their professions.

Since the psychologist applicants were quite familiar with the Rorschach, it was decided to use the Behn-Rorschach. The Behn-Rorschach was developed by Hans Zulliger (1956) in order to have alternate forms of the Rorschach. One of the difficulties in using the Behn is that clear F+ norms are not available and thus we could not compare F+% among groups. Also, as interscorer reliability was too low, we did not analyze the color scores. The scores for which the interscorer consensus was over 80% included the R, W, D, F, Extended F, H, HD, A, M (scored according to both Rapaport and Exner), penetration, and barrier. The penetration across barrier scores were based on the scale in the second edition of *Body Image and Personality* (Fisher & Cleveland, 1968).

RESULTS

A 2×3 factorial analysis of variance of the ratio of penetration to barrier scores was conducted (see Table 6.1). A one-way analysis of variance was performed on the other nine response categories (all except M). The use of a Bonferroni critical value was used in order to avoid an elevated Type I error rate. In Table 6.1, you can see which response categories produced significant differences among the groups.

In order to compare professions individually, a factorial was conducted using a MANOVA program. All contrasts were conducted using Scheffe's contrast method and were tested by a post hoc critical value. Within the scores for which there is a difference by profession, the differences are summarized in Table 6.2.

The M scores were handled differently because there was an interest in comparing M responses when scored by the Exner (1974) and the Rapaport (Rapaport, Gill & Schafer, 1968) systems, as well as comparing the responses given by the three professions. A $2 \times 2 \times 3$ factorial with repeated measures on one factor

TABLE 6.1
Factor Analysis and Analyses of Variance of Behn-Rorschach Scores Across
Professional Groups F Ratios and Levels of Significance

Source	Source	DF	SS	MS	F
Factorial on	Sex	1	9817.980	9817.980	4.117
Penetration to	Profession	2	32806.680	16403.340	6.879*
Barrier Ratio	Sex/Prof.	2	7924.523	3962.262	1.662
	Within Cells	72	171692.938	2384.624	
R	Between Groups	2	981.9656	490.9827	2.608
	Within Groups	75	14121.9531	188.2927	
W	Between Groups	2	1192.2618	596.1309	4.678*
	Within Groups	75	9557.9197	127.4389	
D	Between Groups	2	6747.3678	3373.6838	17.370*
	Within Groups	75	14567.0081	194.2268	
Dr	Between Groups	2	1819.6911	909.8455	6.104**
	Within Groups	75	11178.6160	149.0482	
F	Between Groups	2	107.0693	53.5346	.375
	Within Groups	75	10714.8313	142.8644	
Ext F	Between Groups	2	1489.3978	744.6987	15.017**
	Within Groups	75	3719.2749	49.5903	
H	Between Groups	2	893.6332	446.8164	2.020
	Within Groups	75	16591.1914	221.2159	
Hd	Between Groups	2	3288.8153	1644.4075	12.096**
	Within Groups	75	10195.9905	135.9465	
A	Between Groups	2	1266.9704	633.4851	5.810
	Within Groups	75	8177.8462	109.0379	

$*\ p < .01$
$**\ p < .001$

TABLE 6.2
Comparison of Group Means Across Professional Groups

Score in Percentages					
W	MD	*	MSW		PhD
D	PhD	*	MSW	*	MD
Dr	MD	*	PhD		MSW
Ext F	PhD	*	MD	*	MSW
Hd	PhD	*	MSW		MD
A	MD	*	MSW	*	PhD
Penetration to Barrier Ratio	MD	*	MSW	*	PhD

$*p > .05$

TABLE 6.3
Analysis of Variance for M Responses by Sex and Profession

Source	SS	DF	MS	F
Between Subjects		81		
Sex	.248	1	.248	.005
Profession	961.484	2	480.742	9.184*
Sex by Profession	10.504	2	5.252	.100
Subjects within groups	3978.453	76	52.348	
Within Subjects		82		
System	340.109	1	340.109	56.684**
Sex by System	6.248	1	6.248	1.041
Profession by System	33.360	2	16.680	2.780
Sex by Profession by System	3.272	2	1.636	.273
System by Subject within Groups	456.010	76	6.000	

*$p < .01$
**$p < .001$

was used. Although there was a major effect for system (i.e., there were more Ms with Exner scoring than with Rapaport's at .001 level of probability), this is simply because more content is scored M by Exner than by Rapaport and is not an unexpected finding. Although there were no significant interactions involving sex by system, profession by system, or sex by profession by system, the differences (independent of system) across the three professions were striking ($p<.01$). There was virtually no difference in M between psychiatrists and social workers, but there was a significant difference between these two and psychologists. The psychologists had a significantly greater number of M responses. Also there was no significant difference for sex or sex by profession interaction (see Table 6.3).

DISCUSSION

The study was primarily an empirical and exploratory one. The predictions made come from our collective experiences and biases rather than from a consistent theoretical position. The review of the results in this section is on the significant findings and post hoc explanations. Of course the exploratory nature of the study requires that further study be conducted. A simplifying factor is that there were no sex by profession differences. A limiting factor was that the FC, CF, and C could not be reliably measured.

Only the penetration and barrier scores came out as predicted, that is, the MDs had the highest percent penetration score, the PhDs the least, and the MSWs came out between the other two disciplines. Our prediction had to do with the type of training experienced by the MDs and MSWs (medical model for the MDs and situation and environment model for the MSWs).

As for the D%, the result was the reverse of our prediction. A large D is considered as representing the perception of realistic factors. We thought the MSWs would have the largest amount, the psychologists the least. It was surprising that the psychologists had more Ds than the MSWs and that they both had more Ds than the MDs. This point needs much more clarification.

Our prediction also differed for the A%. The MDs had the highest and the MSWs were second highest, and the psychologists held the lowest A% in relation to the other two disciplines. We had felt that the MSWs were more likely to accept a popular frame of reference. Animals were generally the most easily perceived in the blots. It might be that the psychologists, with their more intellectual frame of reference, did not see or avoided (unconsciously) perceiving animals as frequently as did the other two disciplines. Why the MDs had the highest A% may account for their having a more popular frame of reference than the psychologists but does not account for their surpassing the MSWs in this type of perception. This needs further exploration.

In the analysis of variance, the MDs had higher Dr% than the psychologists, who in turn, had more Dr% than the MSWs. In balanced records, as were those of the individuals in this study, the Dr% might be interpreted as that of rigid compulsive individuals. But since the W% and the D% were high for the MDs (when compared with general norms), this interpretation may not hold. However, some rigidity might be present in their attempt to make a perception more meaningful by the use of greater number of Drs.

Extended F% was scored, but its relevance for the three disciplines was not predicted. In our results the psychologists had the highest extended F%, the MSWs the lowest. Extended F% usually stands for accurate reality testing in which the psychologists in relation to the other two disciplines scored the highest as they did with the Ds.

We made no predictions about H% and Hd%. Our results indicate no difference in the three disciplines in the percent frequency of H, but there was a significant difference on Hd. The psychologists had the highest percent, the MDs the least with the MSWs in between. According to Klopfer (Klopfer, Ainsworth, Klopfer, & Holt, 1954), the emphasis on Hd has to do with intellectualization and compulsion in looking for human details.

The differences in M% (both Rapaport & Exner systems) showed up only in comparing disciplines. The psychologists had a larger M% than did the social workers and physicians. The M seems to signify creativity, kinesthetic perception (seeing movement where there is none), good imagination, and the ability to see the world as peopled, having empathy, a high level of intellectual functioning

(Klopfer et al., 1954). The MDs and MSWs also have these characteristics, but to a lesser degree.

CONCLUSION

Using an analysis of variance, differences in many of the Behn-Rorschach scores showed up among the three disciplines. Some of the results corroborated our predictions, *most* did not. Other unpredicted differences in scores were revealed. MDs, MSWs and PhDs each seem to have certain characteristics typical of their discipline as revealed on the Behn-Rorschach Test. We should note that preferred theoretical orientation was controlled in that all of the candidates were interested in psychoanalytically oriented theory and treatment.

SUMMARY

In order to test for differences across the members of the three major mental health professions, the Behn-Rorschach responses of 82 subjects (30 psychologists, 30 social workers, and 22 psychiatrists) were compared. The subjects had similar theoretical orientations and professional goals as indicated by their successful candidacy for training in psychoanalytic psychotherapy at the Postgraduate Center for Mental Health. The tests were scored independently by readers who did not administer them, and who did not see the candidates or know their professions. The MDs had the highest penetration scores ($p<.01$), and greater Drs than did psychologists and social workers ($p<.05$). The psychologists had a greater percentage of movement responses, scored according to both the Rapaport and Exner systems, than the other groups ($p<.01$), and a greater percentage of Ds ($p<.05$). Explanations were offered for these and other differences across the three professions.

ACKNOWLEDGMENTS

This paper was presented at the 10th Congress of the International Rorschach Society in Washington, D.C., September 4–7, 1981.

REFERENCES

Abel, T. M., Oppenheim, S., & Sager, C. J. (1956). Screening applicants for training in psychoanalytically oriented psychotherapy. *American Journal of Psychotherapy, 10*, 24–39
Carlson, R. (1969). Rorschach prediction of success in clinical training. *Journal of Consulting and Clinical Psychology, 33*, 699–704.

Exner, J. E., Jr. (1974). *The Rorschach: A comprehensive study.* New York: Wiley.

Fisher, S., & Cleveland, S. E. (1968). *Body image and personality* (2nd rev. ed.). New York: Dover.

Holt, R. R., & Luborsky, L. (1958a). *Personality patterns of psychiatrists* (Vol. I). New York: Basic Books.

Holt, R. R., & Luborsky, L. (1958b). *Personality patterns of psychiatrists* (Vol. II). Topeka, KS: Menninger Foundation.

Kelly, E. L., & Fiske, D. W. (1951). *The prediction of performance in clinical psychology.* Ann Arbor: University of Michigan.

Klopfer, B., Ainsworth, M. D., Klopfer, W. G., & Holt, R. R. (1954). *Development in the Rorschach technique* (Vol. 1). Yonkers-on-Hudson, NY: World Book.

Rapaport, D., Gill, M. M., & Schafer, R. (1968). *Diagnostic psychological testing* (rev. ed.). New York: International Universities Press.

Zulliger, H. (1956). *The Behn-Rorschach.* New York: Hans Huber Bern; Grune & Stratton.

7

The Temporal Stability of Acts, Trends, and Patterns

David M. Buss
Harvard University

ABSTRACT

A conceptual framework for examining different facets of temporal stability is proposed. Empirical studies, involving the temporal stability of 200 specific acts subsumed by eight dispositional categories and assessed over time with two data sources in a sample of 130 subjects, are used to illustrate the merits and deficiencies of this framework. Results suggest moderate stability of single acts, as well as robust increments in obtained stability when multiple-act composites or act trends are employed as units of analysis. Individually computed stability coefficients, not dependent on other sample members for meaning, were found to be moderate and similar in magnitude to traditionally computed correlations. Variations in stability magnitudes were reliable across data sources. Three hypothesized moderators of stability differences were operationalized. Eight tests of each hypothesis provided no support for the context specificity or the motive inference hypotheses and moderate support for the cross-method agreement hypothesis. Implications for the conceptual framework and for alternative facets of temporal stability are discussed.

INTRODUCTION: THE CENTRALITY OF TEMPORAL STABILITY

Dispositional concepts, variously formulated, form the core of most approaches to the analysis of personality. Although considerable divergence exists in how dispositions have been conceptualized (e.g., Allport, 1937; Alston, 1975; Buss & Craik, 1980, 1983a; Wiggins, 1974), all invoke some form of enduring tendency, proclivity, or inclination to behave, think, or respond in certain ways over time. Stable plans, expectancies, and competencies (Mischel, 1973) are no less dispositional than are enduring behavioral provlivities of a more overt nature. Dispositions may be broad or narrow, and may span many situations or few. But if humans were not inclined to act or think or respond in certain ways over time, we could dispense with dispositional concepts—a state that would undermine the entire enterprise of personality psychology.

Temporal stability has been explored from a variety of perspectives with an array of assessment devices. Using self-report scales and spouse ratings, Costa and McCrae have demonstrated impressive stability of individual difference dispositions (Costa & McCrae, 1980; Costa, McCrae, & Arenberg, 1980) as well as self-concept (McCrae & Costa, 1982) over a span of decades. Epstein (1979, 1980, 1983) has documented robust temporal stability of emotional states, impulses, and behaviors using daily self-monitoring techniques, aggregated to achieve reliability. Activity level remains moderately stable over a 4-year interval when reliably measured by mechanical recording devices and observer judgments (Buss, Block, & Block, 1980). And personality in general appears to show cross-time stability, whether the data source derives from self-reports (Schuerger, Tait, & Tavernelli, 1982), or from observer judgments and experimental tasks (Block, 1971, 1977; Block & Block, 1980; Moss & Susman, 1980).

In sum, considerable evidence exists that various aspects of personality remain stable over time—a general finding that transcends the particulars of any single data source. This conclusion appears to draw consensus among researchers of widely differing theoretical orientations (Mischel & Peake, 1982). Demonstrations that stability *can* be found should now be transcended by investigations that build on these findings and address more complex questions: Within what conceptual frameworks can findings of temporal stability be placed? At what levels of analysis should temporal stability be sought? By what alternative operations can temporal stability be examined? What specific behavioral domains show relatively more versus less stability? And what factors moderate the magnitudes of obtained temporal stability?

This report attempts to address these questions by presenting a conceptual framework for the analysis of temporal stability deriving from the act frequency approach (Buss & Craik, 1980, 1983a, b, 1984; Buss, 1981a, b). An empirical study involving the temporal stability of 200 specific acts subsumed by eight systematically sampled dispositional categories and assessed over time with two data sources is used to illustrate the merits and deficiencies of this conceptual framework. Alternative operations for indexing consistency are examined. Finally, three hypothesized moderators of temporal stability magnitude are tested.

Three Modes of Evaluating Temporal Stability

From the perspective of the act frequency approach, three modes of dispositional analysis carry relevance for analyzing the everyday stream of behavior: analysis of group trends, analysis of individual differences, and idiographic analysis of persons (Buss & Craik, 1983b). Temporal stability can be evaluated within this framework at each of these three levels. Because the individual difference mode has been a central concern of the field of personality psychology, temporal stability at this level will be examined first.

Temporal stability in the individual difference mode. As with traditional studies of cross-time consistency, evaluating the temporal stability of acts and act trends in the individual difference mode implies indexing the relative position maintenance of individuals on performance frequencies over time. Although these indices do not afford consistency assessments of any single individual, they do provide evaluations of rank order endurance—a crucial facet of temporal stability. Within the individual difference mode, two aspects of temporal stability can be evaluated: single act stability and act trend stability.

From the perspective of the act frequency approach, act trends, as indexed by composites of highly prototypical acts, form fundamental units of analysis in personality psychology (Buss & Craik, 1980, 1981, 1983a). The critical index of temporal stability from this perspective is the overall stability of frequency within each act category, regardless of whether any single specific acts are repeated over time. Comparing the temporal stability of single acts with the temporal stability of act trends provides a test of the effectiveness of aggregation, and of the utility of employing act trends as fundamental units of analysis in personality psychology.

Lamiell (1981) has criticized traditional correlational indices of consistency on the grounds that they do not afford inferences about the specific consistency of any single individual in the sample. Although he suggests abandoning traditional correlational indices of consistency, a more moderate position would be that correlations across subjects between time periods reflect only one facet of consistency—the relative position maintenance of individuals or the endurance of their rank order over time. Deriving measures that accurately reflect the consistency of each individual requires a different index. Thus, the consistency of *specific* individuals and the relative position maintenance of *samples* of individuals are conceptually independent, although perhaps empirically related issues in the evaluation of temporal stability.

Individualized stability coefficients. While correlations reflecting relative position maintenance over time are by far the most prevalent indices in temporal stability studies, such indices, as Lamiell (1981) correctly points out, do not reference the specific consistency of any single individual within the sample. For this purpose, indices are needed that do not require reference to other sample members to derive their meaning. The act frequency approach in the individual mode of analysis provides a means of assessing the temporal stability of each individual without reference to other sample members.

The method for deriving these individualized stability indices is not new, but it has been employed only rarely in personality research (See Block, 1971; Epstein, 1983 for excellent illustrations). In the context of the act frequency approach, one can assess whether an individual who performed a given act during Time Period 1 (T1) also performed that act during Time Period 2 (T2). Across a specified set of acts, the pattern of performance and nonperformance can be correlated with the analogous pattern at T2. Thus, a correlation for each individual can be computed that represents the degree to which the pattern of act performance has remained stable across the two time periods.

One advantage of this individualized stability index is that it can be applied across a set of dispositions. Do individuals who show stability in dominant acts also also show stability in agreeable, arrogant, and ingenuous acts? Are individuals consistently stable? Correlations between similarly calculated individualized stability indices address the issue of the generality or specificity of manifestations of stability.

Individualized stability indices also permit comparative analysis with other conceptual and computational facets of stability. Do individualized indices show temporal stability magnitudes similar to traditionally derived stability correlations? Are traditionally computed stability correlations accurate reflections of the average individualized stability correlations? Analysis of individual consistency through the act frequency approach can address these questions.

A distinct disadvantage of this individualized consistency index should be noted. While assessing stability at the level of single individuals, this index does not yield information about the stability of any single act. Thus, individualized consistency indices are achieved at a cost. Alternative stability indices supplement each other and address different questions. None can serve generally for all facets of the analysis of temporal stability.

Stability of group trends.   Although temporal stability analysis at the individual difference level provides an indication of the endurance of relative rank, and at the individual level an indication of the specific consistency of each individual, the act frequency approach provides a third level for analyzing temporal stability—the consistency of group trends. Over time, does a given population show stability in the relative base rates with which they perform acts within and across a set of dispositional categories? Does the proportion of dominant acts to quarrelsome acts maintain consistency over time throughout the day-to-day stream of behavior? The field of personality psychology encompasses traits that characterize populations, as well as the ways in which individuals within those populations characteristically differ (Buss, 1984b; Buss & Craik, 1983b, 1984). Group level analysis within the act frequency approach provides one method for examining this third aspect of temporal stability.

The importance of the stability of group base rates deserves mention. At present, personality psychology lacks the descriptive richness of biology, in which the variegated behavioral repertoires of species are catalogued and sub-jected to functional analysis. In the development of a personality theory that encompasses both characteristic individual differences as well as population tendencies, it is important to know, for example, that quarrelsome acts, such as hitting others, have fairly low base rates, while dominant acts, such as telling others to perform menial tasks, appear to be relatively common. Documenting the stability of such base rates provides a rich descriptive portrait of the acts that tend to be performed with greater and lesser frequency in everyday conduct. From this perspective, a personality theory lacking an account of group trends would be incomplete.

In sum, the purpose of the present series of studies was to examine the temporal stability of acts and act trends at each of the three levels of analysis provided by the act frequency approach. Individualized indices permit evaluation of the temporal stability of each individual's performance pattern, yet without reliance on the positions of others to provide meaning. Applied across disposi-tions, these indices can address a central theoretical question: Do individuals who show stability on one disposition also display stability across other disposi-tions?

In the individual difference mode, temporal stability can be examined at the level of single acts and at the level of act trends. Comparing these two levels permits examination of the relative gains yielded by the act trend as a basic unit of analysis. In conjunction, these analyses can address the central theoretical issue of whether some acts or act trends show relatively greater temporal stability than do others.

The third mode of analysis pertains to group or population trends. Stability at this level offers the potential of providing insights into the endurance of base-rates of acts throughout the behavioral stream. Finally, comparing the stability coefficients that emerge at all three levels can give an indication of whether traditionally computed stability coefficients (variable-centered correlations across subjects) accurately reflect consistency at the individual level and at the population level.

Hypothesized Moderators of Temporal Stability

A crucial task for personality psychology is the delineation of the acts and act trends that are relatively more or less temporally stable, and the identification of factors that moderate temporal stability magnitudes. In the present program of studies, three variables were hypothesized to moderate obtained temporal sta-bility: context specificity, degree of inference about the motives and intentions required for act assessment, and the degree of cross-method agreement on act performance.

Specific acts, within the act frequency approach, are not viewed as purely physicalistic (cf., e.g., Duncan & Fiske, 1977). Rather, they include aspects of context and interpretation. Assessing the simple act "She danced wildly at the party," for example, specifies a context for the dancing (the party) and requires some knowledge of norms to interpret the dancing style as wild. Act depiction requires at least some minimal specification of context because dispositional standing with respect to prototypicality of membership changes with context (Buss & Craik, 1983a). For example, the act "I displayed no emotion" would probably be considered aloof in the context of being reunited with a long lost friend, but not aloof in the context of a formal ceremony or while watching the news. Because context can be specified at many levels of analysis and abstraction (e.g., physical, social, temporal) with differing degrees of elaboration and complexity, examing various levels of context specificity as they affect the prediction of temporal stability acquires significance.

The first hypothesized moderator of temporal stability was degree of context specificity. It was predicted that acts assessed in the context of highly detailed specificity would show lower temporal stability than would acts assessed in less specific, more generic contexts. Because highly specific contexts have a lower probability of being encountered over time than do less specific contexts, opportunities for act repetition are reduced. Generic act depiction may offer a more reliable index of performance. Therefore, acts assessed in highly specified contexts should show lower temporal stability.

A second issue pertains to the degree to which inferences about internal states, intentions, or motivations of the actor are required for act assessment. That is, act depiction can vary from physical description (e.g., The man traversed a two mile distance in a motor vehicle) to progressive inclusion of inferential elements (e.g., The man raced his hotrod across town to get away from his wife). The second hypothesis was that acts requiring inferences about internal states would display less temporal stability than would acts requiring little or no inference about underlying motivations or intentions.

The rationale for this hypothesis derives from two considerations. First, acts requiring inferences afford greater latitude for alternative construal and interpretation, with attenuation of reliability a likely consequence. Second, the potentially shifting contextual frames provided by temporally dispersed measurement are more likely to alter interpretation of acts requiring inference than those requiring little or no inference about motives and intentions. Both considerations suggest the hypothesis of inference as a moderator of temporal stability.

The third hypothesized moderator of temporal stability is psychometric, and parallels Epstein's (1979, 1980) analysis of the effects of reliability of assessment on temporal stability. Specifically, it is hypothesized that acts that show higher cross-method agreement would display greater temporal stability than those showing lower cross-method agreement. In the present context, correlations between assessments of the same act by different persons (self- and spouse-observer) provide indices of cross-method agreement.

In sum, the present program of studies was conducted to provide a systematic evaluation of temporal stability within each of three modes of analysis offered by the act frequency approach. In addition, these studies sought to evaluate several factors hypothesized to affect or moderate temporal stability magnitudes. Independent assessments of the degree of context specificity, degree of motive and intention inference, and cross-method agreement for each act provide a means to test these hypotheses.

In the present context, it is desirable to have a reasonably comprehensive taxonomy of interpersonal categories from which dispositions and the acts subsumed by them can be drawn. The Wiggins (1979, 1980) circumplex model of the interpersonal domain provides such a taxonomy. It is a structural model that consists of 16 points or interpersonal constructs arrayed in a circular fashion. The relations between each construct and every other construct are specified by position within the model: adjacent constructs are highly positively correlated (e.g., extraverted, gregarious); opposing constructs are highly negatively correlated (e.g., dominance, submissiveness); and orthogonal constructs are uncorrelated (e.g., dominance, agreeableness).

For the purposes of this series of studies, the Wiggins circumplex model has several clear advantages. It provides a relatively comprehensive taxonomic system from which key interpersonal constructs can be taken. Thus, notable gaps in coverage can be avoided by systematic sampling from the model. For these studies, every other point on the circumplex model was chosen for inclusion: dominant, calculating, quarrelsome, introverted, submissive, ingenuous, agreeable, and extraverted. This particular selection has the added advantage that it includes dispositions (e.g., extraversion, dominance) that are widely regarded by other researchers as central dimensions of personality (e.g., Cattell, 1957; Eysenck, 1953; Leary, 1957; Norman, 1963).

Many previous studies of temporal stability have been limited by the use of a single data source, typically self-report. This series of studies sought to employ two data sources—self-reports and spouse-observer reports of each act for each time period. By this dual assessment strategy, temporal stability results can be evaluated in a way that transcends single-source limitations.

METHOD

ACT PERFORMANCE ASSESSMENTS: TIME ONE

Subjects

One hundred and eighty six (186) individuals composing 93 married couples participated in the Time One assessments of act performance. Married couples were employed so that self-reports of act performance could be supplemented by performance reports by an observer in a position of sufficient and prolonged proximity to provide an accurate assessment. Details of the sample and of the method of obtaining the sample are provided in an earlier report (Buss, 1984a).

Materials

Self-Reported Act Performance.   Retrospective reports of the performance frequencies of each of the 800 acts were recorded by each subject. Two forms, each with 400 acts (intermingled from the eight categories), were completed. The instructions were as follows: "The following pages contain 400 human acts beginning with act (1) to act (400). For each act, please indicate how often you have performed it (if at all) *within the past three months.*" A 3-month time frame was chosen to allow enough time for a sufficient number of acts to have occurred.

Spouse-Observer Reports of Act Performance.   In order to obtain an additional assessment of act performance, the spouse of each participant completed a parallel Act Report form on which their spouse's performance frequencies for each of the 800 acts was recorded. Instructions were similar to those for the self-recorded performance forms. For the spouse-observer forms, each act was transformed from the first to the third person singular. Thus, the husband's report of his wife's act performance contained acts that began with "She . . ." (e.g., She rode on a motorcycle); the wife's report of her husband's performance contained acts that began with "He. . . ."

Procedure

Data gathering for the Time One assessments occurred in two sessions, separated by several days. The sessions lasted about 3 hours, although the time needed to complete the procedures varied across individuals. In the first session, participants completed the Self-Recorded Act Reports and a battery of personality measures. In the second session, participants completed the Spouse-Observer Act Reports, and several other measures. Subjects were tested in groups that ranged from 2 (a single couple) to 14 (seven couples). Each couple pair was separated for the duration of the testing session to prevent discussion of the forms.

ACT PERFORMANCE ASSESSMENTS: TIME TWO

Subjects

All subjects who participated in the Time One assessments were contacted by letter or phone six months later and invited to participate in the follow-up sessions. Although only two contacted couples declined to participate in the follow-up, some had moved and left no forwarding address. Several other couples had separated and were undergoing divorce procedures. A few others agreed to participate, yet did not return the forms. In all, 130 of the initial sample of 186 participated in this 6-month follow-up.

Materials

The Time Two assessments employed a subset of the acts used in the initial sessions. Specifically, 25 acts were selected from each of the eight categories on the basis of prototypicality ratings (Buss & Craik, 1980, 1981, 1983a; Buss, 1981a), excluding acts that showed extreme baserates (greater than 90% or less than 10%). These acts were again intermingled, and presented to subjects on Act Report forms similar to those employed in the Time One assessments.

Procedure

Each member of each couple was separately sent two sealed packets of forms, and requested to complete each packet on separate consecutive days (or evenings), without discussion with their spouse. One packet contained the self-recorded Act Reports and several other self-report measures. The second packet contained the observer-spouse Act Report forms, and several other measures. Packets were returned in previously addressed and stamped envelopes.

CONTEXT SPECIFICITY EVALUATIONS

Subjects

Ten university undergraduates rated the context specificity of each of the 800 acts included in Time One Assessments. Each was paid a small sum of money for participation.

Materials

Instructions for the context specificity ratings were as follows: "Please rate each act on the degree to which the context within which the act is set is specified. For example, 'he danced' is an act that involves little specification of context; in contrast, the act 'he danced with his steady partner on Friday night' involves somewhat more specification of context. A '7' means the act statement includes a high degree of context specification; a '1' means that act statement involves *little* specification of context. Use intermediate numbers to indicate intermediate levels of context specification."

RATINGS OF DEGREE OF INFERENCE
ABOUT INTERNAL STATES

Subjects

A separate panel of eight university undergraduates rated the degree of inference entailed in assessing the performance of each act. Subjects were paid a small sum of money for participation.

Materials

Instructions for the inference ratings were as follows: "Please rate each act statement on the degree to which it involves an *inference* about the internal state, intention, or underlying motivation of the actor. A '7' means the act is highly inferential; a '1' means that no inference is needed when an observer is recording the act. Use intermediate numbers to indicate intermediate levels of inference."

RESULTS

Temporal Stability of Acts and Act Trends

Individual difference mode. Tables 7.1–7.8 show the temporal stability results for the 12 most prototypical acts from each of the eight dispositional categories. The first four columns of each table show the base rate with which each act was reported (the percentage of the sample who reported performing the act at least once) for each 3-month period for each data source separately. The next three columns show the cross-time correlations for each act for the self-recorded, spouse-observer recorded, and composite of self and spouse-observer recorded act performance. All temporal stability analyses were conducted twice: once using the full range of frequency scores for reported act performance and once using 0–1 scores that reflect simply nonperformance–performance of each act. The stability coefficients in Tables 7.1–7.8 are based on the 0–1 scores. The results from the two sets of analyses are highly similar.

Several results in these tables merit emphasis. First, the range is substantial: .05 to .63 for self-reported performance, .05 to .65 for spouse-observer reported performance, and .12 to .73 for composited performance. The means across the 200 acts are .37, .39, and .45 for the self, spouse-observer, and composite data sources, respectively.

A second general finding is that the temporal stability coefficients obtained from the self-recorded data source are similar in magnitude to those obtained from the spouse-observer data source. The correlation between the two columns of (z-transformed) correlations is $+.62$ ($p<.001$) across the entire set of 200 acts. This suggests that act to act variability in temporal stability magnitude is

TABLE 7.1
Temporal Stability of Extraverted Acts

Base Rates				Temporal Stability			Acts
S-Data		O-Data					
T1	T2	T1	T2	S x S	O x O	SO x SO	
32	32	37	33	59***	58***	71***	I entertained the party crowd with some jokes.
15	20	15	22	45***	61***	67***	I got people together to play a sport.
17	16	11	12	51***	34***	66***	I flirted with several people at the party.
19	17	19	15	48***	44***	64***	I sang a song in front of a group.
29	20	21	21	53***	38***	62***	I rolled down the car window and talked to the person in the next car.
22	18	29	33	35***	47***	52***	I went to the bar to socialize.
51	50	58	57	32***	48***	49***	I talked to almost everyone at the party.
45	50	38	47	30***	42***	48***	I entered into the conversation of a group I didn't know.
28	23	25	25	28**	43***	43***	I openly discussed my sex life with my friends.
83	87	56	59	33***	36***	39***	I said hi to a stranger on the street.
31	26	30	24	21*	33***	33***	I danced in front of a crowd.
27	20	34	20	25***	25***	31***	I threw a big party.

*** $p < .001$
** $p < .01$
* $p < .05$

175

TABLE 7.2
Temporal Stability of Introverted Acts

Base Rates				Temporal Stability			Acts
S-Data T1	T2	O-Data T1	T2	S x S	O x O	SO x SO	
16	12	15	15	43***	34***	56***	I pretended I was sick to avoid attending the party.
42	46	27	34	51***	40***	53***	I clammed up in the group conversation.
33	20	16	19	53***	53***	51***	I played with the dog rather than interact with the people present.
37	29	32	27	35***	40***	51***	I stayed at home to watch TV rather than attend the party.
40	44	23	32	56***	34***	50***	I avoided eye contact during the conversation.
35	29	29	24	39***	44***	50***	I turned red when someone asked me a personal question.
46	45	27	29	35***	42***	48***	I circled around to avoid someone I knew.
39	28	32	29	36***	26**	44***	I responded to, but did not initiate any conversation at the party.
43	35	24	31	35***	43***	43***	I walked into the room full of people without talking to anyone.
20	16	13	15	30***	45***	42***	I went to the movie alone.
70	52	55	46	30***	28***	40***	I spoke only when someone spoke to me.
29	32	30	23	30***	39***	40***	I changed the subject when my personal feelings were about to be revealed.

*** $p < .001$
** $p < .01$

TABLE 7.3
Temporal Stability of Quarrelsome Acts

| Base Rates | | | | Temporal Stability | | | Quarrelsome Acts |
S-Data T1	T2	O-Data T1	T2	S x S	O x O	SO x SO	
46	37	42	41	51***	61***	66***	I slammed the door when they left the room.
82	74	73	72	57***	44***	62***	I yelled at my partner.
11	12	14	17	43***	42***	55***	I cursed at my parents.
18	13	17	19	21*	54***	54***	I criticised a minority group for being lazy.
41	43	40	47	55***	37***	53***	Even after conceding the point, I continued to argue.
49	52	35	38	44***	35***	52***	I made belittling comments about the people who walked by.
35	30	28	20	38***	37***	48***	I told my friend to "shut up."
53	50	44	43	36***	42***	47***	I gave her the "silent treatment" when I was upset.
22	19	20	25	39***	51***	46***	I ended the conversation by hanging up the phone without saying good-bye.
12	07	11	11	35***	42***	44***	I insisted on playing a record I knew my friend did not like.
19	14	17	17	40***	46***	43***	I hit someone who annoyed me.
29	27	30	25	32***	40***	37***	When someone asked me for a favor, I said "do it yourself."

*** $p < .001$
* $p < .05$

TABLE 7.4

Temporal Stability of Agreeable Acts

Base Rates				Temporal Stability			Agreeable Acts
S-Data		O-Data					
T1	T2	T1	T2	S x S	O x O	SO x SO	
86	89	83	84	53***	40***	65***	I compromised about where to go out to eat.
61	58	46	49	38***	55***	56***	I told a joke to lighten up a tense situation.
57	61	59	62	34***	48***	53***	I watched a different TV show because someone else wanted to.
24	23	27	28	20*	52***	53***	I lent my partner my car when he/she needed it.
53	43	47	30	35***	55***	51***	I offered an older person my seat on the bus.
44	32	32	22	37***	35***	42***	I left the party when my date wanted to, even though I wanted to stay.
30	27	19	20	22*	46***	39***	I offered to help my friend move into the apartment.
91	88	86	87	17	19*	32***	I readily did the dishes after dinner.
72	77	55	68	09	39***	32***	I volunteered to take responsibility when no one else would do so.
65	36	60	32	20*	25**	25**	I helped calm people in the heated debate.
84	86	74	89	26**	27**	24**	I attempted to arrive at a solution that was satisfactory to all.
88	95	88	89	15	13	21*	I smiled and laughed at the jokes that were told.

*** p < .001
** p < .01
* p < .05

TABLE 7.5

Temporal Stability of Dominant Acts

Base Rates				Temporal Stability			Dominant Acts
S-Data		O-Data					
T1	T2	T1	T2	S x S	O x O	SO x SO	
71	74	67	74	35***	62***	60***	I decided which programs we would watch on TV.
43	49	41	45	53***	37***	58***	I issued orders that got the group organized.
54	55	46	53	46***	47***	53***	I set goals for the group.
30	34	34	32	30***	46***	51***	I took charge of things at the committee meeting.
65	68	57	73	41***	34***	49***	I persuaded others to accept my opinion on the issue.
45	57	51	56	45***	38***	48***	I demanded that he run an errand.
44	52	34	39	38***	46***	47***	I told others to perform menial tasks instead of doing them myself.
56	68	51	62	34***	34***	46***	I took the lead in organizing the project.
25	23	22	28	35***	46***	45***	I managed to control the outcome of the meeting without the others being aware of it.
61	61	56	61	29**	42***	44***	I persuaded him to do something he did not want to do.
35	41	38	43	45***	26**	41***	I settled the dispute among other members of the group.
70	71	70	76	29***	51***	37***	I took a stand on the issue without waiting to find out what others thought.

*** $p < .001$
** $p < .01$

179

TABLE 7.6
Temporal Stability of Submissive Acts

| Base Rates | | | | Temporal Stability | | | Submissive Acts |
S-Data T1	S-Data T2	O-Data T1	O-Data T2	S x S	O x O	SO x SO	
51	34	50	40	47***	56***	62***	I made love with my partner when I didn't want to.
39	36	25	25	50***	47***	60***	I did not voice my opinion when I learned that the majority held the opposite viewpoint.
58	59	43	43	48***	42***	51***	I did not tell the man to put out his cigarette, even though it bothered me.
20	20	29	10	36***	23*	44***	I agreed to go out with someone I didn't like.
24	23	15	21	31***	18*	41***	I said "OK" to every suggestion that was made about my project.
32	23	42	30	32***	43***	37***	I accepted verbal abuse without defending myself.
75	68	64	59	37***	38***	33***	I agreed to his plan even though I did not really have confidence in it.
15	16	12	12	10	21*	33***	I let someone cut into the parking space I was waiting for.
23	18	17	20	25**	27**	32***	I let my roommate play the stereo when I was trying to study.
35	22	30	25	16	39***	29**	I said nothing when someone cut in front of me in a long line.
40	27	32	24	29**	23*	29***	I agreed I was wrong, even though I wasn't.
18	12	25	23	39***	19*	23*	I changed my clothes when the others made fun of my attire.

*** $p < .001$
** $p < .01$
* $p < .05$

TABLE 7.7
Temporal Stability of Calculating Acts

Base Rates				Temporal Stability			Calculating Acts
S-Data		O-Data					
T1	T2	T1	T2	S x S	O x O	SO x SO	
24	19	19	21	59***	56***	64***	I changed my mood several times to get my way.
15	07	18	07	63***	54***	58***	I cried to get my way.
30	34	25	22	44***	43***	54***	I complimented someone when I wanted something.
17	14	20	15	34***	60***	51***	I pretended I was hurt to get someone to do me a favor.
12	22	14	20	33***	50***	50***	I made a friend in order to obtain a favor.
39	48	28	33	27**	53***	49***	I planned out the casual conversation.
29	27	28	30	36***	48***	48***	I made others feel guilty to get what I wanted.
25	22	17	18	51***	26**	42***	I flattered a person in order to get ahead.
13	14	07	07	45***	18	35***	I asked "Innocent" questions, intending to use the information against someone.
69	61	48	50	36***	35***	34***	I managed to get my way by appearing cooperative.
12	08	10	11	25***	19*	23*	I pretended I was sick at work, knowing that I would not be there the next day.
12	10	09	07	23*	24*	17	I tricked a friend into giving me personal information.

*** $p < .001$
** $p < .01$
* $p < .05$

TABLE 7.8
Temporal Stability of Ingenuous Acts

| Base Rates | | | | Temporal Stability | | | Ingenuous Acts |
| S-Data | | O-Data | | | | | |
T1	T2	T1	T2	S x S	O x O	SO x SO	
12	08	08	02	43***	56***	70***	I picked up a hitch-hiker.
12	12	14	14	45***	61***	62***	I let an inexperienced friend cut my hair.
22	21	19	17	41***	56***	57***	I left my apartment unlocked at night.
15	19	13	17	43***	46***	52***	I jogged after it became dark.
17	21	18	15	33***	42***	50***	I let someone borrow my car.
38	33	44	38	28**	44***	50***	I trusted someone else to hold my cash for me.
29	22	27	30	35***	34***	46***	I permitted my partner to go out with members of the opposite sex.
12	12	10	07	32***	26**	42***	I told a secret to someone who had previously betrayed my trust.
11	16	10	15	28**	30***	40***	I let someone I hardly knew sleep at my apartment.
26	32	35	35	31***	25***	35***	I let another make an important decision for me.
46	42	42	41	22*	33***	33***	I believed my friend's excuse, even though it sounded unlikely.
20	10	11	12	30***	05	27**	I let a friend stay in my apartment while I was away.

*** p < .001
** p < .01
* p < .001

relatively consistent across data sources. Thus, differences in temporal stability magnitudes appear to be moderately reliable. Systematic stability variations raise a central issue for personality psychology: What factors are responsible for moderating these magnitudes?

A third finding pertains to the potential increment in temporal stability to be gained by compositing act assessments across the two data sources. Across all 200 acts, the mean temporal stability coefficients are $+.37$ and $+.39$ for the self and spouse-observer source, respectively, and $+.45$ for the composite of the two. Thus, a modest increment in temporal stability is found by compositing across data sources—a finding probably deriving from a canceling of error variance associated with each data source combined with cumulation of dependable variance common to each source (Nunnally, 1978).

A fourth finding pertains to the degree to which the two data sources show congruence. Across the 200 acts, the mean correlation at the act level between self- and spouse-observer recordings was .28 for time 1 and .28 for time 2, with ranges of .01 to .78 and .00 to .91. Thus, there appears to be considerable variation in the degree to which self and spouse-observers converge in act assessment—a finding to be taken up under the section on moderators of temporal stability (See Buss, 1984a for a more complete presentation of self-spouse correlations).

Every method has limitations, and the current act report methods are no exception. An alternative interpretation may be raised, for example, that the moderately high temporal stability correlations found here may simply result from subjects or their spouses invoking a general response set or belief system about themselves or their spouse. For example, a subject might believe that his or her spouse is the "extraverted type" or the kind of person who performs extraverted acts. When encountering each instance of an extraverted act, the belief system is activated and performance recorded, rather than veridical documentation that the act has indeed been performed. Obtained temporal stability, therefore, may stem merely from stability of the construct system, and not from stability of act performance over time.

If this interpretation were correct, one would predict a high average between-act correlation within each category. That is, if the construct invocation hypothesis were correct, substantial covariation among similarly categorized acts (e.g., extraverted acts) must be found since similar recordings would be made for each act subsumed by the category. To test the construct invocation hypothesis, the mean inter-act correlations were computed for each category for each data source at each of the two time periods. Table 7.9 shows these results.

Perusal of Table 7.9 reveals that these correlations (termed the tightness or looseness of the manifested *category structure* by Buss & Craik, 1983a) are low in magnitude and not large enough to account for the obtained magnitudes of temporal stability. The correlations for the self and spouse-observer data sources are nearly identical, suggesting that observers are being as differentiated as are

TABLE 7.9
Mean Interact Correlations Within Each Category

Category	S-Data Time 1	S-Data Time 2	O-Data Time 1	O-Data Time 2
Extraverted	.17	.16	.19	.17
Introverted	.16	.18	.17	.15
Quarrelsome	.16	.16	.18	.19
Agreeable	.16	.10	.13	.12
Dominant	.18	.16	.21	.19
Submissive	.15	.12	.14	.09
Calculating	.20	.20	.18	.16
Ingenuous	.14	.09	.10	.13
Mean Across Categories	.17	.15	.16	.15

actors in recording act performance. Thus, the expectation logically derived from the construct invocation hypothesis of a high average between-act correlation within category is not supported by these data. It should also be mentioned that these inter-act correlations are nearly identical to those obtained by other investigators (e.g., Mischel & Peake, 1982), although they are not here interpreted as "cross-situational consistency coefficients" (see Buss & Craik, 1984, for a discussion of the meaning of the inter-act correlation and its relation to cross-situational consistency).

In sum, temporal stability at the level of single acts appears to be moderate in magnitude. Composites across data sources provide a modest increment in temporal stability, suggesting that the present and previous findings may represent lower-bound estimates, being attenuated by unreliability of measurement. Variation across acts in the magnitudes of obtained stabilities are reasonably consistent across data sources ($r = +.62$), suggesting a pattern of reliable differences that might be incorporated and explained by personality formulations. Finally, the hypothesis that the obtained magnitudes of temporal stability can be accounted for by construct or response-set invocation rather than by actual performance consistency is not supported by these data.

As noted previously, the act trend or multiple-act composite is a central unit of analysis in the act-frequency formulation (Buss & Craik, 1980, 1981, 1983a). Thus, a crucial issue pertains to the increment to be derived from such composites over analysis at the single act level. Table 7.10 shows the temporal stabilities of act trends for each of the eight categories for each data source separately and for the composite of the two data sources. Also shown are the corresponding mean single-act stabilities for analogous categories and data sources. In each case, the temporal stability of the act trend is greater than the

TABLE 7.10
Temporal Stability of Acts and Act Rituals

Category	S-Data $\bar{X}$ Act	S-Data Act Trend	O-Data $\bar{X}$ Act	O-Data Act Trend	S + O $\bar{X}$ Acts	Composite Act Trend
Extraverted	.40	.79***	.42	.84***	.52	.86***
Introverted	.38	.72***	.39	.68***	.46	.73***
Quarrelsome	.40	.76***	.43	.74***	.48	.78***
Agreeable	.28	.56***	.36	.72***	.40	.68***
Dominant	.35	.63***	.40	.77***	.46	.74***
Submissive	.32	.73***	.31	.63***	.38	.74***
Calculating	.41	.68***	.39	.65***	.45	.66***
Ingenuous	.37	.54***	.39	.72***	.47	.70***
Mean Correlation	.37	.68	.39	.72	.45	.74

Note: $\bar{X}$ Act refers to the mean single-act temporal stability across the 25 acts within each category.
Note: Act Trend refers to the multiple-act composite of 25 acts within each category.

analogous mean stability at the single-act level. Thus, composites based on multiple-act criteria show substantially higher stability than do single acts, a result that is congruent with the Spearman-Brown prophesy formula, and is consistent with the findings and conceptions of other researchers (e.g., Epstein, 1979; Green, 1978; Jaccard, 1974; McGowan & Gormly, 1976).

Individually computed stability coefficients. As discussed earlier, the traditionally computed stability coefficients (correlations for a sample across time on each variable) do not permit evaluation of the specific consistency of any individual in the sample. The act frequency approach provides a method by which individual consistency coefficients can be computed. For each subject, the pattern of act performance for Time 1 can be correlated with the pattern of act performance for Time 2 separately for each of the eight categories of acts. An alternative would be to standardize each score around the group mean before computing each coefficient. That analysis, however, would artifactually lower obtained stability because any performance stability that an individual shared with the group would be removed. The purpose of the present analysis is to compute individual stability coefficients that do not depend upon reference to other sample members. Table 7.11 shows the results of these analyses: the mean, standard deviation, and range of individually computed consistency coefficients for each of the eight categories for each data source.

The range of individually computed stability correlations is wide for each category, supporting previous contentions that only some of the people are consistent some of the time (Bem & Allen, 1974; Kenrick & Stringfield, 1980). For each category, some individuals showed considerable change in the pattern of act performance. These results suggest that traditionally computed consistency

TABLE 7.11
Individually Computed Temporal Stability Coefficients

Category	Self Report			Observer Report		
	Mean	SD	Range	Mean	SD	Range
Agreeable	.62	.18	-.12 to .89	.64	.18	-.20 to .98
Submissive	.43	.25	-.12 to .89	.39	.28	-.25 to .89
Quarrelsome	.52	.25	-.12 to .93	.54	.27	-.10 to .99
Dominant	.55	.19	-.04 to .93	.51	.22	-.16 to .87
Extraverted	.54	.25	-.12 to .93	.49	.28	-.29 to .92
Ingenuous	.54	.23	-.14 to .96	.50	.29	-.13 to .99
Introvert	.61	.21	-.08 to .95	.57	.23	-.11 to .99
Calculating	.51	.28	-.24 to .99	.53	.32	-.30 to .99
Across 200 Acts	.60	.10	.19 to .81	.59	.13	-.07 to .79

correlations may be averaging or combining individuals who are highly consistent with those who are less consistent, a finding parallel to one reported by Epstein (1983).

The average individually computed consistency correlation, however, is substantial in magnitude for all eight categories. Also of interest is the finding that these individually computed consistency indicies are similar in magnitude to those found with the traditionally computed consistency coefficients (see Table 7.10). Implications of these findings are taken up in the discussion section.

An important issue is whether individuals who are highly stable with respect to one disposition are also highly stable with respect to other dispositions. In other words, is there a general tendency for stability across dispositions? To address this question, the individually computed consistency coefficients were intercorrelated across the eight dispositional categories. Two correlation matrices of consistency coefficients were calculated: one for the self-report data source and one for the spouse-observer data source. Table 7.12 shows these results.

The mean correlation for the self-reported data source is +.09; the parallel average correlation for the spouse-observer data source is also +.09. A few of the correlations in the matrix are significant (e.g., between agreeable and ingenuous for both data sources). However, these results suggest that, overall, there is no general tendency for stability, a finding that conceptually replicates the Chaplin and Goldberg (in press) findings, and is congruent with the findings of Bem and Allen (1974).

Group trend stability.   Endurance of rank and stability of each individual are traditional concerns in personality psychology. A third and less frequently examined level at which stability may be sought pertains to group or sample trends. It should be noted that individually computed stability coefficients and group trend stability coefficients are not independent sources of information: The population profiles are based on individual profiles in the sample. However, it is possible for

TABLE 7.12
Correlations Among Individually Computed Stability Coefficients

	Ext	Int	Quar	Agree	Dom	Sub	Calc	Ingen
Extraverted	---	.04	-.01	.04	-.03	.09	.15	.09
Introverted	.02	---	-.06	.25**	.03	.07	.03	.01
Quarrelsome	.19*	.06	---	.23**	.22**	.00	.07	.09
Agreeable	.06	.21*	.06	---	.23**	.00	.15	.29***
Dominant	.21*	.07	.21*	.20*	---	.14	.07	.13
Submissive	.01	.08	-.04	.21*	-.01	---	.04	.11
Calculating	.13	.08	.12	.11	.19*	.02	---	.15
Ingenuous	-.20	-.03	-.03	.28***	.13	-.01	.00	---

*** $p < .001$
** $p < .01$
* $p < .05$

Note: Correlations above diagonal are for the self-report data source; those below diagonal are for the spouse-observer data source.

population profiles to show high stability even if intra-individual coefficients are low or even zero (e.g., if, over time, different individuals perform given acts, and given individuals tend not to repeat acts). Thus, for the group-oriented psychologist and for sociologists, the stability of population profiles may take on considerable importance, even though they are not independent of individual profiles. To examine stability at this level, the columns of base-rates at the act level at Time 1 were correlated with analogous base rates at Time 2. Table 7.13 shows the results of these analyses for each category for each data source, across the two methods at each time, and across both time and methods. Thus, eight tests are provided for the assessment of population base-rate stability.

All but two of these correlations are in the .90s. These results suggest that base rates of act performance at the population level remain highly stable over time. In addition, this stability is exhibited within each of the eight categories

TABLE 7.13
Temporal Stability of Population Trends

Category	Across Method Time 1	Time 2	Temporal Stability: T1 x T2 S x S	O x O	S x O	O x S
Extraverted	.92	.95	.96	.93	.91	.91
Introverted	.92	.93	.95	.97	.91	.91
Quarrelsome	.96	.95	.96	.98	.93	.95
Agreeable	.96	.97	.95	.93	.91	.92
Dominant	.90	.94	.96	.95	.92	.87
Submissive	.91	.92	.95	.96	.93	.85
Calculating	.94	.95	.95	.96	.93	.90
Ingenuous	.95	.96	.97	.97	.95	.94
Across 200 Acts	.94	.96	.96	.96	.93	.92

Note: All Correlations are significant beyond the .001 level.

examined. It should be noted that these correlations are not inflated by inclusion of acts with unusually high or low base-rates because such acts were not employed in the follow-up Time 2 assessments (see Tables 7.1–7.8).

The importance of these highly stable base-rates warrant emphasis. The base-rates for quarrelsome acts shown in Table 7.3, for example, are striking. The acts "I gave her the 'silent treatment' when I was upset," "I yelled at my partner," and "I made belittling comments about the people who walked by" show surprisingly high base-rates, in spite of their apparent undesireable nature. These stable base-rates provide information about the composition of act repertoires and of the day-to-day acts that occur with relatively greater and lesser frequency throughout the behavioral stream.

Moderators of Temporal Stability

Context specificity. The first hypothesized moderator of temporal stability magnitudes is the specificity of the context with which each act was depicted. The alpha reliability of the context specificity ratings was +.81, indicating that such judgments are quite reliable. Examples of acts rated high on context specificity are "He (she) stayed at home and watched TV alone on a Saturday night" (5.70) and "He (she) paid his (her) bills on the last day that they were due to obtain the highest interest" (5.30). Examples of acts rated low on context specificity are: "He (she) interrupted a conversation" (1.60) and "He (she) walked with his (her) head down" (1.90). Table 7.14 shows the correlations between the mean context specificity ratings and the corresponding temporal stability magni-

TABLE 7.14
Potential Moderators of Temporal Stability
1. Context Specificity

Category	S x S	O x O	SO x SO
Extraverted	.35	.08	.31
Introverted	.08	.19	.37
Quarrelsome	-.18	-.10	-.03
Agreeable	.18	.52	.41
Dominant	.02	.36	.19
Submissive	-.10	.24	.18
Calculating	.00	-.01	.09
Ingenuous	-.20	-.08	-.17
Across 200 Acts	-.04	.04	.07

Note: Correlations are between mean context specificity rating and magnitude of temporal stability computed for each act (see Tables 7.1 through 7.8).

tudes for each act. As shown in Table 7.14, some correlations are slightly negative, and others are slightly positive. Across the 200 acts, there is essentially no covariation between magnitude of temporal stability and degree of context specificity. In sum, the hypothesis that context specificity moderates temporal stability does not appear to be supported by these data. Implications of these results are taken up in the discussion section.

Ratings of inferences about internal states.   The second hypothesized moderator was the degree to which recording act performance required an inference about an internal motivation or intention of the actor. The alpha reliability for the inference ratings was high (+.90), suggesting that reliable judgments can be made about which acts require and do not require such inferences. Examples of acts rated high on requiring inferences about internal motives and intents are: "He (she) asked 'innocent' questions, intending to use the information against someone" (6.13) and "He (she) took the opposite point of view, just to be contrary" (5.27). Acts rated low on requiring inferences are "He (she) rolled down the car window and talked to the person in the next car" (1.00) and "He (she) sang a song in front of a group" (1.00). Table 7.15 shows the correlations between these inference ratings for each act and the corresponding temporal stability coefficients.

As with the context specificity results, the magnitudes are small and account for little variation in temporal stability. Thus, the hypothesized relationship between degree of inference and temporal stability is not supported in these data.

TABLE 7.15
Potential Moderators of Temporal Stability:
II: Inference Ratings

Category	Time 1 x Time 2		
	S x S	O x O	SO x SO
Extraverted	-.15	.01	-.01
Introverted	.18	.26	.19
Quarrelsome	-.13	-.20	-.23
Agreeable	.37	-.10	.14
Dominant	.06	.10	.07
Submissive	.22	.25	.24
Calculating	.08	.08	-.01
Ingenuous	-.32	-.34	-.39
Across 200 Acts	.10	-.02	-.05

Note: Correlations are between mean inference ratings and magnitude of temporal stability for each act (See Tables 7.1 through 7.8).

TABLE 7.16
Potential Moderators of Temporal Stability:
III: Cross-Method Agreement

Category	Time 1 Agreement by:			Time 2 Agreement by:		
	S x S	O x O	SO x SO	S x S	O x O	SO x SO
Extroverted	.08	.29	.24	.16	.33	.26
Introverted	-.16	-.11	-.24	.09	.04	.02
Quarrelsome	.28	.07	.31	.40	.04	.35
Agreeable	-.01	.06	.21	.32	.36	.59
Dominant	.16	.21	.25	.19	.43	.30
Submissive	.23	.20	.30	.31	.09	.19
Calculating	.08	-.15	.00	-.11	.00	.03
Ingenuous	.52	.27	.48	.48	.28	.40
Across 200 Acts	.16	.16	.28	.23	.24	.32

Note: Correlations are between cross-method correlations (S x O) and magnitudes of temporal stability computed for each act (see Tables 7.1 through 7.8).

Cross-method agreement. The third hypothesized moderator was cross-method agreement. It was proposed, paralleling Epstein (1979), that lack of cross-method agreement would attenuate the obtained temporal stability. To test this hypothesis, the cross-method correlations for each act at each time period were correlated with the corresponding temporal stability correlations. Table 7.16 shows the results of these analyses for each data source and for the composites across the two data sources.

The correlations are generally positive, suggesting that acts showing greater cross-method agreement tend to be more temporally stable. This finding is particularly pronounced for the ingenuous and submissive act categories, and weak or absent for the calculating and introverted act categories. In sum, it appears that the acts showing greater agreement across data sources also show higher temporal stability, a finding parallel to Epstein's (1979) results on the effects of reliability on temporal stability. This relationship is weak, however, suggesting that much remains to be discovered about the prediction of variation in degree of stability.

DISCUSSION

Three conceptual modes of stability analysis are proposed and examined empirically—group trends, individual differences, and individualized analysis. Each addresses a facet of temporal stability not indexed by the others. Analysis at the group level provides information about the endurance of performance base-rates over time. Analysis at the level of individual differences yields evidence about endurance of relative position or rank order of individuals within the sample. And at the individual level, information is provided about the stability of the pattern of act performance of each person within the sample.

Each mode is encumbered with limitations. Analysis at the group level does not provide information about endurance of relative position, nor about the consistency of any specific individual within the sample. In the individual differences mode, information about the consistency of specific individuals is lost, and data on group constancies or changes is similarly omitted. In the individual mode, rank order endurance and base-rate maintenance are not indexed. Together, however, the three forms of stability analysis provide unique and complementary forms of information about the temporal stability of acts, act trends, and individual performance patterns.

Empirical examination of these three analytic modes yielded the following major results. At the level of group base-rates, highly robust stability coefficients were found (typically in the + .90s) across a 6-month time span for acts within each of eight dispositional categories. Group base rates remained highly stable using the same methods (e.g., self-report at T1 by self-report at T2), as well as different methods (e.g., self-reports at T1 by observer-reports at T2), suggesting that these results are not method-specific.

In the individual difference mode, analyses were conducted for each act and for act trends (composites of 25 acts within each dispositional category). Moderate stability of relative rank (averaging + .37 and + .39 for self- and spouse-data sources) was found for specific acts within each dispositional category. Stability coefficients were boosted slightly (averaging + .45) by compositing assessments of each act across data sources. Correlations for the stability of multiple-act criteria were + .68 and + .72 for the self- and observer-data sources, respectively, and + .74 when composited across data sources. These results suggest moderate stability at the single act level, as well as substantial gain when multiple-act dispositional composites are employed as the units of analysis.

At the level of specific acts, variations in temporal stability magnitudes were found to be highly reliable across data sources. Such *differences* in temporal stability highlight patterns that warrant attention by personality formulations. Why do members of the same sample *change* in relative position with respect to some acts, yet retain their rank order with respect to other acts?

The present series of studies examined three hypothesized moderators of this form of temporal stability—context specificity of act depiction, degree of inference about internal motives and intentions required for assessment of act performance, and cross-method agreement. These hypothesized moderators were submitted to eight tests—one for each of the dispositional categories employed. Context specificity and degree of inference were not found to moderate temporal stability magnitudes. Cross-method agreement was found to be consistently positively correlated with temporal stability magnitude, a finding particularly pronounced for the categories of ingenuous and submissive. Considerable reliable variation in stability magnitudes, however, remains unexplained.

It should be noted that these findings are limited in that differences in obtained stability attributable to actual performance are confounded with differences due to the method of recording performance. In addition, because considerable reliable variation in temporal stability magnitudes remains unexplained, future investigations could fruitfully examine alternative moderators. Differences in temporal stability suggest previously neglected patterns of stability and change that might be usefully addressed in future personality formulations.

In the individual mode of analysis, these studies found substantial stability (averaging $+.59$ and $+.60$ for the self- and observer-data sources, respectively). These results suggest that traditionally computed stability coefficients may be reasonably accurate reflections of stability at the individual level, in spite of conceptual and computational lack of equivalence. The considerable range of values for individuals within the sample, however, suggest that traditionally computed stability coefficients may be averaging highly-consistent and less-consistent individuals, a point illustrated previously by Bem and Allen (1974) and by Epstein (1983). The present analysis of eight dispositional categories suggests an important theoretical question: Are individuals consistently stable? Correlations among the individual scores for the eight categories were quite low, but positive ($+.09$ for both the self- and observer-data sources). There does not appear to be a general tendency for stability, a finding also noted by Chaplin and Goldberg (in press) in the context of cross-situational consistency.

The proposed tripartite conceptual scheme for stability analysis suggests that the stability question is really an array of questions. The unique contribution of each mode in the context of the act frequency approach highlights features in the study of personality that are generally omitted by more traditional approaches, which focus on dimensional ratings and scale scores. These traditional approaches can usefully abstract and summarize broad personal features and central individual differences in a cogent and concise way. But typically missing are the performance repertoires from which these abstractions are drawn—features that are highlighted in the present framework.

Analysis of the stability of population base-rates yields information, albeit incomplete, about the composition of act repertoires and of the day-to-day acts that occur with greater and lesser frequency throughout the behavioral stream of the population. That more than 70% of this sample report (and whose spouses report about them) that they yelled at their partner (Table 7.3) and less than 20% report hitting someone who annoyed them (Table 7.3) yields information about the frequent or preferred modes of manifesting quarrelsomeness. Through these population base-rates, personality psychology can transcend exclusive focus on individual differences and become more closely linked with psychologies searching for general statements (see, e.g., Bakan, 1967; Buss, 1984b; Cronbach, 1957).

Identifying stable population trends, however, represents only one goal of personality psychology. As Wiggins (1973, 1979), Goldberg (1973), and others have noted, a central task for the field concerns identifying and accounting for the major ways in which individuals differ. Members of this sample were likely to retain their relative position in the frequency of performing acts such as dancing in front of a crowd (extraverted), accepting verbal abuse without defending themselves (submissive), and leaving their apartment unlocked at night (ingenuous). Single-act stability analysis offers a richness of dispositional instantiation not typically captured by summary abstractions.

Within the act frequency approach, act trends, or multiple-act composites of highly prototypical instances, represent a theoretically sanctioned union of the concept of disposition with principles of aggregation and reliability (Buss & Craik, 1983a). It is not surprising, therefore, that stability magnitudes for act trends are substantially higher than for most single acts. This level of analysis illustrates that stability need not be tied exclusively to same-act repetition. Frequencies of dominant act trends, for example, remain highly stable, in spite of individual shifts in manifesting specific dominant acts. Act trend stability, not same-act repetition, is the level at which dispositional analysis emerges most clearly.

Individuals differ, however, in the specific acts used to manifest a given disposition, even with act trend frequency held constant. The *pattern* of performance within each dispositional category is unique to each individual and thus may be used in the idiographic analysis of persons (Buss & Craik, 1983b). The present results indicate that these unique patterns tend to be moderately stable for most people, and thus they provide an empirical foundation for idiographic analysis that does not rely on the scores of other individuals to bear meaning. Thus, each mode of analysis provides unique and complementary information about temporal stability.

Do these three modes exhaust the array of potential types of stability analysis? The answer is clearly no. Although these three modes encompass the range of concerns of most personality researchers, from the single individual to individual differences to population-level analysis, the specific units amenable to analysis within each mode have yet to be fully explored. The temporal stability of dispositional patterns (maintenance of relative frequency of act trend scores), for example, can be analyzed within both the individual and population modes, given a reasonably large array of dispositions. Thus, future studies could fruitfully examine the temporal stability of different units within each of the three analytic modes.

Whether or not stability exists is no longer at issue. The present framework and results, however, suggest an exciting agenda for research on temporal stability: How can reliable differences in temporal stability of acts and act trends be explained? What factors cause individuals to show stability on some dispositions but not on others? How can the various patterns of greater and lesser stability be incorporated into a general formulation of personality? And what aspects, through what methods, and in what domains, are stability and change most cogently displayed?

ACKNOWLEDGMENTS

The author wishes to thank Mike Barnes, Kenneth Craik, Lewis Goldberg, Seymour Epstein, Robert McCrae, Robert Rosenthal, Daniel Ozer, Howard Terry, and Jerry Wiggins for helpful comments on an earlier draft of this work.

REFERENCES

Allport, G. W. (1937). *Personality: A psychological interpretation.* New York: Holt.
Alston, W. P. (1975). Traits, consistency and conceptual alternatives for personality theory. *Journal for the Theory of Social Behavior, 5,* 17–48.
Bakan, D. (1967). *On method: Toward a reconstruction of psychological investigation.* San Francisco: Jossey-Bass.
Bem, D. J., & Allen, A. (1974). On predicting some of the people some of the time: The search for cross-situational consistencies in behavior. *Psychological Review, 81,* 506–520.
Block, J. (1971). *Lives through time.* Berkeley, CA: Bancroft.
Block, J. (1977). Advancing the psychology of personality: Paradigmatic shift or improving the quality of research? In D. Magnusson & N. S. Endler (Eds.), *Personality at the crossroads: Current issues in interactional psychology* (pp. 37–64). Hillsdale, NJ: Lawrence Erlbaum Associates.
Block, J. H., & Block, J. (1980). The role of ego-control and ego-resiliency in the organization of behavior. In W. A. Collins (Ed.), *Minnesota Symposium on Child Psychology* (Vol. 13, pp. 39–101). Hillsdale, NJ: Lawrence Erlbaum Associates.
Buss, D. M. (1981a). *The act frequency analysis of interpersonal dispositions.* Unpublished doctoral dissertation, University of California, Berkeley.
Buss, D. M. (1981b). Sex differences in the evaluation and performance of dominant acts. *Journal of Personality and Social Psychology, 40,* 147–154.
Buss, D. M. (1984a). Toward a psychology of person-environment (PE) correlation: The role of spouse selection. *Journal of Personality and Social Psychology, 47,* 361–377.
Buss, D. M. (1984b). Evolutionary biology and personality psychology: Toward a conception of human nature and individual differences. *American Psychologist.*
Buss, D. M., Block, J. J., & Block, J. (1980). Preschool activity level: Personality correlates and developmental implications. *Child Development, 51,* 401–408.
Buss, D. M., & Craik, K. H. (1980). The frequency concept of disposition: Dominance and prototypically dominant acts. *Journal of Personality, 48,* 379–392.
Buss, D. M., & Craik, K. H. (1981). The act frequency analysis of interpersonal dispositions: Aloofness, gregariousness, dominance, and submissiveness. *Journal of Personality, 49,* 174–192.

Buss, D. M., & Craik, K. H. (1983a). The act frequency approach to personality. *Psychological Review, 90,* 105–126.

Buss, D. M., & Craik, K. H. (1983b). The dispositional analysis of everyday conduct. *Journal of Personality, 51,* 393–412.

Buss, D. M., & Craik, K. H. (1984). Acts, dispositions, and personality. In B. A. Maher and W. B. Maher (Eds.), *Progress in experimental personality research: Normal personality processes, Vol. 13*(pp. 241–301). New York: Academic.

Cattell, R. B. (1957). *Personality and motivation: Structure and measurement.* Yonkers-on-Hudson, NY: World Books.

Chaplin, W. F., & Goldberg, L. R. (in press). A failure to replicate the Bem and Allen study of individual differences in cross-situational consistency. *Journal of Personality and Social Psychology.*

Costa, P. T., & McCrae, R. R. (1980). Still stable after all these years: Personality as a key to some issues in aging. In P. B. Baltes & O. G. Brim (Eds.), *Life span development and behavior* (Vol. 3, pp. 65–102). New York: Academic.

Costa, P. T., McCrae, R., & Arenberg, D. (1980). Enduring dispositions in adult males. *Journal of Personality and Social Psychology, 38,* 793–800.

Cronbach, L. J. (1957). The two diciplines of scientific psychology. *American Psychologist, 12,* 671–684.

Duncan, S., & Fiske, D. W. (1977). *Face-to-face interaction: Research, methods, and theory.* Hillsdale, NJ: Lawrence Erlbaum Associates.

Epstein, S. (1979). The stability of behavior: I. On predicting most of the people much of the time. *Journal of Personality and Social Psychology, 37,* 1097–1126.

Epstein, S. (1980). The stability of behavior: II. Implications for psychological research. *American Psychologist, 35,* 790–806.

Epstein, S. (1983). A research paradigm for the study of personality and emotions. In M. Page (Ed.), *Nebraska Symposium on Motivation* (pp. 91–154). Lincoln, NB: University of Nebraska Press.

Eysenck, H. J. (1953). *The structure of human personality.* New York: Wiley.

Goldberg, L. R. (1972). Some recent trends in personality assessment. *Journal of Personality Assessment, 36,* 547–560.

Green, B. F. (1978). In defense of measurement. *American psychologist, 33,* 664–670.

Jaccard, J. J. (1974). Predicting social behavior from personality traits. *Journal of Research in Personality, 7,* 358–367.

Kenrick, D. T., & Stringfield, D. O. (1980). Personality traits in the eye of the beholder: Crossing some traditional philosophical boundaries in the search for consistency in all of the people. *Psychological Review, 87,* 88–104.

Lamiell, J. T. (1981). Toward an idiothetic psychology of personality. *American Psychologist, 36,* 276–289.

Leary, T. (1957). *Interpersonal diagnosis of personality.* New York: Ronald.

McCrae, R. R., & Costa, P. T. (1982). Self-concept and the stability of personality: Cross-sectional comparisons of self-reports and ratings. *Journal of Personality and Social Psychology, 43,* 1282–1292.

McGowan, J., & Gormly, J. (1976). Validation of personality traits: A multicriteria approach. *Journal of Personality and Social Psychology, 34*(5), 791–795.

Mischel, W. (1973). Toward a cognitive social learning reconceptualization of personality. *Psychological Review, 80,* 252–283.

Mischel, W., & Peake, P. K. (1982). Beyond deja vu in the search for cross-situational consistency. *Psychological Review, 89,* 730–755.

Moss, H. A., & Susman, E. J. (1980). Longitudinal study of personality development. In O. G.

Brim, Jr. & J. Kagan (Eds.), *Constancy and change in human development*. Cambridge, MA: Harvard University Press.

Norman, W. T. (1963). Toward an adequate taxonomy of personality attributes: Replicated factor structure in peer nomination personality ratings. *Journal of Abnormal and Social Psychology, 66,* 574–583.

Nunnally, J. (1978). *Psychometric theory*. New York: McGraw-Hill.

Schuerger, J. M., Tait, E., & Tavernelli, M. (1982). Temporal stability of personality by questionnaire. *Journal of Personality and Social Psychology, 43,* 176–182.

Wiggins, J. S. (1973). *Personality and prediction: Principles of personality assessment*. Reading, MA: Addison-Wesley.

Wiggins, J. S. (1974). *In defense of traits*. Invited address to the Ninth Annual Symposium on Recent Developments in the Use of the MMPI, Los Angeles, February 18.

Wiggins, J. S. (1979). A psychological taxonomy of trait descriptive terms: The interpersonal domain. *Journal of Personality and Social Psychology, 37,* 395–412.

Wiggins, J. S. (1980). Circumplex models of interpersonal behavior. In L. Wheeler (Ed.), *Review of Personality and Social Psychology, Vol. 1* (pp. 265–294). Beverly Hills, CA: Sage.

Author Index

Numbers in *italics* indicate pages with complete bibliographic information.

Subject Index